To
Mary, my dear
friend, with all
good wishes !
Much love,
Jeannie

ISBN: 1494408740
ISBN-13: 9781494408749

TEN HOURS 'TIL SPRING

BY

JEANNIE HUDSON

Can you hear the wild awaking from rest
Can you be eased when you haven't a nest
Can you smell the aroma the flowers emit
As I do, yes we do together we sit
Time as we know yields another indeed
As life emerges from one sown seed
When all else is pointless, somehow we grew
Into one-and-one, yes that makes two
Daytime grows longer, night takes its place
Mother Nature the bearer of blessings called Grace
Longing, striving, the strength of the weak
Life bearing life, isn't that what you seek
And time moving forward, the birds too shall sing
For time's of the essence, ten more hours 'til spring

Raquel Heiderscheidt

DEDICATION

To Jill Schad, the best friend anyone could ever have.

Cover watercolor by Jeannie Hudson

ACKNOWLEDGMENTS

Once again, I wish to thank my dear friend Jill Schad for her generous help with the technical processes in the publication of this book. Also I owe much appreciation to my husband Adam for his extensive proof reading.

I'm grateful to Barb Trotz, RN, Pediatric Leukemia Coordinator, University of Minnesota Amplatz Children's Hospital, for her information on leukemia and bone marrow transplants.

Many people at the Arabian Horse Trust assisted me with information about Arabian Horse breeding and showing. My huge thanks.

CHAPTER ONE

Jeremy Foxworth surveyed the *Radbourne* grounds below the Big Horns. Seated at his desk, he let his gaze settle on Evelyn's portrait and acknowledged his constant grief, tinged today with new worry. Francine's granddaughter was arriving that afternoon.

Would this phantom make the old woman happy or miserable?

He glanced at the ceiling. Francine's bedroom occupied the third level of the manor's tower because it let her view much of her domain. Jeremy wondered if second thoughts troubled her this morning.

As for him, Katherine Meade's imminent arrival stirred only anger. Now she stood to inherit all he had assumed would be his.

In truth, Francine's only living relative was a threat to the very heartbeat of *Radbourne*. Likely, she would cause the dying woman more grief that she'd bargained for when suddenly, she summoned her to *Radbourne*.

Jeremy rose and paced to the nearest window, searching for Bordeaux. As though conjured, the old stallion appeared beyond the stream, ghostlike in the box elder and willow. Bordeaux was the first Arabian foal he helped Francine deliver after Jeremy came to live at *Radbourne* as a frightened twelve-year-old.

The sun warmed him now. Each night, winter drew nearer. It was barely September yet yellow streaked the cottonwoods and new snow lay on the slopes of the mountains.

Out of loyalty and love, and a bond of gratitude, Jeremy would protect Francine as fiercely now as he had since he became the son she had never borne. She had been a widow for a year when she arrived in Denver, one day after his bankrupt father committed suicide, and brought him home with her to *Radbourne* a week later.

It was Francine's grandfather from Nottinghamshire who established the *Radbourne* as a cattle ranch in 1872. Tyson Chamberlain wasn't content to settle among the cattle barons in the south. With a perversity that even today ruled Francine's judgment, he headed into Wyoming Territory's untamed north still overrun by Sioux in mortal combat with the Cavalry. The Indians burned Tyson's cabin twice. Nonetheless, his ranch endured and over time, Herefords phased out the longhorns. After Francine inherited the *Radbourne* from her father Thomas Chamberlain in 1959, she and her husband Boyd Gellis imported the first Arabian horses. The hardy, elegant breed was a fitting extension of the Chamberlain saga rooted in a stalwart albeit refined heritage. Although Francine refused her husband's name, her marriage was apparently successful while it lasted, producing a daughter, the mother of the inexplicably absent Katherine Meade.

After Gellis' early death, Francine nurtured their dream of breeding the finest Arabs in the mountain states. Years later, after Jeremy became her ally, they produced national champions and built an international reputation.

What did Katherine Meade from Boston know of this commitment? Nothing, Jeremy would bet.

Katie Meade came awake with a jolt, pressing fingertips to throbbing temples. Travel through time zones and interminable delays in Chicago and Denver had left her exhausted and hurting.

The taxi had collected her at four a.m. so she'd have ample time to deal with the new maze of airport security in place since the terrorist attacks last week. She shivered, recalling the panic that pursued her to Boston Logan terminal, her nerves already frayed by the need to fly so soon after the hijackings.

Now as the commuter plane neared Sheridan, no memories guided her. She recalled nothing of the hastily arranged trip to Boston after her mother's sudden death.

When Katie was five, her Aunt Jessie came to collect her. For weeks after, she was too ill to know what was happening to her.

Once she was aware again, she'd been robbed of an entire year. Yet, even as a dark puzzle was still insinuating itself deep in her subconscious, she felt stronger, eager, and curious about first grade.

The Beacon Hill townhouse offered its own security and some happiness, yet she remained haunted by what she couldn't remember. A particular nightmare besieged her girlhood.

Nothing remained of Wyoming as years

passed. The hideous dream beset her less often but when it came, its power to sicken and terrorize strengthened. Now when she crawled her way up through the horror, she felt as helpless as the child whose screams woke her night after night, and brought Aunt Jessie running

The dream varied little. Enervated, Katie stood in a circle of light watching someone step through a doorway. It was all so dark and dim, she could never see who'd come and she always woke just before they came closer. She hugged herself, rocking until she could cry no more, moaning through teeth that wouldn't stop chattering. Suspended, she was paralyzed beneath mystifying guilt. Only waves of nausea broke the spell, and she rushed to the bathroom to vomit.

With adolescence, she managed to banish the dread for longer and longer intervals. There was no more tragedy until Aunt Jessie died a month after Katie graduated from Wellesley.

She was ninety-nine. Death only brought gratitude in Katie for a very kind woman who'd lived long and cared well for her.

Katie excelled in photo journalism while her life took expected turns. She married and gave birth to a daughter. Marriage was never what she expected, but she delighted in Ursel.

When calamity struck a second time, it hurled Katie back into the void of huge loss. While she was away on a photo assignment, Zachary took Ursel to the hotel where he was headlining with his clarinet. When the fire started at two a.m., both he and their daughter died in the space of minutes.

This time, it took Katie three years to

recover, but when she'd healed, she was possessed of previously untapped strength and purpose. Well before Francine Chamberlain's letter arrived, fresh panic fueled by the recurring nightmare pulled her focus to the past.

She considered searching for other relatives but didn't know where to look, plus the revulsion and fear in Aunt Jessie's eyes had silenced her questions long ago. Nevertheless, she had been losing ground to the terror recently. Along with new resolve to learn the truth, she had discovered anger she hadn't acknowledged before – rage at whomever had banished her. The tone of the letter demanding her immediate appearance at *Radbourne Arabians* did nothing to appease her. She wasn't accustomed to taking orders.

In the end, her desperation forced her compliance. Her grandmother was terminally ill and evidently having second thoughts about dying before seeing her only living relative.

The letter's hint of monetary reward was no enticement. Aunt Jessie's estate was vast, as was the death benefit from Zachary's life insurance. Katie wanted only to know why she'd been shut out of Francine Chamberlain's life.

As the plane descended, Katie searched for something familiar. She was astonished by the freshly cultivated plots spreading in all directions. The acreages were likely called ranches here but the overall effect of the low, rolling hills wasn't so different from the farm country of Massachusetts.

Probably from geography class, Katie had come to think of Wyoming as barren, nothing like this fertile land rising toward hovering mountains.

She stared out the window as the runway rushed up to meet the plane.

A sturdy woman waited at the bottom of the steps. "Mrs. Meade?"

"Yes." Katie offered her hand.

The homely, weathered face eased into a warm smile. "I'm Pearl Carter. My husband and I work for your grandmother. I was doing errands in town so Jeremy asked me to meet your plane."

Katie suspected from her tone that no one would have come for her if there hadn't been another reason for driving into town. At least, she mused, she had been granted a reprieve from dealing firsthand with her grandmother.

"We'll find your bags over here." Pearl led the way toward a metal building.

"Who's Jeremy?" Katie asked as they walked.

"Mrs. Chamberlain's foreman. He's been with her so long, he's more like a son."

Katie considered this while her luggage was stashed beside rows of grocery bags in a battered station wagon. In minutes, Pearl left the airport via a narrow highway that bypassed the outskirts of Sheridan before continuing into the country.

"How was your trip? Were they as strict with security as they said?"

"It took forever at times. They even checked my shoes – twice."

Pearl glanced at her. "How odd."

Once they turned onto a gravel road where a sign announced *Radbourne Arabians* two miles ahead, Katie studied the fields intermittently visible beyond banks of trees on either side. She could see so little except encroaching vegetation that she gasped when they emerged into a wide valley. As they crossed a wooden bridge over a shallow stream, she questioned whether her reaction might be an instinctive recollection of *Radbourne*.

They passed a number of the elegant Arabs in small railed pastures. Wrought iron gates ushered them onto manicured grounds where acres of lawn swept down to the stream, then dropped toward a great complex of barns and paddocks barricaded by rock retaining walls. Katie imagined the back-breaking labor required to gather the stone from adjacent fields. The barns were a mix of past and present. Brick-fronted wooden stables offered a picturesque foreground for sleek modern facilities.

They proceeded along a cobbled drive toward a Gothic manor crowning the hillside. Again, Katie was at a loss. Surely she should remember this. There likely wasn't another house like this in all of Wyoming.

Green slate roofs over the main structure as well as balconies, and a massive round tower tempered the gray sandstone. Stone arches framing every window from first floor to third lent the hulking edifice a saving grace.

Katie shivered as she visualized the hostile look of the place in winter when the cottonwoods had gone stark and gray. Was it within these walls that she had lived through the nightmare?

Pearl inspected her while she parked. "Have you been to Wyoming before?"

"I lived here at *Radbourne* as a small child." Katie followed her up granite steps, past a wide, open porch. Bronze medallions inlaid double oak doors.

"Gives a body a start, don't it?" Pearl offered a smile."Were you too young to remember?"

"Yes."

They stepped into a vestibule opening into a wide hallway. A short way along the corridor, an oak staircase rose toward upper stories.

"Jeremy will see you now."

Anger shot through Katie at the idea of being cleared by the foreman before getting to the business she had come for. "I'll see my grandmother first."

"I'm sorry but Mrs. Chamberlain will still be sleeping. She naps much of the afternoon."

Katie pushed aside her impatience. "Oh, very well, I'll see the foreman then."

"He'll be in his office." Pearl forged ahead up the stairs.

Katie's heels clicked on the parquet floor. "What is it you do for my grandmother?"

"I keep house and prepare meals. When I'm needed, I help with her care."

Continuing, Katie noted the bronze ceiling in the hall *Which of her relatives was responsible for the bizarre decorating style?* On the landing, the steps veered to the right. A huge stained glass window filled much of the outside wall. "Mrs. Chamberlain is very proud that *Radbourne's* been in the same family since 1872," Pearl said. She halted before a door at the end of a wainscoted corridor.

At her knock, a tall, slightly built man appeared, his hand lingering on the doorknob while he inspected Katie.

She decided he was in his mid-thirties. For an instant something suggesting joyful recognition slid into his hard gray gaze before he stepped back.

Inside the tower's second level, Katie was entranced by the view of the mountains, drawn from window to window until she'd taken it all in. Only when she stopped at the last opening, did she realize Jeremy Foxworth still observed her with an intensity that made her look at him.

No smile softened his mouth, yet his voice brushed across her senses. "Was flying a royal pain today, Mrs. Meade?"

"Pretty much." She pulled her gaze toward a large grouping of Arabian photos against pale burlap. The framed prints had caught an awesome spirit and sexuality. She heard the foreman shifting his feet behind her. "Who took these?"

"Various photographers. Why?"

"I'm always comparing my work with others. I'm a photographer with a magazine in Boston."

"Are you?" The question conveyed no interest.

Katie watched him walk to the desk. He wore a tapered oxford cloth shirt, tan riding breeches, knee-high boots, all emphasizing the litheness of his lean frame. His clothing was another surprise. She'd hardly expected the foreman of the Wyoming ranch to be dressed for fox hunting. His bronzed face gave evidence of much time spent outdoors.

He busied himself with some papers, then sat on the corner of the desk. "Have a seat." He nodded toward an armchair.

Settled, she saw the portrait.

"My wife."

Katie didn't know whether to be dismayed or relieved. Ultimately, she was confused. She could see how much she resembled the woman. Why should that have caused this man to look at her the way he had when she first entered the office? His wife possessed Katie's narrow, finely drawn face and the same dark, dark tumble of hair, this woman's swept up in an Edwardian Pompadour. "Are her eyes blue?" Glancing up, she caught a startling depth of torment in his face.

"No, hers are violet. Yours are more Wedgewood blue." Once more, the fanciful observation held no emotion.

She wanted to run but held her ground. "You asked to see me."

He stood and circled the desk to sit in the chair behind. "Why have you come here, Mrs. Meade?"

"I'm curious about my life here."

He frowned. "You *lived* here?"

"Until I was five. Until my mother died."

"Why did you leave?"

"That's what I've come to find out."

He raised an eyebrow. "Why haven't you come back before? Why now when your grandmother's dying?"

Katie barely contained her anger. "Because I didn't even know my grandmother's name until I got her letter."

Slender fingers stroked his chin. "I find that hard to believe." His voice was low, almost menacing.

"Actually, I'm not concerned about what you believe. And I most definitely didn't come here so I'll be on hand when my grandmother dies. I wouldn't touch her money if I didn't have a cent to my name. But what business is that of yours?" She leapt from the chair and stood gripping the back.

"Francine's affairs are my business."

"Well, my affairs aren't, Mr. Foxworth. I'll thank you to remember that."

"There again, if you stir up old business that will cause Francine grief, it's my concern." Perplexity knit his brow. "I believe you've come for another reason. It's understandable that *Radbourne* would hold appeal now as it never did in the past..."

"You clearly don't intend to hear anything I tell you," Katie broke in, "so feel free to think whatever you like!" She spun toward the nearest window. "Please tend to whatever you do around here and stay out of what you know nothing about."

"Mrs Meade, I can't believe you're that naive. Until two weeks ago, I didn't know Francine had a granddaughter, let alone that she'd asked you here. If you think I'll step aside and let you take what's mine, hurting Francine in the process, you're sorely mistaken."

"Mr. Foxworth, hell-O! I just told you I'm not interested in my grandmother's money."

"I know what you told me. Now let me tell you this." He leaned forward, elbows on the desk, his look assessing. "To save us both a great deal of bother, I'm willing to make it worth your while, Mrs. Meade, to leave *Radbourne* right now, without seeing Francine. I'll drive you to the airport myself. You go back to Boston and think of this as a brief vacation." He smiled as though he amazed himself by coming up with such a clever solution.

"I'll leave when I've finished what I came for, but thanks so much for offering to bribe me. I'm sure my grandmother is very impressed with your resourcefulness."

Hands folded beneath his chin, he glared at her for at least a minute, then rose. "Very well, I think we understand each other, Mrs. Meade. I'll show you to your room."

Katie thought he might as well have shouted, "Let the games begin!" Though he escorted her into the hall with perfect manners, she had the impression that he would make her stay as difficult as possible.

Indeed, despite the fleeting awareness that had passed between them, a more unpleasant man she had yet to meet. She was amazed that she had felt the slightest attraction, let alone keen sexual tension. All the more bewildering because it had been years since any man had stirred a similar reaction.

Now Jeremy Foxworth marched down the corridor, and only paused at the landing to wait impatiently for her to catch up. "Francine has given you a bedroom on the third floor." He gestured up the steps. "Things are usually very casual around here," he continued as they climbed, "but Francine has always enjoyed dressing for dinner. So whenever she comes down, we humor her."

"What exactly do you mean by dressing for

dinner?"

"I'd have thought, coming from Boston, you'd know enough to wear something a bit formal. You did bring a dress or two."

"Of course. But what's the point? This is a Wyoming ranch."

"Ergo, those of us living here haven't been touched by civilization?" His faint smile mocked her. "If you want to discuss her eccentricities, do it with her. I'm just the messenger here."

Before Katie could comment further, she heard running footsteps on the stairs. Jeremy leaned over the banister and, as a child and a German shepherd bounded around the newel post, Katie thought she actually heard him chuckle.

"Daddy!" the little girl called, pigtails flying.

"Hi, Sweetheart." When the child dressed in riding breeches, boots and T-shirt, had bounced up the steps, he hugged her with one hand as she beamed up at him. "My daughter, Rebecca."

"Daddy, no one calls me that."

He shrugged. "We call her Becca."

"Hello, Becca." Katie smiled at the girl who examined her solemnly for a moment before her impish face broke into a gap-toothed grin.

"This is Mrs. Meade, Francine's granddaughter from Boston."

The grin widened, revealing more missing teeth. She possessed her father's light brown hair and the same gray eyes. She draped an arm over the huge, panting dog, eyeing him benignly. "Daddy, Patrick says I ride well enough to go out of the arena. May I?" She hopped up and down.

"Not by yourself."

The high spirits fled. "You've been saying that *forever.*"

"Next time I ride up in the hills, you may go with me. Okay?"

"Without the lead rope?"

He tugged one pigtail. "Without the lead rope."

"Oh, cool! Thank you, Daddy! I love you so much!" She stood on tiptoe as he bent to kiss her, both laughing at her restored good humor. "Want to go with us?" Her merry eyes consulted Katie.

"Perhaps Mrs. Meade doesn't ride." The thrust of Jeremy's chin announced he doubted she knew one end of a horse from the other.

"We do have horses in Boston, Mr. Foxworth." Katie smiled at Becca. I'd love to ride with you and see some of the ranch."

Becca observed her with new admiration.

"There's not that much land," Jeremy allowed.

"Then we'll see all of it."

Becca grinned. "May we go tomorrow, Daddy?"

"I don't know when I'll have time. And you have to work really hard with Patrick."

"I know that." She glanced at Katie and managed to look persecuted. "Riding in the arena is really boring."

"That's how future champions are made," he father reminded her. "Now go change. Remember, you have to wear a dress." The tolerant affection was gone, leaving tension.

She wrinkled her nose, then shrugged and

turned up the stairs with Jekyll ambling behind.

Watching her, Katie was swamped by memories. She had thought she was beyond reacting to reminders of another time and tried to pull herself together before Jeremy noticed.

No luck there. He studied her with new curiosity as they continued on but made no comment..

"Why's it such a big deal that Becca have formal riding lessons?"

"The number one reason is she loves the Arabians and riding.

"This is hardly Virginia or England. Wouldn't she be happier just riding through the hills?"

"I'm sure that will be her next favorite thing to do." He swung around. "Mrs. Meade, I appreciate your candid opinion, particularly since you're no doubt an authority on both ranch life and child rearing. But during your stay, you may find things aren't always what they seem." His eyes narrowed. "While we're on the subject, Mrs. Meade, you might want to research the Arabian horse." The final comment shouted his contempt.

"I'll get right on that." She made no effort to disguise her sarcasm.

He strode ahead to swing open a door. "Here you are." Turning on his heel, he retreated.

CHAPTER TWO

Katie fled into the bedroom and slammed the door. She tried to think why Jeremy assumed she was here to steal Francine's money.

Sinking into a wicker armchair, she noted the room's charm and urbanity. Not even an overly ornate brass bed defeated the magic. Like Jeremy's study, the furnishings created harmony among several periods and styles. Katie loved it.

She had planned to escape back to Boston the second she knew the truth. Now, she threw up her hands in acceptance. Jeremy hadn't called her here but his attitude might prove beneficial. A longer stay held its own appeal. She might stay long enough to gain a real perspective on her heritage.

She leaned down to unbuckle her sandals, spotted a vase of peach roses and wondered who had bothered to order a welcoming bouquet? Certainly not Jeremy. Her grandmother? Maybe but more likely Pearl doing her job as housekeeper.

Katie's laptop, camera case and tote bag sat on a table beside an old radiator. She found the rest of her luggage already in the closet. The bath was another time-warp space where antique fixtures looked at home with modern. Late sunshine streamed through stained glass windows, reflecting off lemon wallpaper. It was lovely.

Smiling at her change of mood, she headed for the shower. She was, in fact, looking forward to dinner and whatever adventure that promised.

Half an hour later, she stood before a cheval mirror dressed in white silk that fell softly to her ankles. She wore her hair down, dark and rippling over her shoulders. She selected blue earrings. Wedgewood blue. Renewed fury at Jeremy's comment jammed all circuits. Why should that iceberg throw out such a pleasing description and, more to the point, why should remembering undo her all over again?

With a deep breath, she seized the doorknob and stepped into the hush of the waiting house. Only a few steps along the hall, she was overcome by foreboding. Icy fingers of perspiration touched her neck and she was already running even as she looked back. The corridor was empty, yet a palpable energy pursued her past closed doors and on toward the landing.

She grabbed the banister above the stairs, staring at the carved panels of double oak doors, voices and images racing in the recesses of her memory, sounds and pictures she's heard and seen thousands of times. The focus was no clearer than in her nightmare, yet she was drawn closer until she touched one brass lever, her pulse hammering.

Even as the cold metal moved beneath her hand, she was fleeing toward the stairs. *My God, Oh, my God! That's where it happened! Behind those doors.*

Lurching to the banister, she leaned against it, over it, panting, afraid she was going to vomit. *How would she ever face whatever lay inside that room?* Already it had diminished her.

It was some minutes before she regained her equilibrium. Her breathing finally slowed and she shoved the encounter to the place where she kept the horror shackled. *How had she managed to do that all these years?* Shivering, she smoothed her dress and blotted the damp from her face with the back of her hand.

As she descended to the second floor, she heard Becca somewhere near Jeremy's office. A woman was practically screaming at the child. Anger rose in Katie. Evidently, Becca's mother was as ill tempered as her father.

Katie kept on, dismissing her own prick of pain. She must stop thinking of her own daughter every time she saw Becca, or her stay here would be as miserable as Jeremy wished.

The reminder of the foreman made her unwilling to encounter him before dinner so she took the rear stairs. When she stepped into the kitchen, Pearl jerked up her head from stirring something on the range.

"My goodness, Mrs. Meade, you gave me a start! Do you need something?"

"I wanted to thank you for the roses you put in my room. That was very thoughtful. They're gorgeous." Katie wondered why she was so flustered.

"I'd like to take credit but your grandmother ordered the roses and Jeremy put them in your bedroom."

Katie covered her disquiet at this news by walking to a wide window overlooking the rear grounds.

"You scared me coming through that door

from the stairs. No one uses that shortcut. Did you remember it from when you were little?"

Katie hadn't a clue. "Could be, I guess." She stared outside until she realized Pearl was talking and turned back.

"...after all these years. Your grandmother is making the supreme effort to meet you outside of her bedroom. Lately, she takes nearly all her meals there. Perhaps Jeremy told you her bedroom is the top of the tower."

"Why is that?"

She chuckled. "She *must* see everything that goes on down below."

"What's wrong with her exactly?"

"Heart disease. Her doctor can give you the details."

"How old is she?"

"Her attorney has determined she's seventy-nine." Pearl carried the pan from the stove to a butcher block where she paused to appraise Katie. "If Mrs. Chamberlain intends to intimidate you, she'll have her work cut out for her."

"I had no idea anyone in Wyoming felt obliged to dress for dinner."

"Mrs. Chamberlain puts great store in the glorious past. Her grandfather was among the elegant English who settled a lot of the country around here. The way I understand it, they decked themselves out in their finery at the slightest excuse. Your grandmother never took it that far, but she did enjoy the novelty from time to time. Now it's very much an occasion when she comes down." She began opening drawers to remove linens that she stacked on the counter. "It's fun serving dinner in the dining room as I rarely get Jeremy and the others out of the sun porch..."

As if on cue, Jeremy appeared, dressed in a gray flannel jacket the precise color of his eyes. "I thought I might find you here." His tone insinuated that she'd been hiding. "Would you like to join me for a drink before Francine comes down?"

Katie's stomach pitched at the thought but she realized Pearl would probably prefer giving her full attention to dinner, so she gave her a little nod and followed Jeremy into a front parlor.

"Pretty ghastly, isn't it?" He noted her disenchantment with the Victorian furniture upholstered in burgundy velvet.

"Unbelievable."

He raised the glass in his hand. "What would you like?"

"Bourbon."

He'd stepped to a sideboard that served as a bar when Becca, wearing a green dress, walked in, head down, arms folded tightly, the remnant of tears on her cheeks. Her hair, crimpy from being braided all day, fell past her waist. She went straight to her father, reached for his hand, leaning her head against him.

What's wrong with this picture? After seeing her earlier spark of mischief and fun, Katie could hardly bear Becca's dejection.

"Hi, sweetie." Jeremy cupped her chin, tipping it so he look at her before he handed Katie her drink.

More tears trembled at the edge of Becca's eyelids and she followed him to a loveseat where he sat down and she crawled into his lap, snuggling close.

Watching them, Katie couldn't fathom how Jeremy could stand by while his wife tormented their daughter. Renewed fury at him acerbated her headache, making her nauseous all over again.

Aware that she would throw up for sure if the bourbon came anywhere near her nose or mouth, she abandoned the glass on a window sill and chose a seat opposite the others.

Becca's head lay on Jeremy's shoulder. He held a glass of bourbon in one hand and stroked his daughter's hair with the other. "Was your grandmother giving you a hard time again?"

"Pearl was too busy to help me and Grandma was in such a hurry, she pulled my hair."

Katie felt instant sympathy, though she didn't understand Becca's plight. A new layer of anger mixed in with the rest – if Francine was well enough to care for Becca, she couldn't be on her deathbed.

"I'll talk to her."

"She won't listen." Before he could reply, a tall bony woman swept in as though she owned everything in sight. Her black dress hung on her like a sack. She stopped short, staring wild-eyed at Katie.

Jeremy made no move to get the new arrival a drink but proceeded to make introductions. "This is Katherine Meade, Francine's granddaughter. Cheryl is my mother-in-law. She's Francine's nurse and helps me with Becca."

"Hello." Katie was no less puzzled. *Where was Jeremy's wife?"* Nothing about this gaunt creature resembled the lovely portrait.

Ignoring her, Cheryl rounded on her son-in-law. "Jeremy, I want to talk to you about Becca. I'm becoming less and less amused by her theatrics. She needs to be taken in hand."

"Actually, I've been meaning to discuss Becca's care with you." His look was as frosty as his voice. "But this isn't the time. Is Francine down yet?"

"In the drawing room." Cheryl helped herself to a sizable bourbon. "She wants to see Mrs. Meade alone before dinner."

Katie stood up. "Great." To her astonishment, as she followed Cheryl out, Jeremy gave her a thumb's up and Becca grinned from ear to ear. The unexpected encouragement warmed her. Still, once Cheryl jabbed her finger toward the heavy pocket doors, she fought the impulse to flee. After perhaps a minute, she squared her shoulders and entered.

Her attention instantly riveted on Francine Chamberlain, seated grandly on a Victorian settee before the fireplace. Black chiffon with antique lace at the collar and cuffs camouflaged her ravaged body. Her blue-veined hands were heavy with diamonds and sapphires. Manicured nails were polished with bright pink polish. She'd obviously prepared for the meeting with great care. Snowy hair was well cut and freshly styled. Still, rouge on sunken cheeks did little to hide the pallor of illness.

Katie longed to remember a time when Francine was as familiar to her as Cheryl was to Becca. But she recalled nothing. The ancient, regal figure was a stranger.

Katie's own cerulean eyes was the sole feature she recognized. She considered whether her grandmother's white hair had once been as dark as hers.

"You are the spitting image of your mother." Francine's voice was steady and cultured.

How those eyes must have once manipulated men, Katie mused. Her grandmother had surely been a tall, striking woman. That realization reassured Katie somehow and she relaxed ever so slightly.

"I do not care to talk to you while you tower over me, so kindly sit."

Katie's anger flashed back. "Why have you sent for me?" She remained standing.

"I wonder." Francine continued her inspection. "You have a strength I did not expect. Why do I find that surprising? Perhaps because as a child, you resembled your mother but behaved like your father."

She didn't speak again for such a long time, Katie forgot herself and sat on a bench before the settee.

Francine's mouth twitched and Katie felt even more defensive. "The bigger question is, why have you come?"

"To find out why I was banished from my home."

"You need not concern yourself with the past."

Katie stared at her. "What an insulting thing to say! My past was entirely orchestrated by you, and I shouldn't concern myself with it? Have you lost your mind as well as your health?"

Ice glinted in the blue eyes. "I will thank you to mind your tone with me! We are blood whether we like it or not. And believe me I would have preferred leaving you in Boston where you couldn't hurt me."

Katie sensed Francine feared her somehow which was ludicrous considering it was Katie who was hurt nearly beyond healing. "Then why did you send for me?" She hated the ill-natured sparring that had begun so quickly.

"Because I'm dying. I won't see Christmas."

"What does that have to do with me? I probably loved it here until you exiled me. I hate you. Save for one reason, I don't want to be here."

She nodded with satisfaction that further set Katie's teeth on edge. "You want to know why I sent you away."

"How astute you are?"

"Well, there is no reason for you to know." She moved her hands restlessly, then folded them once more in her lap. "Believe me when I say you do not want to know. It took every ounce of fortitude and courage I still possess to write you that letter."

Now Katie was bewildered.

"You are my sole blood relative and my only means to insure the continuity of *Radbourne*. That is why you are here. I want you to stay long enough for me to know you. I want to learn if the strength I see is real. If it is and you have the courage, I will know you are up to the responsibility of my bequest...."

"I know nothing about Arabian horses and the last thing I want is to be stuck in this mausoleum." She realized she was shouting and took a visceral pleasure in it.

"Whether you care to acknowledge your responsibility, it exists. *Radbourne* belongs to you for no other reason than the blood in your veins. You look almost identical to what I looked like sixty years ago. You appear to have my grit and irreverence which is a compliment. Only time will tell if there is enough steel under all that beauty."

"I can't believe your...."

"Balls?"

Katie rolled her eyes but couldn't help giggling when her grandmother burst out in a peal of laughter."

"Oh, I do amuse myself." Francine fanned herself with her handkerchief.

"You're a riot." Katie regretted laughing. Now she felt like an idiot. "I'll not cool my heels here while you decide whether you find me worthy of your land. I don't give a damn about *Radbourne,* or the Chamberlain heritage. The only Chamberlain I know is you. What kind of woman lets her grandchild grow up with strangers? What loyalty do I owe you or *Radbourne?*"

"Do not tell me how maligned you were. If you knew why I sent you away, you would start screaming and maybe never stop. I doubt you would survive the shock of knowing. Just let it be. It took me over twenty years to reach a place where I could stomach contacting you. Twenty years of fighting my revulsion at being reminded of the past. Now I will not have you leave until I know if you are a Chamberlain or not."

Katie's mind reeled. "You'll not have me leave! Well, let me tell you this, madam. I'll leave whenever I choose. I'm not some pauper clamoring for cash."

"Ah, yes, you're quite the little heiress, aren't you?" Her gentian eyes glittered. "Tell me, have you recovered from the death of your *musician* husband?" The inflection spoke volumes on her prejudices.

"Quite."

"I understand you bore a daughter."

"I did." What a cross examination; clearly the woman had missed her calling.

"Wealth offers its own rewards, does it not? One need do nothing to support oneself. But then you chose not to be one of the idle rich. You have a respected career in your own right...."

"How do you know that?"

"I had you investigated, of course. I had lost track after Jessie died. Up until then, she sent me an update from time to time, though I must say, I never replied...."

"How fair was that? I knew nothing of you but you got your regular updates about me."

"As I said, wealth has its own rewards. When a miracle is needed, it is easy to come by. I wanted my granddaughter found and here you are. But for all I know, your estate may surpass my own, what with the hotel's settlement."

"How dare you speak of my family's death that way. Making it sound like I was happy to profit. You truly are revolting."

The old woman actually appeared taken

aback at that and seemed to have drifted off somewhere for a minute or two. "I went too far," she said at last. "I apologize. Was your marriage a success?"

"You're impossible! Anyone ever notice that but me?"

"Never mind." Francine continued looking past her into some unseen place. "In the end, family is all important. Only love and the memory of it endure. All else is fleeting."

"I've come here for one reason. You won't tell me the truth, so what possible reason did I have to stay? I'll go on line later and have my return ticket changed to tomorrow."

Francine was quiet, taking her measure for a time. "So we have reached a stalemate, have we? I brought you here for one reason. You came for another. You will only stay if I tell you something I cannot. It is quite a dilemma we find ourselves in, is it not?" Sadness crept into her voice. Her body slumped with exhaustion. "Katherine, believe me when I say the past must be left alone. If it meant nothing, you would have grown up here. There would be no question of your loyalty. You must let all this die with me!"

"If that is your stand, why in the name of God, did you send for me?"

"I've told you my reasons."

"I can't let the truth die with you. It's haunted me since I woke up in Boston desperately ill. I was sick for months and tormented by an ungodly nightmare that still terrifies me. For years, I wasn't strong enough to deal with the truth. But since I lost my family, I am."

Francine appraised her without comment, evidently calculating how far she could push..

Katie waited, daring to savor a tiny victory.

"Would you consider a compromise? If you will stay long enough for me to know you, know who my granddaughter is, I promise I will tell you what happened." She held up one bejeweled finger. "Providing I feel you are strong enough to know. I will never tell you if I am convinced it will destroy you."

New outrage rocked Katie. "What a bargain! I stay here while you fulfill your deathbed fantasy of rallying your family around you at the eleventh hour. How do I know you won't change your mind? After I've wasted my time, you'll still decide it's best if I don't know."

"I daresay we have to trust each other just a bit. If you care to know, I am no more enchanted with you than you are with me. Up until the moment you came through that door, I was positive I had made a dreadful mistake. But seeing myself in you encourages me."

"What about Jeremy Foxworth? I gather until I showed up, he assumed he would inherit *Radbourne.*"

"And he may. Only you will determine who is my final heir."

"I don't want to be put in that position! Jeremy loves this place and understands its value as I never will. Yet he sees me as a personal threat."

"Your insight is quite accurate. Jeremy is only concerned that *Radbourne* remain safe."

Katie considered this.

"I love Jeremy like a son but blood is

stronger in the end." Her gaze softened a little. "Jeremy and Becca are wealthy as it is so in that respect, it is immaterial whether you or he ends up owning *Radbourne*."

"What about his wife?"

"I am not at liberty to discuss Jeremy's personal life."

Katie barely managed to remain silent.

"You are the last of my blood."

Katie felt the trap snap shut. "We'll do it your way," she heard herself say. "I'll stay for awhile."

Francine betrayed little reaction, as though Katie's capitulation was no more than she expected. "I will do all I can to make your stay enjoyable. Even this house you dislike so much can be a pleasant place to spend one's time."

Katie decided to take her lead and concentrate on the mundane. "I've been wondering why the downstairs looks like a Victorian museum while the rooms I've seen upstairs actually have some taste."

Her grandmother appeared pleased to launch into explanation. "This may as well be your first lesson in *Radbourne* priorities. This house is a fine reminder of Wyoming's most colorful history. Over the years, Bill Cody, Teddy Roosevelt, John Pershing, Ernest Hemingway and other notables stayed at the Inn in Sheridan and visited *Radbourne* as well. The memory of that exciting past must never die!" A more pronounced tremor in her voice drew Katie's attention from inspecting the room's furnishings.

"There were so many beautiful homes when

young men made vast fortunes driving longhorns from Texas," she carried on, but *Radbourne* is the only place that survived in one family for three generations." Her eyes snapped. "So you see, my dear, it would be criminal to change a direct link with a grand past. Still, I am no more inspired by this ornamentation and gilt than you. So in the upper stories, I have allowed Jeremy to redo most every room we use. I have no talent for design myself but I admire what he has done with some truly hideous spaces."

Even as Katie felt a slight empathy toward Francine who wasn't so taken with the vulgar decoration after all, she was incredulous that Jeremy had such an eye for color and harmony.

"Unlike you, I cherish my heritage and will fight to preserve it."

Declining the challenge, Katie waited but apparently her grandmother was winding down.

"I will not keep you longer. I cannot have dinner after all." She clutched the arm of the settee, her face ashen beneath the rouge. "I am plumb done in."

"Shall I get Cheryl?"

"Just ring the bell there." She nodded at a button on the wall.

Katie complied, understanding the charade. Francine had been intent on overpowering her with her autocratic bearing even though it was a facade. Now that she'd gotten her way, her will had deserted her.

A muscular man entered without knocking, followed by a teenager pushing a wheelchair. There would be no spectacle. While Jeremy and Cheryl waited in the parlor, others would transfer Francine back to her tower.

"You may go now, Katie. I will see you tomorrow." She managed a wan smile. "I look forward to it. Go, go, now. Do not keep these good men waiting."

Torn between vexation and admiration for the woman who insisted the dreary routines of her illness be performed on her terms, Katie retreated into the hall. Quickly, before her grandmother emerged, she stepped through the next doorway. From that sanctuary, she watched as Francine was borne up the steps, all the while surveying her realm with a hauteur that made Katie smile.

The others emerged from the parlor, Jeremy glancing up the stairs. As she joined them, Katie decided it was standard procedure to allow Francine to play lady of the manor even though she was an invalid. She felt Jeremy's assessing look.

"How'd it go?"

"It was a start."

"Well, then, let's have dinner." He hurried down the corridor with Cheryl and Becca behind with the ever present shepherd. Katie brought up the rear.

They entered a dining room as grandiose as the rest of the ground floor. Jeremy seated Cheryl and Katie before ringing for Pearl.

As the meal proceeded in silence, Katie avoided Jeremy's brooding regard from the head of the table. The entree was poached salmon with dilled hollandaise. Considering Katie had expected a slab of roast beef or a thick, bloody steak, seafood for dinner at *Radbourne* was a nice surprise.

Becca remained out of sorts. Cheryl made no attempt to be civil to her or anyone else. The moment Pearl appeared with coffee, Cheryl announced it was Becca's bedtime.

"But, Daddy, I haven't had dessert."

"Francine's finished with dinner by now," Cheryl said, small black eyes holding the child in their cold stare. "If I don't get up there, she'll be ranting 'til hell won't have it."

"Go ahead." Jeremy's voice was very weary. "Becca can have dessert, then I'll put her to bed tonight."

With an annoying shrug, Cheryl departed. Katie excused herself and wandered into the front parlor. Her head felt like something was tearing things apart inside. She opened French doors onto a wide verandah. She stepped outside and leaned against the railing, watching the sun set over the Big Horns.

She drew a deep breath, letting the quiet ease her tension. There was an inviting serenity as the ranch fell under the spell of night. She would've loved to linger there longer but the autumn chill soon drove her back inside.

When she went past the dining room, Pearl was clearing the table. She wondered where the woman lived and what time she got home after serving dinner to Francine Chamberlain and her subjects. Turning up the stairs, she noted the faint, rosy glow through the stained glass window. At that moment, the house revealed a subdued grace that overshadowed its excesses.

She was stopped on the landing by Becca's voice, tired, yet defiant. Pulled against her will, she walked toward the child's bedroom. At the door, she saw that Jeremy had discarded his jacket and sat on another brass bed.

Propped on one elbow, he leaned toward Becca, already under a comforter. "...understand. Your grandmother's very sad so we have to be patient with her.

"She's sad because of my mom."

"That's right, sweet thing."

"But why's she so mean?"

"She's so worried about your mom she sometimes forgets how we feel. Neither she nor I behave well at times. Can you be patient with both of us?"

"I just want my mom to come home...."

"Becca, maybe she can't. I've told you that."

"I know...but I want her to."

"Come here." Jeremy opened his arms and she sought their haven.

She gazed up at him. "May I go see her?"

"No, no, no, you cannot go see your mom...not now." He tapped her head with one finger. "Is your memory gone? I've told you this many times before...." He rested his chin against her hair, his face haggard with fatigue and something else.

Katie remained in the hall. *What had happened to Jeremy's beautiful wife to cause this torment. Where was she?*

He held Becca until she slept. When he'd settled her under the covers, he sat looking at her for a long time.

Katie lost track of everything save the pain

in her head and her own sorrow. She became lost in thoughts of Ursel and was no longer aware of Jeremy until he stood beside her.

"Mrs. Meade, is it too much to ask that while you're
here, you don't spy on us?"

She ran from him, barely able to see through her tears. In her room, she collapsed on the bed, panicked by the turmoil in her brain. Her grief for Ursel had bordered on madness but when healing came, she thought it was complete. Now she was chilled with dread.

CHAPTER THREE

Despite Katie's exhaustion, the dream invaded her rest. When she'd crawled from the maze, she lay awake and trembling. Dawn seeped around her bed before she slept again. It was after eight when she woke to the sound of rain on the windows. Out of bed, she looked out at a foggy gray morning, the gloom deepening her frustration. What was she doing here?

After a shower, she felt a bit more reconciled to her plight. Recalling the dream, she knew she was there for the duration. No matter how long it took, she couldn't leave until she unraveled the puzzle.

Dressed in jeans and fisherman knit sweater, she ventured into the hall. The aroma of coffee led her down the rear stairs to the kitchen where Pearl again looked slightly unnerved by her entrance.

"Good morning, Mrs. Meade."

"Please call me Katie."

Pearl pointed toward a dining area in a solarium. "I'll bring coffee right along."

Katie approached a charming arrangement of rattan table and chairs among inviting palms and ferns that were a surprise in arid Wyoming. "Where is everyone?" she asked when she'd been served oatmeal and orange juice."Mrs.

Chamberlain's in her bedroom and Becca's off to school. Jeremy called the vet for a sick stallion. I believe Cheryl went to visit her daughter."

"Jeremy's wife?"

"Yes." Her manner was hesitant, almost guarded.

Katie was struck again by the air of mystery surrounding Jeremy's wife. "I understand she's ill."

"She has multiple sclerosis so she's in a nursing home in Sheridan. It's heartbreaking."

Katie's fingers tightened on her coffee cup. "When did she get sick?"

"Two years ago; she was only twenty-six."

"Then surely her condition can't have deteriorated that much."

"In Evelyn's case, it's happened much, much faster than usual...." Pearl turned back to the kitchen as though just realizing she'd said way too much about the matter.

While she ate, Katie considered what she'd learned. Knowing of his wife's illness, she could almost forgive Jeremy for his attitude yesterday.

After her second cup of coffee, she asked how she could get an email hookup in her bedroom

Pearl hurried to bring a notepad and pen. "Just jot down your address and I'll take care of it. Do you need a phone?"

"Not right away." Katie wrote what she thought might be a small joke for friends in Boston. *WAY WEST.*

Once Pearl left, Katie wandered through the downstairs, marveling anew at the time warp quality. After an hour or two, she went to the library.

Now there was no alarm today, only curiosity. Without hesitation, she walked into the oak-paneled room, leaving the door ajar. Her gaze slid over book-filled shelves. She stepped to a massive table centered on an antique Aubusson rug, noting a glass display case in the center.

With heavy drapes still closed, the room was dim and Katie had to lean close to make out the pistol inside the box. She shivered. She hated guns and hurried toward the door, but cold and weakness overtook her before she reached the hall. Her stomach convulsed and she couldn't pull free from whatever force shoved her back. Loud, garbled sounds assaulted her. Dark shadows moved just beyond her reach.

A voice broke the sickening enchantment. Shocked, she swung to face Jeremy beside her. She had no idea what he'd just said. As she sought the dubious solace of his eyes, she caught a shifting in his demeanor.

"I missed breakfast so Pearl's serving lunch early. If you'd care to join me...."

"Thanks, but I need to email the magazine."

He mulled over her excuse with an air of not being convinced. "All right, then." After observing her a moment longer, he turned to go.

"Maybe I'll look up the Arabian horse on the Internet," she said to his retreating back.

"There'll be a quiz later." He saluted her with two fingers as he strode out.

Katie still felt more charitable toward him. Because he'd freed her from the deja vu, she was even grateful for his intrusion.

She soon went to her room. After she'd

emailed her editor, she searched the web for information about Arabians. She located the Arabian Horse Trust that provided endless data. One article held her interest. *The Bedouin tribes of the desert, believing the horse to be a gift from God, told many romantic tales of the Arabian's beginnings. One such legend claims God created the desert south wind into a creature who "shall fly without wings...."*

She raised her eyes to the nearest window, surveying the foggy grounds. The mystical description delighted her. Maybe, she mused, if she hung around here long enough, she'd revere Arabs as the rest did. She continued reading until she eventually decided to visit her grandmother.

Her knock on Francine's door brought an instant, "Come in!" that sounded much like an order. When she stepped closer, no reaction invaded the blue eyes. Dressed in a pink robe, the old woman sat propped against pillows in her own brass bed.

"Did you buy your brass beds in bulk?"

Francine ignored her sarcasm. "Some people collect teapots. I collect brass beds. I want one for each bedroom and only need seven more. Perhaps I will get them before they carry me out feet first."

Katie could think of no reply so she inspected the room, the theme of which was roses – on the bedspread, drapes and wallpaper. Vases of fresh roses sat on nightstands and every mahogany chest and table

"Do you approve, or is this still too Victorian

for your taste?"

"I approve."

"I am charmed. I daresay you think I'm mad with all these roses."

"Do a zillion roses make one mad?"

"Old women are entitled to their eccentricities. Did Jeremy put roses in your bedroom as I asked?"

"Yes, thank you." Katie pulled a Windsor chair near the bed.

"You shall always have roses. Is your bedroom comfortable?"

"It's lovely."

"In Tyson Chamberlain's day that room was used by six maids."

"Tyson Chamberlain was your grandfather?"

Francine nodded. "From Nottinghamshire. He refused to marry my grandmother or let her come with him initially. He brought only Morgan, his valet, and it was more luck than good management the poor lad survived. Still, he proved to be as hardy as Tyson and killed two Indians himself. You can see their cabin out that window."

Katie rose and went closer. "That little place by the stream?"

"Correct. It must have been character building, two men living for ten years in a space not much bigger than my bedroom. It was not until 1882 that this house was finished. Tyson finally sent for my grandmother and twelve servants."

"Once she got here, your grandmother must've thought she was still in England. The lifestyle must've been pretty grand if twelve servants were required."

Francine studied her. "I think you might be correct about that."

Katie remained at the window. "What's the building that's the same design as this house?"

"Originally it was a carriage house. Now we use it as a garage but in a bit of whimsy, we still call it the carriage house."

Directly below the tower, a stone staircase angled down to a huge terrace. Jeremy descended more stone steps to a cobbled driveway, then strode across the lawn to a white rail fence beside the stream. A pale horse trotted out of the trees and hung its head over his shoulder.

"Bordeaux has decided to brave the rain for his carrots."

Katie saw that Jeremy was feeding the horse from a bunch of carrots in his hand.

"Bordeaux is Jeremy's stallion," Francine said. The year Jeremy turned twenty, the two of them took thirty-seven championships across the country. Bordeaux has done more to make *Radbourne* what it is today than anything else." The contentment in her voice sent unexpected warmth through Katie. "Now Bordeaux is retired and serves no purpose whatsoever except as comfort for Jeremy."

"Pearl told me about Evelyn Foxworth."

"Jeremy's affairs are none of your concern unless he tells you himself. Remember that."

Had she waited for Jeremy to tell her, Katie still wouldn't know why he roamed the place in such a foul humor. "How long has he lived here?"

"Since he was twelve. I almost married his father before I met your grandfather. As a girl I often visited an aunt in Denver. Charles Foxworth lived across the street. We fancied ourselves in love but while I attended Wellesley, I met Boyd Gellis in Boston."

"Excuse me, you went to Wellesley? I went there too."

"I would assume Jessie would have steered you in that direction."

"No, by fifth grade, I'd already decided to go there. Aunt Jessie just always knew that's where I wanted to go."

Francine pondered her with something suggesting approval. "That's quite remarkable, considering your mother was a graduate. Makes one think."

Katie was stunned by the coincidence. "You were talking about Jeremy's father," she presently prompted.

"Charles and I shared nothing but deep friendship. A little like Jo and Laurie in *Little Women*. Only Charles accepted the truth more readily than Laurie and we remained devoted even after we married others. He often visited here and when luck went against him, I couldn't save him, but I could take in Jeremy. His mother died in childbirth, so Jeremy is my son in every way but blood. Our bond is all the greater because his father and I loved and respected each other."

Now Katie understood Jeremy's animosity. If their places were reversed, she knew she'd feel the same. "He must be thrilled that you're talking of giving me what he's worked toward since he was twelve."

Francine's gaze darkened. "I haven't made

my final decision. Rest assured Jeremy has not been so devoted to me all these years because he was looking to line his pockets."

"Why don't you use your husband's name?"

"For the same reason you are here. Tyson Chamberlain risked his life for *Radbourne*; Boyd Gellis only had a half interest because he married me. If you prove worthy, a Chamberlain will carry on after I'm gone."

"If you think I'm going to start calling myself Katherine Chamberlain, you're crazy."

"That's hardly feasible since your maiden name was not Chamberlain. Tell me, did your daughter resemble you?"

"No. Ursel looked like her father. Very fair."

Apparently Francine wanted no more information about Zachary Meade. "Were you happy with Jessie?"

"Eventually. She tried hard to give me what I needed, but she wasn't my mother. When she took me away from here, she was a stranger. It was like I'd been kidnapped. She told me nothing about my family."

"She understood me when I told her to keep quiet."

Katie's anger was building but she knew Francine wouldn't be bullied into telling her anything. So the need to begin piecing the puzzle together herself gave her some control. She tried to sound offhand when she asked about the gun in the library.

"It belonged to Boyd."

"Is it one of the famous Colt .45s?"

"No, it is a good bit older, a Colt .44-40. The B Westerns were wrong to emphasize the .45. It did not come on the scene until the rowdy days here in the West were nearly finished."

"Why the locked case?"

"My husband never had a gun in the house that was not loaded, a common practice out here." She fell silent, studying Katie. "What were you doing in the library?"

"I spent the morning looking around the mansion. It's like a museum." She forced a teasing smile.

"Do you remember the library?"

"Should I?"

"While you lived here, your grandfather used it as an office. He doted on you. He had you up there with him a good part of the day and the night as well. He was truly incorrigible. When your mother put you to bed, you usually got up and ran to the library. Your grandfather let you stay and while he worked, you looked at books or curled up to sleep, with his coat as a blanket. When Christina marched in, ready for battle, Boyd invariably looked up like he had no idea what she was talking about. After she pointed you out, he feigned surprise and offered to carry you back to bed. She never did stop him from spoiling you. He thought you hung the moon and believed you would grow up to be *Radbourne's* premier show woman. Toward that end, when he rode out to check the mares and foals, he put you in front of him. By the time, you were five, you had likely ridden three hundred miles." The corner of her mouth twitched at the memory.

"My mother's name was Christina?"

"Did you not know that?:

"No, how would I? Aunt Jessie kept me totally in the dark."

 Glinting tears reflected the full measure of the old
woman's hostility but it was Katie who was left floundering, sitting still under her grandmother's silent censure.

She finally realized Francine wasn't likely to volunteer anything further unless Katie offered her something...but what? What were the rules of engagement between her and this ridiculous situation? This maddening
old woman?

As she'd listened to the talk of her grandfather's mild corruption of her as a small child, she had heard fondness in Francine's voice. Now she wanted to run away
from her accusations. Instead, she held her wintry gaze. Her grandmother's enmity confirmed her gut feeling that the library held the source of her nightmare. "I remember my grandfather."

"Do you?" The words felt like shards of steel.

"He was tall with a beard and wore tall boots. And he smelled of peppermint."

Francine wrinkled her nose. "An astute memory there. He was overly fond of peppermint schnapps."

"I don't remember my father."

"No loss in that. You were two when he died of cirrhosis. He was an utter wastrel and never supported your mother after the first year of their marriage. That is why they lived here. I, for one, was delighted when he died. If I had known what he was, I would have had the marriage annulled at the altar." She folded her hands under her chin, lost in the past. "Christina was so level headed, I could not fathom her falling for a rounder. In truth, I was as beguiled by him as she. He was exquisite, the handsomest man I have seen before or since. As fair as Christina was dark, with eyes blue as delft china. Beneath all that beauty and charm, he was hollow." Her gaze pierced still deeper. "What has brought you here, Katherine? You want to know why you were sent away when your mother died. After all these years, why is that so important? You appear to be capable young woman, with an admirable career...and an abundance of romantic opportunities I should think. Why bother with this...this obsession now?"

Katie told her about the nightmare.

Francine listened without a quiver of response. "Have you seen a psychiatrist?"

"Not since I was a child."

"Why not?"

Katie had no answer. She knew her grandmother would be unimpressed if she told her about all the times she'd longed to see someone then failed to make an appointment. Sometimes enough happiness returned to push back the dread. Sometimes she was in such despair, she couldn't function.

"If you had seen a competent doctor, you might have your answer now," Francine said after a time. "And I would have no means to keep you here."

Was that true? If Katie had learned the truth earlier, would she have avoided coming back? She searched her grandmother's face for the answer, but weariness had eroded her regal bearing. The damage of time and illness was all the more visible today. There was still little warmth or compassion.

Maybe Francine was right. Without the leverage of ignorance, Katie would've remained in Boston. Perhaps destiny was the final player. "What's wrong with you exactly?"

Her grandmother swung her face around as though the question was an interruption of her reverie. "My heart has worn out. There are all manner of symptoms we might discuss, but there's no point."

Katie didn't comment. Neither she nor Francine had more to say just then, yet they continued taking each other's measure for awhile longer. There was nothing companionable in their silence but more of a circling of adversaries hunting for vulnerable spots to attack in future. Finally, Cheryl arrived.

"You might let us know you're here instead of barging in without knocking," Francine snapped.

"Nurses don't knock." She brought water and some pills to the bed. "You know it's time for your nap. Take these or Dr. Remington will come deal with you himself."

There was apparently some truth in the threat because Francine swallowed the medication without further argument.

Cheryl turned to Katie. "She won't be talking much longer, so you can leave now."

Katie wondered how long she and Cheryl would cross paths before she said something truly profane to the woman.. "I was just leaving."

"When you want more sport, come beard the old lioness in her den." Francine managed a little wave of dismissal.

Katie smiled and let herself out. Perhaps she'd made a start with the irascible old woman but it was hard to tell.

Despite the pain stirred by this most recent exchange, she found herself intrigued anew and looked forward her next visit with her grandmother. She knew one thing for sure. Talking to her was never dull.

CHAPTER FOUR

While Katie ate lunch in the solarium the next day, Pearl told her Francine was so fatigued she'd been sleeping all morning. "The past couple weeks have taken more of a toll than Mrs. Chamberlain likes to admit. You must know she's been tuckered out since she wrote you that letter."

Katie thought her grandmother had disguised her exhaustion remarkably well. "Is that her lunch?" She nodded toward a tray Pearl had brought from the kitchen. "I can take it up."

"Thanks so much but I'll take her something later. This is for Cheryl."

"Is she with my grandmother?"

"She's in her own room. Why do you ask?"

"I was curious why she doesn't come down for lunch?"

"We've wondered the same thing." Pearl shrugged. "She seems to prefer eating alone."

Lucky for everyone else, Katie decided. Finished with her lunch, she wondered anew at Francine's choice of a nurse. Cheryl clearly saw herself more as queen than hired help. She promenaded around the house, dispensing cutting remarks to whomever she encountered. Katie assumed she'd ensconced herself at *Radbourne* because she was related to Jeremy's sick wife.

Cheryl had no rapport with anyone in the

house. She spent so much time in Sheridan, she avoided most of her nursing duties. More often than not, when Katie stopped by Francine's room, she found Pearl sitting with her. Francine was so heavily sedated now that Katie couldn't talk to her again all week. No big mystery why she was fatigued.

Though Pearl insisted such a long stretch of rain was rare in Wyoming, it continued for six days. With Cheryl and the Foxworths out of the house most days and Francine sleeping, Katie was on her own.

She was drawn to the library. Now she found serenity there instead of terror. She spent each morning curled in an armchair reading. One day, she found the picture books that had entertained her when she visited her grandfather twenty years ago.

After lunch, she holed up with her computer and continued researching Arabians. She soon received a message from Paula Quinn of the Arabian Horse Trust who enlightened her on many obscure horse-breeding subjects. Occasionally, from the computer table in her bedroom, she watched Jeremy and another man riding in the rain along the drive converging with the main road. Noting how nervous the horses were, she assumed they were youngsters being schooled to accept traffic and other scary challenges.

She found herself wishing she was out there with them. She hadn't ridden in five years but felt the old pull of exhilaration. She was forever grateful for the riding lessons Aunt Jessie had arranged that went on through college.

She longed to explore the ranch on horseback, but decided to forego sloshing around in the wet. Besides, she needed riding clothes since she hadn't packed her own. She lost no time finding a website that sold used English riding apparel.

These days, she rarely saw Jeremy in person except at dinner served in the sun porch. Candlelight cast shadows among the potted plants and rattan furniture. With rain dripping into the vines outside, the setting was pleasant. The company was not.

If Cheryl ate with them, Becca was silent. Cheryl made only rude comments. There was no warming of Jeremy's attitude toward Katie. He treated her and the others with a politeness that suggested he was miles away.

Saturday morning, Katie woke to sunshine pouring through her windows. She hurried out of bed, excited at the prospect of freedom outdoors. After a quick shower, she dressed in a T-shirt and sweater then pulled on the canvas riding breeches she had ordered. Once laundered and pressed, the pants looked like they'd been tailored for her. The English riding boots fit equally well. Katie was so anxious to find a horse, she escaped the manor without breakfast.

Outside, she walked down over the lawn toward the stream, pulling on riding gloves. She tipped her face to the sun. The air was cool and fresh-washed.

Bypassing the log cabin, she approached the rail fence where Bordeaux waited for her.

Nickering, Jeremy's old friend pushed his head against her, clearly expecting her to produce carrots.

"Sorry to disappoint you." She patted his neck, delighted with his friendly nature. There was evidence of his aristocratic bloodlines in the fluid, powerful contours of his body that belied his age. "Next time, buddy," she promised, moving on toward the wooden bridge spanning the stream, high and turbulent after the rain.

She followed a stone walkway to the barns, eventually finding the arena where Becca rode a small chestnut gelding around her instructor, the young man, Katie had seen schooling horses with Jeremy. Jekyll lay in the sawdust, his eyes never leaving Becca.

Watching, Katie saw that Becca rode well. Her impish face often so close to tears was relaxed and happy now. Katie saw that her pigtails were gone and her hair fell in soft blonde layers beneath her helmet.

Becca's high spirits encouraged Katie. Her fisherman knit sweater over faded jeans tucked into rubber riding boots might have been miniatures of Katie's. The scene reminded her of her own riding lessons years before.

The instructor spotted Katie and after motioning Becca to continue, came closer. "May I help you?" Friendly brown eyes inspected her.

She extended her hand. "Hi, I'm Katie Meade. Here visiting my grandmother."

Perception dawned in his narrow face. "Ah, yes, I was told you were here." He took her hand. "I'm so happy to meet you. I'm Patrick Morris, resident trainer and riding instructor." He glanced at Becca. "There we have *Radbourne Arabians'* future show person."

"I've been watching you and Jeremy riding out on the road this week."

"No kidding. We've been working some geldings that will be shipped to New York in two weeks. The time frame is a little tight so Jeremy took pity on me even though it meant working out in the rain."

"What will happen to those horses?"

"They're going to a facility on Long Island where they'll be in Park and English Pleasure training for a year or two. They'll be getting their Master's degrees so to speak. Ultimately, owners on the show circuit will pay amazing prices for them."

Because of her investigation on the internet, Katie knew what he was talking about. "I gather *Radbourne* horses are shown a great deal."

"We take at least two vans, often more, to over fifty shows every year."

"Do you ride in Park?" Katie recalled a breathtaking video of Park horses she'd found yesterday. "Park's my favorite event. All that fire and strutting." His eyes lit up. "Riding a seasoned Park horse is a trip – just a whole new dimension."

"I'd love to do that," Katie confided. "I've always ridden Hunt Seat. After seeing Park classes on the Web, that's one of my secret wishes."

"I can arrange that." Patrick appraised her. "Just let me know when."

"Thanks, I will."

He glanced at Becca. "I'll be happy when

that one can start showing. She's got what it takes, tenacity and that certain spark." He considered Katie musingly. "A young girl and a horse make a formidable team. Take two young riders, a boy and girl – I'll put my money on the girl every time." He watched Becca for a minute or so before gesturing for her to reverse directions which she did without missing a beat.

"Would you believe I didn't know people rode English out here?" Katie asked.

He laughed. "Nothing new there. People think we still get around by stagecoach. The truth is most riders in the West wouldn't use English tack on a bet. They think the whole idea is terribly funny. Besides, without a saddle horn, they'd be in trouble." He winked. "I thank God every day, Tyson Chamberlain hailed from England."

"So ranchers don't use Arabians?"

"Oh, Lord, no!" He put up one hand. "That's not entirely true. There are a few enlightened souls but not many who will give them a chance. That's ironic because Arabs can do just about anything the other breeds can, only much better." His smile grew rueful. "Let me tell you a little story. "Last spring, Jeremy and Mrs. Chamberlain sponsored an endurance ride. Know what that is?"

"The horses race to complete long courses in the shortest time."

"The distances vary. Ours was fifty miles with thirty entries. We had twenty-five Arabs which is pretty typical because endurance is their long suit. All those centuries in the desert created formidable stamina. So we thought the Arabs would be all over the top three places. We were dumbfounded when a kid on a Quarter Horse won. The rest of the day, we heard all the usual bull. Mrs. Chamberlain was in her wheelchair on the terrace, arguing with everyone, swearing there'd been some funny business somewhere during the ride."

He shook his head at the memory. "Jeremy was trying to keep her quiet but she kept on, pretty much accusing the winner of cheating. So the kid's parents loaded up him and the Quarter Horse and went home. By then, Jeremy was mad as hell, worried about the bad publicity but he was the first to admit Mrs. Chamberlain was probably right. He asked me to help him with a little investigation.

"It all cleared up pretty fast. The last half of the ride crossed land bordering *Radbourne* that belonged to the kid's parents. When Jeremy was putting the ride together, he paid a big fee to use their land. They wanted their son to enter and that was fine with Jeremy. The day before the ride, they asked if they could help us mark the trail. Later they showed the kid where he could cut across and still make the checkpoints." He spread his hands, palms up. "No more mystery."

"Mrs. Chamberlain wanted to call the media and set the record straight, but Jeremy would have none of that. He said it wouldn't change anyone's mind, and he didn't want to embarrass the kid. He didn't give a rip about the money, but he wanted to make a point with the parents. So he picked up the trophy and cash prize and told them not to discuss it with anyone. You'll find they're both ethical to a fault, but Jeremy's more tolerant of people's frailties than Mrs. Chamberlain."

Katie had seen no such leniency in Jeremy.

"So," Patrick continued, "the Arab remains principally a show animal. I personally think that's a tragedy, but that's our reality and why I have a job."

"Are *Radbourne* horses only shown in English classes?"

"Primarily. We enter the odd Western Pleasure class, but an Arab can flaunt his athletic ability so much better under English tack." He beckoned to Becca. "Want to say hi to my number one student?"

"Katie," Becca said, riding closer, "were you watching me?"

"Yes, and I think you're a fabulous rider."

She grinned. "This is Juniper." She leaned over to pat his sweaty neck.

"He's very pretty. When did you get your hair cut? I like it."

"Me too. Daddy took me this morning. Now Grandma can't pull my hair all the time. I can brush it myself," she finished with a jut of her chin, then concentrated on Katie. "Did you come to take me riding?"

"Take you riding?"

"Up in the hills. You said you'd go with me."

"I said I'd like to go when your dad takes you riding."

She frowned. "But he'll never get around to it...."

"Becca, I'm sure he'll take you soon."

She shook her head. "He wouldn't know if we went right now. He's visiting my mom and won't be back until after lunch. Couldn't we go, please?"

Katie implored Patrick who merely shrugged. "I'll probably get in big trouble with your dad."

"No, you won't. We'll just ride up the mountain a little way and then come right back."

"Make a note," Katie said to Patrick. "My good sense has just deserted me. Are you about finished with her?"

He grinned. "You're a brave soul. She's been out here for a couple hours and did a great job today. Shall I saddle another horse then?"

"Why not?" She could think of several reasons actually.

Becca whooped with delight and Katie reached up to give her a high five. "This is going to be so great."

Within minutes, Patrick brought out a second chestnut gelding. "This is Murphy. He's a sweet guy."

Katie hoped this didn't mean he was the resident plug.

Patrick adjusted her stirrups and walked them to the door. "Have fun."

With Jekyll trotting alongside, they rode up a trail that went past a small community of employees' cottages. They had nearly reached an open meadow when someone behind them shouted Becca's name.

Katie pulled up. "Damn! Here we go."

Becca whimpered beside her.

Jeremy strode along the trail, his open trench coat billowing behind him like Superman's cape. "What the hell do you think you're dong?" he demanded, coming abreast the horses.

"Going riding."

"Mrs. Meade, you were with me the other night when I told Becca I didn't want her riding outside the arena until I can go with her."

"Daddy, I made Katie do it. Don't blame her...." Becca trailed off in a flood of tears.

"I assumed you were merely concerned she not go alone!" said Katie. "And I'm sure you remember what little patience you had when you were seven."

"Mrs. Meade, when was I supposed to take Becca riding when it's been raining every day this week?"

"Stop calling me, Mrs. Meade! I don't think you're all that concerned about Becca going without you. You just don't want her riding with the enemy who's here to run you out." She stared him straight in the eye for several seconds. "Jeremy, I've told you I don't want this ranch. I've never been more adamant about anything in my life." She leaned back, still taking his measure. "Now, do we have your permission to finish our ride?"

"No." Noticing for the first time that Becca was crying, he put his arms on either side of her saddle.

"I...I asked, Katie," she said bleakly. "It wasn't her idea, so don't be mad at her, Daddy."

His shoulders relaxed slightly. "Sweetheart, I don't want to be mad at anyone, but you disobeyed me."

"I...I know." She scrubbed at her face with the back of her gloved hand. "I didn't think you'd ever have time to take us." Her arms went around his neck.

"Well, I would have, and I will." He inspected her a moment. "Will you forgive me for yelling, and go with me tomorrow?"

Her face brightened. "Really?"

"I promise."

"Katie too?"

He consulted her over his shoulder. "Katie too?" His look was almost apologetic.

His swift change of mood and the hint of warmth in his eyes threw Katie off balance. "I wouldn't want to miss the chance to look over the ranch."

"Wonderful," he said, sarcasm seeping through now. He lifted Becca down.

"You can still ride if you want," she said to Katie, pulling off her helmet.

"No, I'd rather wait until tomorrow." She dismounted, and the three of them walked the horses back toward the barns. Halfway there, Jeremy and Becca veered off along a converging walkway. Katie continued toward Patrick, who leaned on a wall of the arena. He came forward to take Murphy.

"That didn't work out too great," Katie said. "No wrath like a father scorned...or something."

"Jeremy's got a lot on his mind. He's not usually so damned rude." He led the horses through a wide doorway. "It's still early. Want to try riding a Park horse?"

After a moment's thought, she knew his suggestion was just what she wanted to do. "That'd be terrific!" She nodded in the direction Jeremy had gone. "Might the master take offense?"

"I won't tell if you don't. Now wait here and I'll be right back."

"Thanks." She realized he was an ally and found that reassuring.

He soon returned with an exquisite stallion, pure black, his huge velvet eyes filled with wisdom. "Here's Bohjalian." While Patrick adjusted the bridle, the long neck arched playfully against the bits.

This creature might have been sculpted from a huge block of ebony, every bone and muscle finely etched. "My God, he's gorgeous! Absolutely breathtaking!"

"He's been in school a long time, so he's quite the showman."

"I've never ridden a stallion," Katie said, a little nervous at the prospect.

"He's a perfect gentleman and won't give you any trouble. Arabs are the only stallions children under twelve are allowed to show."

"Really? I had no idea."

"In ancient Arabia, stallions shared their owners' tents with the family."

Katie imagined this pleasant picture of harmony between man and beast.

Patrick gave her a leg-up. "You'll find this English Pleasure saddle a little different from Hunt Seat."

"Once astride, Katie realized that was an understatement. She was accustomed to pushing against knee rolls; now she felt like she was sitting in a rocking chair.

"Ever ride bareback?" Patrick asked,

handing her a long riding whip.

"When I first started lessons, the instructor said it was the only way to learn balance. She wouldn't let us use saddles for two months."

"Wise lady. Now," he continued as though she was one of his students, "remember how it felt when you got the hang of riding bareback?"

"I do. When I learned to use my tailbone as my center of gravity, I had perfect balance. I loved it. I'd probably still be riding bareback if that woman hadn't decided it was time to master Hunt Seat and jumping."

He glanced at her one last time. "All set?"

"Ready for takeoff."

He laughed, gave a grand bow and gestured toward the arena. The stallion moved out with style, settling into a slow, rocking trot. She tapped him with the whip, pushing him forward while collecting him with light pressure on the reins. She was soon suspended in total bliss just as Patrick had described. Her heart soared. Leaning slightly to the left, she glanced down, astonished to see Boh's left leg extending straight out from his chest with each stride.

After half an hour, her legs were tired and the horse's hide glistened with sweat. She rode back to Patrick. Becca had rejoined him and both were clapping.

"You were magnificent!" Patrick said, holding Boh while she dismounted.

Becca ran over to take her hand. "You ride so great! Did you have an amazing teacher like Patrick?"

"I did." She noted with amusement that

Jeremy stood nearby, puzzled by what he had seen.

"I see the estranged heir can ride after all," he said. "Francine will be positively giddy."

Katie turned to Patrick. "Thank you so much for the ride. I loved it!" With a parting pat to Boh's shoulder, she turned to go. She heard Becca behind, then her warm little hand slipped into hers again. Jeremy followed a few paces back.

When they reached the manor, Katie leaned down to look at Becca. "I love your haircut. You look totally awesome." She kissed her fingertips and touched the end of her nose. "See you guys later."

Katie was brushing her hair into a loose ponytail the next morning when Becca knocked on her door. "I take it we're going to get an early start." She inspected her visitor while she affixed a clip to her hair.

"Yes, we are." Becca stepped inside, holding her helmet. "We're going to have a picnic on the mountain."

"Who's idea was that?"

"Mine." Becca beamed at her. "And Daddy agreed."

"I see." Katie collected her camera. "Is it cold up there?"

Becca nodded. "It's already snowed. Better take something nice and warm."

Katie grabbed her parka while Becca ran to hold the door. When they rounded the corner in the hall, Jekyll leapt out at them. Becca shrieked in delight and threw her arms around his neck.

Katie cringed. She'd nearly forgotten how

shrill little girls' voices could be.

Downstairs, sunshine flooded the solarium with warmth. Having finished breakfast, Jeremy sat drinking coffee. He rose and circled the table to hold Katie's chair, his manner guarded.

Katie unfolded her napkin and thanked Pearl who brought her oatmeal. She decided since Jeremy couldn't delay any longer showing her the ranch, he'd adopted a new neutrality. "How's my grandmother feeling?"

"No real change. It usually takes awhile for her to come around after a bad spell." He poured another cup of coffee and stared out through the vines, his weariness evident today.

"My mom's birthday is next week," Becca said, her spoon in the air. "May I go see her that day? Can we have a party? When Andrew broke his leg, he had a party in his hospital room." She waited for her father's reaction.

Katie let her gaze drift to Jeremy who sat studying Becca, a vein throbbing in his throat.

"Your mom's not up to a party this year. She's very tired and needs lots of sleep." He touched Becca's hand. "You and I'll go shopping for her present and you can make a beautiful card for me to take to her. That way, she'll know how much you love her."

Something in his eyes told Katie she'd know nothing of the kind. It was now clear that the multiple sclerosis had affected Evelyn's mind as well as her body." She shuddered at the thought.

Becca retreated, apparently unwilling to risk ruining their ride. "She loves my birthday cards."

He smiled, squeezing her hand. "Yes, she

does, sweetie, and she loves you."

What a confusing maze he was forced to navigate every day. Katie had a new awareness of his profound love for his daughter and the measures he'd take to protect her.

Becca finished her cereal and headed outside with Jekyll, donning her helmet as she went. Kathie gathered her things and stepped past Jeremy holding the door for her. He carried their lunch in saddlebags slung over his shoulder.

The autumn morning was gold perfection. Warm sunshine was delicious after so much rain. Even yesterday's clearing skies had come with a sharp wind that had now dissipated.

Katie laughed at Becca and Jekyll gamboling across the lawn toward the bridge. Jeremy stopped to give Bordeaux his carrots.

After the stallion crunched his snack, Jeremy hugged him, rubbing at dried mud clinging to his white hide. "Damn, you're such a pig." He turned a droll look at Katie. "One of the perks of retirement – rolling in the mud whenever he wants which is whenever there's mud." He gave the horse a farewell smack on the rump. "Knock yourself out, big guy."

They caught up with Becca and Jekyll on the footbridge where they stood looking down at the rushing water.

"Would Jekyll rescue her if she fell in?"

"In a heartbeat."

"Daddy, are there snapping turtles in this water?"

"I'm not sure. Maybe." He rested a hand on her shoulder as she walked beside him.

"Could we try to catch one? We could eat it. Andrew says it tastes like shrimp."

"Do you know what we'd have to do between the catching and eating?"

"We'd have to chop it or something."

"We'd have to butcher it." He hugged her against. "I don't know about you but I don't even want to think about butchering. Sawing bones, and the smell and all that blood. I'd just as soon have Pearl buy some shrimp. What do you think? If it's really important, I guess we could try catching a turtle."

Becca eyed him second. "I get it, Daddy. You don't want to catch a turtle, or eat it, or butcher it." She burst out laughing. "I don't either. *Grrrooosss!* But duhh, Daddy, don't patronize me."

"Excuse me." He grabbed her hands, swung her in a circle, then pulled her into his arms to plant a kiss on her lips. "I'll never patronize you again, my darling daughter."

"Yeah, sure, Daddy." She wrapped her arms around his neck.

When he put her down, Katie lowered her camera. She'd shot several pictures, catching the bond of respect and delight between Jeremy and his intrepid daughter. This lighthearted connection left her filled with a new sense of belonging. There was much for her to enjoy as she journeyed toward her resolution.

Becca gripped Jeremy's hand and soon took Katie's as well. Within minutes of arriving at the barns, they were underway with Becca in the lead on Juniper. Katie chose Murphy again because she'd discovered he was far from the slouch she'd feared but had an edgy spirit she liked. Jeremy rode a nervy gelding from the consignment bound for New York.

They were soon in thick woods above the barns, following a trail that intersected the trees and meadowland. Occasionally, they heard migrating geese overhead. When they came upon a herd of *Radbourne* broodmares, Katie turned her camera on them.

Jeremy watched her with interest. "When did you get into photography?"

"In boarding school, Aunt Jessie gave me a camera and I was hooked. I had no talent for anything else, except riding, and I couldn't imagine how I'd make a career from that."

"Little did you know your riding ability was in your genes."

"It's uncanny, I'll admit."

"I believe there're no coincidences."

"I tend to believe that also." Suddenly desperate to escape the turmoil in her mind, she urged Murphy into a canter."

Jeremy pulled abreast. As they climbed, the terrain grew rougher, the trail more obscure. The peaks of the Big Horns seemed to hang in the blue. When they stopped for Katie to take more pictures, she noticed a solitary cabin perhaps a half mile ahead. This one wasn't made of logs so it looked more like a cottage.

Jeremy noted her inspection. "Francine's hideaway. She had it built a few years after she married your grandfather. She brought him up here for a wild weekend every chance she got." His eyes teased Katie, underscoring the sexual implication.

"Seems a little remote." She focused her lens.

"That's the appeal, don't you think? She claimed she loved the cabin because no one could hear her." He winked.

"Maybe that's more than I need to know about my grandmother's sex life."

He laughed.

They cantered across the pasture land.

"Where are we going, Daddy?" Becca shouted.

"We'll ride part way up to the summit. We'll see if there's snow up there yet."

"I think there is," Becca said gravely.

They presently slowed their pace when they entered the higher foothills of the mountains, the trail narrowing until they rode single file with Jeremy in the lead, Becca next, and Katie bringing up the rear. Fog rolled in around them, obscuring the rocky ramparts higher up. After a time, spitting snow swirled about the thickening pines as they climbed. Katie was grateful she had heeded Becca's warning and worn a heavy coat.

They continued for an hour with the weather growing worse with each mile. Katie felt invigorated by the worsening conditions, the challenge of heading straight into potential danger, yet, confident in Jeremy's experience to keep them safe.

"We should head down," he said at last, stopping his horse beside the trail drifted over with accumulating snow now.

Katie took a few shots of the deteriorating weather before they headed back down. Becca looked around in amazement, catching the snow flakes on her tongue. "It's winter up here," she observed happily. "I told you."

They descended through clouds that slowly gave way to the fog once again. After awhile, shafts of sunlight pierced the billowing haze. Eventually, the clouds disintegrated into tatters that swept across the deepening blue of the sky.

After a time, they entered the open meadow again and stopped for lunch. They found a sizable flat rock that would serve as table and bench. Becca laid out chicken, salad, bread and cheese along with a thermos of hot chocolate and a bottle of peppermint schnapps.

Now that they were out of the cold above, the weather was still and fine, and Katie had the vague impression of being in a vacuum. She watched Jeremy pour hot chocolate into three paper cups, then he added schnapps to two before he gave the other to Becca.

Katie sat on the outcropping of the rock and he came to sit beside her. His hand brushed hers as he passed her a cup. She thought of her grandfather's affection for peppermint schnapps. *No coincidences?*

"That was amazing," she said.

Jeremy grinned. "I love to ride up there this time of year. Gives a whole new perspective."

Becca was so excited about all they had seen, she chattered nonstop through most of the meal, eliminating the chance for more real conversation. Nonetheless, it was one of the few enjoyable meals Katie had shared with the Foxworths. She savored the serenity, marveling at the difference in Becca whenever she was away from Cheryl.

"If I'm not a vet, I might be a photographer someday." Finished with her lunch, Becca sat in the curve of her father's arm, watching Katie snap their picture. "Do you make a lot of money?"

Katie laughed at Jeremy's groan. "Some photographers do. Why don't you take some pictures now?" She set the camera on Auto and passed it to her as she scrambled to her feet.

Becca peered through the lens. "I'll take a picture of you guys, but you have to move together more."

Katie glanced at Jeremy who watched her with a faint dare to a raised eyebrow that prompted her to slide closer. She called Jekyll who sat decorously against their knees. "That's very good," Becca declared and pressed the shutter. "This is sort of like painting pictures, isn't it?" She returned with the camera.

"It is. Both are a form of art. Take some more if you like. Get totally creative."

"Okay." She was soon posing Jekyll atop a rock.

"She is a treasure," Katie said. "A credit to her raising as Aunt Jessie would have said."

"I thank God for her every day. She's having a really hard time with her mother's illness."

"Like you?"

He nodded, watching Becca in silence for a time. "At least I have an adult's perception."

Without thinking, Katie put her hand on his. "I'm so sorry."

He squeezed her fingers. "Thanks."

Becca brought the camera back again. "Thanks so much, Katie," she said before turning to her father. "Can I ride Juniper now?"

"Yes, you *may* if you stay where we can see you." He pulled her down for a kiss. "Have fun, sweetie." When she'd ridden off across the meadow, he mixed two more hot drinks. "Now that she's been liberated, I may never get her back in the arena." He slid down, resting his back against the boulder. After Katie did the same, he observed her for a minute or so without speaking.

She was drawn into the depths of his compelling eyes.

"I think I've misjudged you, Katie. I refused to look beyond my prejudices and see why you've come here."

"I told you I'm not interested in Francine's money."

He sipped his drink, his gaze still steady. "You did but I wasn't listening. I'd already drawn my own conclusions." He smiled. "I'm trying to apologize. By way of explanation, I've lived at *Radbourne* for nineteen years but knew nothing about you until Francine asked me to mail that letter."

"Did you think about not mailing it?"

"No." His voice held more gravity than she expected. "She told me what was in it and why she was sending it. She even asked me if I thought she should. I said if it was important to her, yes. But I couldn't bear the thought of her being hurt."

"She hurt me."

"I can see something has hurt you badly. If it was Francine, how did she do it?"

"She sent me away when my mother died. I went to live with my Aunt Jessie who told me nothing about my life here. If it weren't for the nightmare, I might never have cared." She told him about the dream. "Now, I want to know."

"Have you talked to Francine since you got here?"

"She insists I don't want to know, implying something truly sinister about my mother's death." She watched Becca on the other side of the pasture. "Sometimes I'm terrified of remembering, but I have to or I'll never be free of it. I'm hoping with time, it will come back. I already know the library is where it happened."

"Is that old Colt in your dream?"

"No. Why?"

"When I found you looking at it the other day, you were in a total panic. That's when I knew I'd been wrong about your reasons for coming here."

"That episode makes no more sense than the rest of it." She shrugged. "I've reached a stalemate with my grandmother. She's promised to tell me if I stay long enough." She held up one finger. "That is, she will tell me *if* she decides I can handle the truth."

Amusement came into Jeremy's eyes. "That's our Francine. She can be the most impossible woman you or I will ever know. I've felt like strangling her on more than one occasion."

Katie nodded musingly "My guess is, she'll renege, but one thing's for sure, I'll not let her dump this ranch on me."

"If she decides to make you her heir, you'll

find she can be stubborn."

"So can I."

"A week ago, I was ready to do battle to protect Francine from you. Now it appears I don't know as much about the woman I've lived with since I was twelve, as I thought I did." His concerned look was like a caress, easing Katie's confusion. "I'm sorry she hurt you. Nonetheless, she saved me from a horrendous situation and has given me nothing but love and the opportunity to make the most of my life. I owe her my loyalty. So I must tell you, I won't let you wound her when she has so little time left." He reached for Katie's hand. "That said, I'll do whatever I can to help you." He pressed her palm to his mouth. "Don't be afraid to talk to me."

Katie wasn't angered by his frankness. Actually, she felt as though she'd gained a bit of firm ground among the shifting sands of her grandmother's moods.

"Francine told me you're a widow. What happened to your husband?"

She hadn't expected this sudden detour into personal territory. "He and our daughter, Ursel, died in a hotel fire. He was a musician playing in the lounge that night. I'd gone out of town on assignment so left Ursel with Zachary and a baby sitter. In the middle of the night, the police were at my door."

Jeremy digested the account, pain in his eyes. "I wonder if instant severing isn't kinder." He still looked at her intently when he realized what he'd just said and grasped her arms. "Oh, Katie, I'm sorry! What a stupid thing to say."

"It's okay, I know what you meant and I think you're right." She waited, unsure if he'd confide the rest. "Pearl told me Evelyn's illness is already advanced," she said when he didn't elaborate.

"It's been bizarre. After she got sick, she was in a wheelchair in six months, bedridden in nine."

"How long has she been in the nursing home?"

"Two years. Cheryl and I kept her at *Radbourne* longer than we should have."

"Cheryl's lived at *Radbourne* for awhile then?"

"Since Evelyn got sick. I met Evelyn at Harvard and got to know her mother who was working as a private nurse. Cheryl's a bad mother and a worse mother-in-law. Still, we've come to understand each other to some degree."

Katie didn't want to argue with him about Cheryl so she made no comment.

After awhile, he turned to appraise her. "Katie, I've very much enjoyed our talk and getting to know you."

"Thank you for a lovely time."

He smiled. "You're welcome. Now we should start back." He got to his feet in one lithe motion and reached down to pull Katie up, then began gathering the remnants of lunch into the saddlebags.

Katie stood looking across the meadow where Becca still rode in sedate circles. "She gives me a glimpse of my life if I hadn't lost Ursel," she said when he came to stand beside her.

"That must hurt."

"It did at first. When I heard you talking to Becca in her bedroom the night I arrived, I thought I'd die."

"Katie, I'm so sorry I was so obnoxious that night. I'm usually not such an ass."

"There was no way you could know." This man she had thought incapable of warmth was looking at her with such sensitivity now. "You're raising a delightful little girl."

"Thanks." He caught her in a quick one-armed hug as they walked to the horses.

When they were mounted, they sat watching Becca on the other side of the field.

"I was stunned to see how you rode Boh. I wanted to tell you."

Katie smiled at the memory, snuggling into the fur-lined hood of her parka. A frigid wind had come up again. "I'm proud I could do it."

He waited.

"I took riding lessons forever and became proficient enough to enter and win Dressage and Hunt Seat classes in major shows. I even had aspirations for awhile of trying to make the U.S. Olympic Team but that didn't work out and other matters intruded. So the day I decided to ride Boh, I hadn't ridden any horse for a long time."

"Could've fooled me," Jeremy said.

"All that training must have stayed with me somehow. I saw a Park Horse class on the Web and it just blew my mind." She pressed her fists together under her chin, still reliving the pure joy of her ride on the black stallion.

"I hope I didn't ruin it for you yesterday

with my horrible attitude. I can be an insensitive bastard."

"You hurt my feelings because you made it sound like I had some ulterior motive for not telling you I could ride."

He shook his head and reached between the horses for her hand. "I've nothing but admiration for your riding skill. It seems pretty miraculous to me that you grew up two thousand miles from *Radbourne,* yet turn out a better rider than anyone here."

"Maybe destiny means more than we know."

He stared toward the distant mountains before looking back. "I think I said this already, but I believe nothing happens by chance. Know what I mean?"

"Yes, I do. Your theory creates a whole new value system for life." She felt a new sense of goodwill at the easy way they were talking. "Do you believe in reincarnation?"

"I'm not sure about that, though I've always leaned in that direction. I do know there's an afterlife, not some patch of clouds where everyone's playing harps, but a real world similar to ours. Only without pain, and unlimited opportunity for spiritual growth."

"How do you know that?"

"Because Francine's father came back to tell her. A week or so after he died, he showed up in the kitchen and they talked for ten minutes. She didn't have a maid at the time so she was washing dishes."

"That would be Thomas?"

"Yes, your great-grandfather. He believed in predestination so evidently wasn't surprised when he died young. I share his belief that everything is laid out for us before we're born. You know the story of Jesus counting every hair on our heads?"

Katie nodded. "So you believe Evelyn got sick because it was preordained?"

"Yes."

"Does that help you accept it?"

"When I stop railing against God and accept what I can't change. But you might have noticed I'm quite fond of tilting at windmills." He squeezed her hand. "I'm working on it."

Becca had come closer, pulling up the gelding. "Isn't it nice here, Daddy? Can we come again soon?"

"Yes, we can, sweet thing. You ready to go home now?"

Nodding, she urged Juniper into a canter, heading for the trail.

Jeremy and Katie followed at a brisk walk that still allowed conversation.

"Francine told me you and Bordeaux won a ton of trophies when you were twenty. Weren't you at Harvard then?"

"Your grandmother and I had one hell of a battle over where I was going to college. I thought the whole idea was a colossal waste of time but she was a brick wall. Eventually, I agreed on Harvard if I took Bordeaux with me. We finally had a stallion to put us on the map and I wasn't about to screw that up."

"You must have been so proud of him and yourself for having the vision to use him to show everyone how magnificent *Radbourne* horses are."

He slanted a quick glance at her that was difficult to read. They soon picked up the pace to catch Becca already descending toward the ranch.

When they'd reached the bottom of the trail, he pointed out the cottage where Pearl lived, and identified the homes of other ranch employees. They dismounted in front of the arena where stable boys collected the horses.

As Jeremy and Katie walked to the manor, Becca skipped between them. "That was so fun!"

"I thought so too," Katie said.

Once the three of them reached the manor and parted upstairs, Katie continued to her bedroom, her thoughts sliding back through the day. There was no denying the emotional rapport between her and Jeremy, not to mention an undercurrent of physical attraction.

Mixed with the torment, his gray eyes had held unguarded desire. Even now, she felt her own response.

Apart from her basic female reaction, she hadn't a clue how she felt about him. During her marriage and after, she couldn't fathom the appeal of casual sex. But after she healed from Zachary's death, she'd thought an uncomplicated affair might hold its own rewards.

Should she ever set aside reservations long enough to accept what she'd read in Jeremy's eyes, she knew the liaison wouldn't be casual but very complicated.

CHAPTER FIVE

Francine rallied from her fatigue more slowly than Pearl predicted. For many days, whenever Katie went to her room, she found her sleeping, but finally, she could talk a little again.

As before, Francine was jovial at times, on other occasions, irascible, spoiling for a fight. Despite misgivings, Katie was beginning to like her. The old woman was no longer the faceless mystery she'd come to despise but more a stranger becoming familiar as layers of personality were revealed. Katie perceived a mellowing in her grandmother as well.

Still, Francine tired quickly and sent Katie away after only a few minutes. Most days, Katie left the sickroom frustrated, filled with impatience. But over the span of a week or two, although there was still no foreseeable end to the waiting, she made peace with it, aware that what she'd come for couldn't be hurried.

She was drawn outside, into Indian summer. The ranch was suspended in the drama of changing seasons. Katie was accustomed to New England's spectacular autumn. Here the transformation of cottonwoods and willows, aspen and box elders was subtle, yet somehow more stark and final.

Katie had no memory of Wyoming in

winter, yet she sensed the violence to come and hungered for it. What would a blizzard be like here below the mountains? Would she still be here when the first one swept over *Radbourne?*

She explored the ranch on foot and horseback, taking hundreds of pictures, always searching, struggling to find some image to help her decipher the puzzle. The land affected her in ways she hadn't expected. The stillness flowed through her, bringing a serenity she'd never experienced before. There was a fierce pull as well, something primal and all-consuming. The raw power shouted its challenge to her but she felt inadequate to face it....this was Jeremy's world.

After their outing on the mountain, Jeremy had drawn away from Katie. He avoided being alone with her and this increased her loneliness, even as she welcomed the opportunity to put the situation into perspective.

Though she still rarely saw Jeremy except at meals, Becca seldom left her side unless asleep or in school. Sometimes Patrick excused his pupil from the arena so she and Katie could ride up the mountain. Every evening before dinner, Becca brought her magic markers and school assignments to Katie's room.

Tonight Katie sat curled in the wicker armchair, watching Becca stretched out on the rug, drawing a purple dragon. Jekyll lay sleeping beside her.

"My mom didn't like the card we made for her birthday."

"Really?" Katie thought back to the hour spent on design and execution of the giant poster board card. She had provided photos that Becca glued among her drawings – flamboyant images of family, Jekyll and Juniper.

"If she'd liked it, she'd have called me." Her concentration told Katie she knew that an impossible fantasy. Still, she pressed on. "Sick people have phones right by their beds." She bent over her drawing for a space of minutes before looking up, her face taut with longing. "Every night when I say my prayers, I ask Jesus to let her get better. And every day, I wish it."

Katie's heart contracted.

"You have kids?"

"No."

"You act like a mother. Lots of people don't. Like Grandma. You think she was mean to my mom when she was little?"

"I hope not." Katie wished she could span the breach in Becca's understanding. "I had a husband once and a little girl. They died."

Becca's head jerked up. "What was her name?"

"Ursel."

"Was she sick?" A trace of fear hovered in her eyes.

"No, it was an accident."

"I'm sorry." Becca closed the sketchbook. "Please tell me about her." She hugged her drawn-up knees.

Katie was caught off guard but let her mind edge back. She wanted to share Ursel, the delight of one splendid year when she'd glimpsed what her baby would become.

She told her about Ursel's bright, quick

mind that was enchanted by Zachary's music and so much else day to day. She talked about her daughter's death and the long months of grief. Now instead of pain so crippling it robbed her of will, she was thankful for having known pure joy and she shared this as well.

When she fell silent, she noticed Becca had resumed her drawing.

"Is my mom going to die?"

"Honey, I don't know."

"Daddy won't tell me when she's coming home. She's really, really sick, isn't she?"

"Yes."

"She couldn't ever get out of bed before they took her away. Sometimes when I went into her room, she didn't know I was her little girl, Becca. She just got scared and yelled." Tears ran down her cheeks. "I didn't mean to scare her. But she scared me when she yelled."

Katie drew her onto her lap. "She didn't mean to scare you either. It was only because she was so sick." She smoothed back the silky hair, resting her cheek against it.

Becca eventually lifted her face, consulting Katie through her tears. "Did it hurt this much when Ursel died? And her daddy?"

"Yes, it did." She handed her a tissue.

"My mom had to go away because of me."

"Oh, no, Becca. Why do you think that?"

"Because Grandma said I had to be quiet and not run in the hall with Jekyll. I forgot and was too noisy. My mom couldn't get well.."

Katie wrapped her close again. "It wasn't anyone's fault that your mom got sicker. Not yours, not your dad's. It just happened. No one knows why." She remembered Jeremy's theory of preordination.

Becca shuddered.

Rage at Cheryl moved through Katie. She set Becca back a little, searching her weary eyes. "For awhile, I thought I was to blame when my family died but I finally understood I wasn't."

Becca watched her tensely.

"Did you ever tell your dad what you told me?"

She shook her head.

"I think telling him would make you feel better. I know he'll say just what I did."

As Becca let her head drop against her shoulder, Katie dared hope she might have won a tiny battle against her demons. Nonetheless, she was uneasy. In only a few days, she had picked up on the growing bond of dependency in Becca The pull of it unsettled Katie and she knew she should probably push her away. Otherwise, she would only add to Becca's pain when she returned to Boston. Nevertheless, she knew she wouldn't extricate herself from this charming child who allowed her to recapture something of Ursel.

Becca snuggled closer. "I won't think that anymore."

"I'm glad." Katie kissed the top of her head.

Despite her good intentions, Becca shivered again. "It was so scary. All that blood and yelling."

Before Katie could inquire about that, Jeremy appeared in the doorway. He came every night recently to escort them to dinner and always watched them briefly with a pensive, searching expression. Now he sat on the end of Katie's bed. "Is this how we do homework these days?"

"I'm all finished." Becca jumped down and showed him the purple dragon. "And I drew a picture for Francine." She picked up her sketchbook "It's Ursel, Katie's baby. Francine's granddaughter." She stood beside Jeremy as he looked at the drawing.

"Great-granddaughter," he corrected gently, lifting his hands to wipe away her tears with his thumbs. "It's beautiful, hon. She'll love it."

"May I visit Francine tomorrow with Katie so I can give it to her?"

"Of course, Katie said. "We'll take her breakfast before you go to school."

"Cool." She put the picture away, then skipped into the hall with Jekyll on her heels.

Katie felt Jeremy's gaze, steady, thoughtful as she stepped past him to door.

Cheryl waited beside the dinner table. Becca's high spirits instantly evaporated.

Futility filled Katie anew. *Why didn't Jeremy see?* Studying him once they were seated, she realized he did see but was helpless to change anything.

Cheryl was employed by Francine. Jeremy would run interference to protect Becca but beyond that, he wouldn't venture. It wasn't weakness that restrained him. Katie couldn't find the correct label. As always she was relieved when the meal ended.

Cheryl turned to Becca who was scooping up the last of her raspberry sherbet. "Come on!

It's time for your bath." She wrinkled her nose. "Which you should have had when you came in from the barn. The odor of horse is distinctly unappealing at the dinner table."

Becca squirmed, beseeching Jeremy who crossed his eyes, instantly sending her into a fit of giggles. Katie was so surprised she nearly choked on her iced tea. She watched Jeremy lean close, whispering something to Becca that stopped her laughter but left her grinning.

For several nights, Jeremy had tended to Becca's bath and bedtime himself, a ploy Katie suspected was to ensure he wasn't alone with *her.* Something had shifted tonight, and Becca was being sent upstairs with Cheryl.

"I couldn't have my bath before," Becca said. "I was doing my homework."

"Indeed." Cheryl wrenched back her chair and stood up.

"I'd be happy to take care of Becca," Katie said.

The black eyes locked on her. "That won't be necessary!"

"Becca and I are reading the new *Harry Potter*," Jeremy said. "Be sure to read another chapter tonight."

Cheryl's bony hands seized the back of her chair. "I won't have time, what with settling Francine as well."

"Make time, after you've seen to Francine. Becca can play until you're finished." His steel gray gaze conveyed open challenge.

Cheryl's smile was forced, but still an improvement. "Very well, young lady, we'll have a chapter of *Harry.*"

Becca wasn't encouraged but slid from her chair, and after kissing Jeremy, threw her arms around Katie. "Will you have breakfast with Daddy and me?" she whispered.

Over her shoulder, Katie noted Cheryl's annoyance. "Of course I will, then we'll take breakfast to Francine. Goodnight, sweetheart."

Becca drew away to look at her once more, kissed her cheek and was gone.

Katie sipped her tea, wondering at Jeremy's change of mood. "Why do you think I'm a threat to Cheryl?"

"Because Becca loves you."

"But Cheryl's her grandmother. I'm her new best friend, a passing fancy who'll soon be leaving."

An unreadable emotion crept into Jeremy's gaze. "By nature, Cheryl is a woman of hard angles, mentally and physically. But she does love Becca and I think it's important that they spend time together."

Katie could have offered her own opinion of the subject but declined.

Jeremy finished his coffee. "There's a splendid moon tonight. Come with me to visit Bordeaux."

They went to the kitchen for carrots, then stepped onto the rear terrace bathed in silver-white moon glow. Jeremy gripped Katie's hand as they walked down the stone steps. At the bottom, she stopped and looked back at the moon suspended in cottonwoods behind the manor. An interweaving of black and white created enchantment.

They'd nearly crossed the lawn when Bordeaux crashed out of the trees.

"Social guy, isn't he?"

He chuckled. "He's always liked being the center of attention," he said when the stallion thrust his head over the fence, a pale phantom in the moonlight. "He was glorious in his prime and he knew it. You can still see it in the fire in his eyes and the way he moves."

The awe and respect in his voice stirred wonder in Katie. She'd never felt any particular empathy for the cycles of nature. Now she could comprehend the force that made Bordeaux an unparalleled show and breeding animal.

She was struck by the blatant sexuality and power. Caught in the peculiar spell, she was acutely conscious of Jeremy's masculinity, a mix of leather, soap and lemon aftershave. The current between them that had ebbed and flowed was now a tangible allure that left her trembling.

She knew she should run from him and all the drama in his life. Despite the heat in her blood, she shivered and his arms went around her, holding her to him. She knew he would kiss her seconds before his hands came up to cradle her face. She wanted it, longed to feel, to be touched.

At first his mouth was tender, unbearably sweet as he molded her against him. But then came the violence of need and danger, and he set her away, looking hard into her face. Finally, he leaned his forehead against hers a moment, then tucked her arm through his as they headed back to the house. Inside, standing at the bottom of the stairs, his eyes were guarded even as he smiled at her. "Come have a brandy with me." Without waiting for her response, he guided her to the drawing room.

While he lit the prepared kindling on the fireplace hearth, she settled on the settee where her grandmother had sat so regally. Once the flames warmed the cold space, it didn't seem so forbidding.

Jeremy soon joined her, bringing snifters of brandy from the mahogany bar between two rear windows. He tapped his glass against hers. "You must've been unnerved by your audience with Francine."

"Yes, but I was determined not to let it show."

"I remember. Think she's going to tell you what you need to know?"

"We haven't talked a lot since she's been sleeping so much."

"She's doing a lot better now so maybe you'll somewhere with her soon."

"You'll miss her terribly, won't you?"

"Like a mother." He sat watching her. "Do you resent what I had with Francine, what you couldn't? What you can't remember with your mother?"

"As an adult I know that's ridiculous, but there's the child in me who hates it."

He lifted her hand, holding it between both of his. "It must have been hell for you. I think about Becca when she was five and I can't imagine what that kind of pain would've done to her. She's having a dreadful enough time now and she's seven and her mother's alive."

"I know it was hell for me, yet there's no clear memory, even of the suffering. I was terribly ill and alone and so afraid, but I was somehow detached from it all. When I finally surfaced, I'd forgotten everything. A professor at college told me that forgetting is the mind's safety valve, a way to siphon off some of the agony."

"Do you remember your grandfather?"

"Vaguely. Seems he was the one person who thought I hung the moon."

Jeremy smiled.

"How about you? Were you close to your father?"

"Not really. He was a kind, gentle man and did his best by me, but my mother's death was the beginning of the end for him. He tried hard to hide it, but he blamed me. When I came here, I hauled along a huge load of guilt. Francine, however, cleared it away in short order. She gave me permission to really think about my mother and grieve for her. My father never talked about her, so I didn't either. I talked to Francine for hours and hours, and that saved me."

"Becca said something earlier, when we were talking about her mom....something about a lot of blood and yelling. What's that about?"

A grim smile twisted his mouth as he leaned forward, fingers steepled under his chin. "Becca never misses a thing, bless her heart. During the last few months Evelyn was still here at *Radbourne*, her cycle was really screwed up. A couple times she hemorrhaged. As I recall, Becca's got it right.

Cheryl and I did plenty of yelling while we waited for the ambulance that last day. And the blood...Jesus! I don't even remember Becca being with us. She must've thought her mom was going to die right then."

"She told me Cheryl blames her for her mom being sick."

Jeremy's back stiffened. "That's not true!"

She shrugged. "She said Cheryl told her she had to be quiet so her mom could get well. But sometimes she forgot and ran in the hall with Jekyll."

He lifted his gaze to the ceiling, blowing his breath out. "This is all so damn hard." He looked at Katie. "Why would Cheryl say that to her?"

"Because everyone needs someone to blame."

"But her granddaughter she loves so dearly?"

"It's no different than what your father did to you?"

He didn't disagree. He stood and moved to the fireplace where he stood with one arm propped against the mantel. "It was stupid keeping Evelyn here so long but I couldn't let go and give up. Toward the end, she was also going blind, and whenever anyone went near, she basically freaked. After we got a hospital bed, I slept beside her on a futon. If I coughed or made any sound, she started screaming." He turned his head to consult Katie who'd come to stand beside him. "Why didn't I see what it was doing to Becca? What else didn't I see? The remission she's reached now might have come sooner." The despair in his voice reminded Katie of what she was spared by Zachary's quick death. The swift end had been agony, yet in time, she tapped into a reservoir of strength and confidence, and finally a place of peace.

Now caught between the past and future, bereft of hope and reason, Jeremy was denied such healing. For some time, he seemed oblivious to her. Finally, he reached out and drew her to him with one arm.

CHAPTER SIX

The next morning, Katie opened her eyes to find Becca's face inches from hers. Jekyll sat close by, studying her curiously, his tail beating a happy cadence on the floor.

"I thought maybe you wanted to sleep some more."

Katie fondled Jekyll's ears. "What time is it?"

"The sun's up."

Katie glanced at the bedside clock with a sigh. Five to six. "Why are you up so early?"

"You said we would go see Francine."

"Not at six in the morning. Why don't you go tell Pearl we'll take Francine's breakfast to her later. Tell her to let Cheryl know." By using Pearl as intermediary, she hoped to avoid a skirmish with Cheryll. "Okay? I'll be down soon."

"Okay!" Becca threw out her arms and spun in circles into the hall.

Katie shook her head ruefully, then got out of bed. While she showered, her thoughts edged back to last night and the hours she had spent with Jeremy. She could no longer deny what was happening between them.

She had to admit to herself that the idea of a relationship with Jeremy had lain in the back of her mind for awhile now. A notion to be taken out and examined at odd moments, a fanciful consideration. Last night, when he let her close, let her see into his heart, the matter had taken on a more significant dimension.

Presently she dressed in a slim cashmere suit. She'd decided to do what had been a vague plan for several days, with no idea whether it would untangle her confusion or confound it.

Downstairs, Jeremy sat in the solarium, his face drawn. He watched her enter with open male admiration.. Smiling, he poured her coffee. There was much to say after last night but neither could find the words.

"I'm going shopping," she said before he could ask what she was up to. "May I borrow a car?"

"Of course, or I can drive you in. We could have lunch at the Sheridan Inn. It's a wonderful old hotel where Buffalo Bill Cody auditioned acts for his Wild West Show from the front porch." He quirked a smile. "Are we on?"

"I'll meet you there. That way I won't subject you to the leisurely trek through the shops I have in mind. I want to find gifts for my friends at the magazine."

Jeremy stroked his chin. "I'll be there at one. Some of the shops and galleries have nice Western art. And they're happy to do the shipping."

"I'll take everything back with me."

His gaze narrowed.

"I was naive thinking in a matter of days or weeks, I could unravel what's haunted me for twenty years. I'll arrange a leave of absence and sublet my condo. Then I can see things through here." She caught a subdued elation in Jeremy, as well as the same misgivings that pursued her.

"When will you go?"

"Next week." She glanced into the hall. "Where's Becca?"

"Feeding Jekyll and making sure Pearl fixes Francine's breakfast tray to her liking."

"So Cheryl didn't veto the plan?"

"She's always so anxious to get to the nursing home, she's happy with whatever help she can get."

"For a fulltime nurse, she doesn't spend much time with Francine."

"I think Francine prefers it that way. Cheryl isn't the most pleasant company."

Katie raised her coffee cup, toasting the statement.

The tinny squeak of Pearl's teacart preceded Becca from the kitchen, Jekyll in her wake.

"Come tell me when to put on Mrs. Chamberlain's hot cakes," Pearl instructed Becca with a wink before taking her leave.

"I want *you* to read *Harry Potter*," Becca told her father after she'd eaten two pancakes. "Grandma makes it boring. Can you believe that? *Harry Potter* boring? Duh." She grinned. "Oh, yeah, I almost forgot. When she stood up last night, she stepped on Jekyll's tail and he growled at her." She giggled at the memory.

Jeremy's mouth twitched. "I hope you scolded him."

Becca looked askance. "It wasn't his fault."

Katie stifled her own inclination to laugh and settled back with a second cup of coffee. She acknowledged contentment that was becoming more and more familiar, albeit elusive.

Half an hour later, she and Becca climbed the stairs to Francine's bedroom.

After Katie tapped on the door, Becca marched to Francine and leaned her elbows on her bed, peering at her. "I came to see you. Grandma said I couldn't but Katie let me."

"Your grandmother is very tiresome."

"I know." Becca whipped out the picture she'd brought. "Look what I painted for you. It's Ursel, Katie's little girl. Isn't she pretty?"

Francine adjusted her spectacles and studied the blonde image. "Yes, she is. Thank you so much. But how do you know what she looked like?"

"Katie told me all about her."

"Thank you for sharing her with me," she said to Katie who still held the breakfast tray.

"She was your great-granddaughter." Katie observed.

Anger flashed in the blue eyes before she dropped her gaze.

As Katie situated the food in front of Francine, she saw a single tear roll down her wrinkled cheek and felt tears welling in her own eyes.

Becca surveyed the tray, grinning. "See, we gave you a rose." She sniffed the pink blossom.

Francine raised the plate cover, handing it to Katie. "This is a very nice change from the ghastly gruel Cheryl packs up here every blessed day." She brought a forkful to her mouth. "Where's your friend Jekyll?"

"Out in the hall. Katie thought he might bother you."

"Bullrushes." She stabbed her fork at Katie. "Let him in."

Katie complied. Jekyll walked to the bed, no more intimidated by Francine's inspection than Becca.

Katie watched the mutual fascination between Becca and the old woman as they carried on a lively conversation. Her heart ached and she frantically wiped her eyes, swamped by grief that Ursel had been robbed of ever knowing her great-grandmother.

By the time Francine dismissed Becca to catch the bus, Katie had pulled herself together. She took a chair beside the bed.

Francine still smiled, her gaze wistful as she still looked at the door where the small whirlwind had just disappeared. "She is filled with so much joy. Funny it has not all been blighted with her living here with two people drowning in sorrow, and a broken down old woman." Sudden cruelty invaded her voice. "Do you suppose she will blank out all the hurt like you did?"

"She knows what causes the pain, and her father adores her. He won't let others wound her in their ignorance."

"You know what caused your pain." She averted her eyes.

"Is that a clue?" Despite their evolving goodwill, all Katie's animosity was back.

"It's the truth." Francine was silent for some time. "I apologize," she said at last. "I didn't mean to ignore you when I was looking at Becca's picture of your daughter and Becca said she is my great-granddaughter. I want you to know I acknowledge that fact. And I'm very sorry for your loss...for my loss...." She clasped Katie's hand. "I can't say why I've become an emotional wreck over this. I am not an emotional woman as you have likely noticed." She tightened her fingers on Katie's, looking at her through tears. "But right now, I dearly wish I could know your daughter." She lifted her arms to Katie who moved into her embrace.

Katie hugged her, her own tears mingling with the wetness on the lined cheek. "Thank you so much. That means the world to me." She put her hands at either side of her face, looking into the cerulean depths. "She was so beautiful and she had your eyes."

Gnarled fingers patted her hand against her face. "My darling, Katie. That is a handsome suit. What's the occasion?"

"I'm going shopping in town."

"That should cause quite a sensation in Sheridan. We rarely see designer suits on Main Street." She smiled as Katie retrieved the tray and bent to kiss her still damp cheek. "Have a lovely time, dear."

As she made her way downstairs, Katie marveled at the unexpected goodwill in her grandmother. She had a new appreciation for her high regard for blood ties.

She retrieved her bag from where she had left it in the solarium and Jeremy walked her to the waiting Mercedes in the driveway. He leaned in to squeeze her hand before closing the door.

Within fifteen minutes, Katie parked beside one of three nursing homes in Sheridan, this one providing care for the area's worst geriatric and neurological cases. She took her camera case from the backseat and hurried inside. By showing her press pass at a reception desk, she gained full access.

She navigated a path through residents staring at her without a flicker of curiosity. Nurses, aides and orderlies moved among them, occasionally pausing to straighten a teetering body, offer a smile, touch, or a bit of conversation.

Katie once did the photos for an article about Boston nursing homes, and was now flooded with the same sadness that possessed her during that assignment. She wondered again what had snuffed out personality in these people, leaving them bent, unthinking shadows of themselves.

Further along a branching hallway, the inner walls gave way to large, open wards where beds were placed in a haphazard arrangement. No trace of health or normalcy here. Still bundles tied in the beds. Swaying bodies tied into wheelchairs. Here and there, a screen shielded the suffering from prying eyes.

Katie thought she wouldn't recognize Evelyn but some faint reminder of Jeremy's portrait guided her. Yet, as she stepped closer, her brain denied this was the same woman.

The skeletal figure slumped in a converted wheelchair, head thrown back, vacant eyes fixed on the ceiling. An arm with clenched fist lay across her chest and Katie realized from the way the sleeve was altered that the limb was frozen there. Evelyn's other arm rested uselessly in her lap. A sheet covered her lower body.

A familiar grating voice cut through Katie's bewilderment and she watched Cheryl approach the bed where a nurse's aide changed Evelyn's linens. Katie looked for a hiding place and settled on a screen beside another bed. Cheryl's back was to her and she managed to reach the dubious sanctuary where she leaned against the edge of the mattress to ease her trembling.

Glancing over her shoulder, her gaze fell on an ancient wraith lying against the pillow. The old woman had no teeth and her jaw gaped as she snored softly.

A shiver crept up Katie's spine. She glanced again at Evelyn. She had no idea what she'd expected coming here but it wasn't this. Last night Jeremy had talked about his wife being in remission.

Katie's hands ached from gripping her camera as she stared around the edge of the screen. Evelyn's bed was ready. Cheryl sat staring at her with an expression Katie tried hard to read. She needed to know what Cheryl thought about the wild, staring eyes.

Cheryl remained impassive. Soon enough, she took out a tabloid, infuriating Katie with her indifference even as she knew Evelyn was beyond any interaction her mother might attempt.

Katie didn't know how much time had passed before Cheryl folded her paper and stuffed it back in her tote bag. Again she looked searchingly at Evelyn until a nurse appeared.

"You may take her down the hall, or outside. It's warm today."

Cheryl still examined the cocked and

distorted face. "It wouldn't matter, would it?"

"We like to think it does. Who are we to say what she feels."

Cheryl's features took on her customary cold, pinched look. At last Katie thought she knew the reason.

"Well, personally, I don't think she feels a goddamned thing. If she's taken out, someone else is going to do it."

"Of course, Mrs. Menefree. I think we'll put her back to bed then."

"Goodbye!" Cheryl sang out before sashaying into the hall, her heels clacking on the black and white tile.

As soon as the nurse left, Katie ventured out. Again she was drawn to Evelyn. By what? Curiosity? Pity? Horror? She couldn't decide.

She stopped beside the wheelchair, compelled to look into the sightless eyes and speak quietly Evelyn's name. She touched the balled fist flung across her cadaverous frame at such an awkward angle.

She adjusted her camera settings and took several shots, her hands moving instinctively. Torn between the urge to escape and her need to know more, she remained there when another nurse appeared beside her.

"This is one of our sadder cases. Advanced M.S. A great tragedy for her family."

And probably for her too, don't you think? Katie wanted to shout at the stupid woman. "Will she get better?"

"No. She'll remain the same or decline."

Katie wondered how she could be so

certain. "Why is this arm twisted while her legs and other arm are straight?"

"Only one arm was affected by severe muscle contractions. The tendons in her legs were surgically severed so she can lie flat."

Katie's mind recoiled from the answers the woman recited so calmly, yet she continued asking questions. "Does she ever speak or react to things around her?"

"When she first came here she was quite vocal but no more. She doesn't even respond to her husband anymore. It was always just a pull toward his voice, I think. Apparently they had a marvelous romance. I've seen old photographs in the society pages. She was so lovely. Hardly a day passes when Jeremy doesn't visit. He's very loyal." She glanced up as two aides approached with a contraption Katie realized was a hydraulic hoist. "They're here to put her to bed. Can I do anything for you?"

"Thanks. I'm fine."

The pair with the hoist moved in and attached chains to a canvas sling Katie now saw was beneath Evelyn in the wheelchair. Evelyn moaned as the hydraulic mechanism gathered and lifted her into the clean bed where she lay still, staring at the ceiling.

Alone with her again, it occurred to Katie that Jeremy might come there before lunch. To stay was risky but she decided to wait nonetheless. She stepped back behind the screen. The old lady in the bed cried out, evidently reacting to the slight jostling of the mattress.

Katie froze, waiting as the gray head

burrowed into the pillow and quiet came down around them. Her thoughts mixed with the blend of sounds from the ward, turning back to Jeremy. Since coming there, she hadn't let herself imagine his part in this. Now she opened her heart to his pain. *Dear God, what must he feel when he sees this parody of the woman he loved?*

She felt dizzy and leaned her hands on the mattress, taking care not to disturb the sleeper. By the time her nausea had retreated a little, Jeremy appeared.

He went to Evelyn and stood looking down at her. Anguish tracked over his features in a rush that struck Katie like a slap.

He sat backwards on the chair Cheryl had used, resting his chin against his folded arms. Katie saw a part of him that was carefully guarded away from this place. She'd seen his distant sadness. Once or twice he had let her glimpse the terror and dread, but, even then, he was in control. Now the constraint had dropped away. Throbbing tears pricked behind Katie's eyes.

Jeremy scanned Evelyn's face that he'd turned toward him slightly, as one might an adjustable doll. Now she looked like any hospital patient listening to a visitor, only she stared past him. Katie wondered what she saw in that secret place. She hoped there were happy pictures and memories but knew there weren't.

Jeremy finally spoke to her. "Evelyn, I don't know what to do anymore. I don't know what to tell Becca. I can't say you're getting better. I can't tell her she can visit you soon."

His voice became easy, conversational, an

echo from another time. He poured out his worry for Becca, as well as assurance, sharing some of her happy mischief.

Katie longed to see some stirring in Evelyn, some sign that she heard and understood. But nothing. And eventually, Jeremy fell silent. He looked so tired as he rose and bent over the bed. One hand tenderly cradled Evelyn's disfigured arm while he braced the other beside her pillow. He brought his face close, searching one last time for what wasn't there, then pressed his mouth to her cheek.

When he straightened, his calm was back in place. He turned away, clearly anxious to escape as Cheryl had before. Without looking back, he hurried through the ward, a striking, self-possessed man who drew the attention of staff and patients.

Katie felt disoriented, lonely. She couldn't imagine meeting Jeremy so soon after witnessing how deep and open his wounds were. Soon enough, her turmoil pursued her to the front entrance and out into sunshine. Minutes later, she drove down a winding drive with no idea where she was going. After following tree-lined streets for a time, she checked her watch and found it way past one o'clock.

She longed to keep going out of town. She might stop and walk and maybe make some sense of the morning. But there wasn't time and she knew this was best. If she postponed confronting Jeremy, she would lose sight of her conviction and anger now intermingled with shock.

She turned toward the downtown business district, barely aware of the traffic and businesses around her. At length she came out of her fog long enough to recognize the Sheridan Inn by the formation of small dormers marching across the roofline.

She soon walked along the wooden porch fronting the imposing hotel. As she looked out over a huge tract of lawn, she tried visualizing the auditioning cowboys. She continued past a line of empty rocking chairs and through an entrance into a lounge.

Jeremy waited beside a stone fireplace, his expression undecipherable. "I thought we'd have a drink before we eat." He guided her to a nearby table. "I also wanted to show you the bar they shipped from England."

Seated, Katie inspected the grand mahogany structure that took up the entire length of the room. Jeremy described the ordeal of hauling the massive creation by ox cart from the town of Gillette, there being no railroad to Sheridan at the time. Katie hardly heard anything he said but found herself making more inquiries. The ploy worked only until a girl served them both bourbon, then Jeremy fell silent and Katie realized he knew.

"I saw the Mercedes in the parking lot. You had no right to go there behind my back. I resent the intrusion, Katie."

"Really? How else would I learn the truth? You clearly wouldn't tell me."

Their eyes met in challenge.

"Why isn't she cared for better? Just what does Cheryl accomplish there every day reading the *National Enquirer*? If the staff won't do their job properly, why can't Cheryl do the few things that would give Evelyn more dignity?"

Jeremy sighed. "For months Cheryl and I took turns caring for her intimate needs. We bathed her and brushed her hair and teeth. When she grew facial hair from the medication, we were desperate to keep it trimmed. We helped her with a bedpan, and when she became incontinent, we changed her diapers." He swallowed more bourbon. "But she was completely smothering us so we put her in the nursing home.

"And that part of it was over. We could no longer do all we had at home. I despised what I thought mistakenly was the staff's apathy. The first year I yelled constantly, demanding they do everything we had." He shook his head ruefully. They didn't show it but I'm sure they hated the sight of me. Gradually, I gained perspective and I figured out that most of the nurses and aides care deeply but they're usually short-staffed, under paid, and so tired it's sometimes hard to keep moving. They tend to give more of their time to residents who are still thinking, still responding. Finally, I knew it didn't matter. I couldn't rage against it any longer."

Katie looked away from his bewilderment. "Jeremy, please forgive me. I didn't know."

"Only experience teaches certain realities."

She searched for the right words. "You said before that when Evelyn was still home, she was smothering you. Isn't it the same now?"

He remained silent.

"On days you can't go see her, it must seem like a betrayal. You talk to Becca like her mother will get better." She clenched her hands. "How long can you keep on before facing the truth? Evelyn's not getting better."

He folded his arms, his eyes dark and dangerous. "Do you have a medical degree I don't know about?"

She refused the bait.

He leaned closer. "Damn it, Katie, I know Evelyn can't get well. My God, they've cut the tendons in her legs and removed her uterus. She's blind and her mind's gone. But I have to play the game for Becca, and, to keep my sanity, I try believing it myself. When I'm talking about Evelyn to someone who doesn't know how ill she is, I say we all hope to have her home again. Occasionally, part of me has faith for a moment or two that it will happen."

He sank back in his chair and raised his hands. "I liked having you in the dark. It fed the delusion and that's all I have now. Last night I talked about remission, and there by the fire, with you believing what I said, it almost seemed real. You don't have to tell me this isn't a healthy way of dealing with the truth. Right now, I can't find anything better. It's like treading water after a shipwreck, not rescued but not yet drowning."

"Have you thought about talking to someone?"

"A therapist?" He quirked an eyebrow. "No, have you?"

Katie laughed.

"I've thought about it but so far, I haven't."

Considering her own avoidance of psychiatric help as an adult, she could empathize. "Maybe you underestimate Becca. Perhaps it's harder for her living with false hope, the vague promises that come to nothing. I think she knows more than you realize. But no one's told her that her mother's never coming home. Isn't that unfair?"

Jeremy drained his glass, all his tension back. "If I told her the truth, it would destroy her."

"I doubt that."

He stood and paced to the bar. "Could you have abandoned your husband?" he demanded when he was back with fresh drinks.

"I can't say how I'd deal with pain like this. I do know one can't abandon what's no longer here. There's nothing left of Evelyn."

"Only an ideal, a commitment." He traced patterns on the table, finally looking at her again. "I'm sorry. I was wrong putting you in a position where you felt you had to see Evelyn, to see where my life is headed. I had no right. I think we misinterpreted each other. We each wanted what the other can't give. My final loyalty stays with Evelyn."

Katie's anger had seeped out of reach again. "I think I knew that from the start. It was tempting to see nothing but the here and now."

He said no more but merely sat still, regarding her with open regret and sadness.

To stay there was agony.

"I'm sorry I can't have lunch." Katie hurriedly gathered her bag.

He offered no protest as she took her leave.

CHAPTER SEVEN

Katie tried calming her thoughts as she rushed from the Sheridan Inn, and on to the Mercedes in the parking lot. Once inside, she moved methodically, adjusted the mirror and smoothed her hair before she turned the car into traffic.

She drove toward the hill country she'd seen from the plane that first day, her mind concentrating on the road ahead. Presently she turned from the highway and came upon a rambling stream flowing between stands of willows and cottonwood. After a time, she found a turnout and parked.

After locking the car, she moved through the deep shade toward the sound of the water and upon reaching the bank, sank down on a wide, mossy rock. Resting her elbows on her knees, she watched the hypnotic motion of the stream that slowed her thoughts. It suddenly occurred to her that while she was in Sheridan, she hadn't made a single purchase of art for her friends.

Her frustration gave way to tears even though she could not decide for whom she cried. Was it Jeremy or Evelyn? Herself?

She still had no clue by the time the shadows crept from under the rocks but at least, the disassembled sensation of the morning was gone. And she knew she would leave for Boston sooner than she's planned. The respite from *Radbourne* might guide her toward acceptance and restore the clarity of purpose that brought her here.

Alarm cut into Jeremy's sleep. Instantly, he was out of bed, pulling on a robe.

In seconds, he'd crossed the hall to Becca's room. "Daddy!" She still sobbed for him even as he sat on her bed, gathering her into his lap.

"Sweetheart, I'm here." He stroked her hair while the shaky length of her burrowed closer. As usual, he soon carried her to a rocking chair bathed in a pool of moonlight. Jekyll arrived and lay down with his head resting on Jeremy's foot.

"Daddy...." The misery in her voice wrenched at him.

"Try to go back to sleep now. I'll hold you." He spread an afghan over her.

"I had an awful dream. I couldn't find my mom...I looked and looked..." The words grew softer and more halting before her breathing became shallow and she slept.

Jeremy felt his body relax. Her face was serene now in the moon glow. If only his own demons were defeated so easily.

A cloud obscured the moon, leaving the room dark save for a dim night light. How many hours had he sat here holding Becca, watching the moon chart its course through the apple tree branches outside?

When Becca was a baby, Evelyn rarely heard her at night. Jeremy never minded because he loved the solitary quiet with his tiny daughter. Indeed, when she outgrew nighttime feedings, he missed their time there. Becca slept without incident for several years before Evelyn's illness sent her into a cycle of nightmares and fear of the dark. A night light and Jekyll sleeping on her bed had eased the dread but didn't banish it.

Only Jeremy could coax her back into untroubled sleep. Cheryl thought rushing to comfort her whenever she cried out did her more harm than good. She argued that if Becca was left to cry it out a few nights, she'd stop disturbing Jeremy's sleep.

There was a pattern to Becca's behavior. When she suffered an upset or disappointment, she digressed into night trauma. There was no mystery about this latest episode. When Katie announced at dinner that she was leaving for Boston the next day and might be away for a month, Becca betrayed no reaction. Yet, Jeremy sensed her growing terror, not so different from what he'd seen in her the day the ambulance came for her mother.

He closed his eyes. Why was he so angry with Katie? Resentment had lain within him since the very first day he looked into her face and glimpsed Evelyn. Now she'd become a threat. It was no longer possible to think no further than seeing Evelyn one more day, his heart closed, his body numb. Katie had torn apart his dispassion, stirring in him a hunger he'd thought dead.

He'd concluded early on that Katie and Evelyn were nothing alike. While Evelyn was passive, the scope of her existence anchored within the boundaries of her husband's life, Katie was a free spirit. Timid, Evelyn depended on him for her strength and direction. Katie wasn't afraid, period, save for her nightmare perhaps.

Still, the two women merged. Often, late at night, the abstraction overwhelmed him. Before Evelyn got sick,
this was their time for passion, tenderness and talk. Lately
when he lay alone in their bed, he ached with longing. Sometimes he fled to the terrace where the night air eased his sweating body.

Now he shifted Becca a little as the moonlight spilled around them once more. *Evelyn, I miss you so goddamned much*....

His eyes found her framed in lamp glow from the hall, a tall, graceful figure. He smiled, reaching his hand to her. How many times had he teased her about her delayed alarm clock? Some nights, like tonight, long after he'd settled with Becca in the rocking chair, she joined them. When she stepped nearer, he caught her hand.

"I couldn't sleep. I kept thinking about how Becca looked when I said I was going to Boston. I came to check on her." Katie looked down at the child's sleeping face. "Is she okay?"

Jeremy stared at her in dismay. Cold crept through him. *Sweet Jesus, was he losing his mind?*

Still holding his hand, Katie sat on a footstool close by the rocking chair.

Gradually Jeremy's mind cleared and reality slid back into place. "She had a bad dream. This happens a lot since her mom's been sick." He laughed softly. "Actually, I've sat here with her a lot since she was a baby. I'm very good at sleeping in this chair."

Katie read the quiet pleasure in his voice.

"I used to work out my best ideas for photo layouts while I nursed Ursel at two in the morning."

"Evelyn didn't nurse Becca. So I was usually with her at night. Middle-of-the-night feedings are good for the soul."

Katie acknowledged the renewed sharing between them, a spanning of the day's tension. She watched him settle Becca against his shoulder and stand.

When his daughter was settled beneath the covers, he kissed her. "Sleep well, my darling."

Observing his tenderness, Katie thought of Zachery. How was it possible to still miss a man who'd been dead for three years, and rarely stirred any depth of emotion in her when he was alive?

She felt Jeremy's probing gaze. "Are you all right?"

"Yes," she said, shaking off her sadness.

"Maybe a little brandy will help you sleep." He came to help her up and led the way into the hall.

There was risk in his suggestion, but she couldn't refuse and they'd soon descended to the drawing room. Was it only last night when they lingered there for hours? Curled on the sofa, she accepted the snifter he brought her.

"May I drive you to the airport tomorrow?"

She hunted for the anger that had ignited the very first day when she met the steel of his gaze and felt vibrations of something threatening, guarded, yet beguiling. It was gone tonight, replaced by new fascination, the lure of his commanding personality. "I'd hate it if you didn't," she said.

Like the previous night when their

conversation was intimate, exploring, their talk soon entered this same zone. They discussed food and music and Dr. Seuss.

Katie laughed with the understanding that they were sharing like old friends. The restraint and confusion of recent weeks had given way to this.

Perhaps an hour passed before Katie grew drowsy. Jeremy sat observing her. "I feel pretty much the way Becca does about you going to Boston."

This knocked Katie's contentment askew. He wasn't playing fair. "I won't be gone that long."

"No," he said dismissively. "And I'd better let you get some sleep." He rose and pulled her up from the couch.

As Katie followed, she saw his humorous ease had evaporated, leaving his features tight. She thought they'd put to rest what lay unspoken, yet tangible between them. They'd talked and laughed here in the wee hours without the impediment of lust.

Now she knew the illusion was false. She saw his arousal and returned his deep kiss with an abandon she hadn't felt in years, straining against the muscled length of him. When they finally continued to the stairs, their arms remained around each other as they climbed.

On the landing, she stepped back into his arms where it felt very safe. It would be so easy to give in to her reckless and rash frame of mind.

Jeremy leaned his forehead against hers. "You are the most amazing lady," he said, then his mouth claimed hers again and he took her tongue inside while his hands moved lower, hard and demanding.

Her arms circled his neck and she held him, wanting his passion, his tenderness and all the complications. Then his hands came up and he gently pulled her arms away from him until he held both her hands in his, studying her with eyes still hot, dark with want. He lifted one hand to kiss her palm. "I guess there's nothing I can say to make you stay?"

She shook her head, tears threatening..

He folded her back in his arms, rocking her. "I know. Don't cry. Go do what you must and I'll be here when you get back." He held her until she stopped trembling. "Off you go now." He winked and led her to her door. His mouth grazed her cheek, then turned and strode down the corridor.

In her room, Katie switched off the lamp and slid into bed. Quickly, she slept.

The next morning, Francine considered Katie over her reading glasses. "So you really are running out on me? It is not some peculiar joke you're foisting on me?"

Katie met her stabbing appraisal. "I had no idea this would be such an extended campaign. So I have to go to Boston."

"What is to prevent you from staying there?"

"Nothing but my word. And my need to know the secret you keep guarding so rabidly."

Her grandmother cocked her head, a tiny smile easing the hard line of her lips. "Well, since it is not practical to lock you in the attic, I am obliged to believe you." Her words were equable but her gaze narrowed and Katie knew some unnerving revelation was forthcoming. "Contrary to what your cronies in Boston may believe, we do have telephones here. There is nothing there you couldn't handle from here. So it's not business taking you away. My guess is it's Jeremy...." She waited for reaction.

"Do you know something I don't?"

"Don't be tiresome. Blindness is not one of my infirmities. You have had Jeremy in a state from the moment you walked in. And from the looks of you lately, I would say the feeling is mutual."

Katie sat still, amazed and annoyed by her awareness.

There was concern in Francine's voice when she spoke again. "I don't wonder you need to get away. But let me say this – there is a way through this if you want it. First, you must understand Jeremy. Understand the man he is. When he married Evelyn, he gave her everything, including his soul. Now not even his love can save her. My advice is, while you're counting up the things Jeremy can't give you, remember what he can."

Katie knew she was telling her that Jeremy might always be married to Evelyn, but she could have the rest of him. She held her ground beneath the old woman's scrutiny.

Francine inclined toward her. "Come here, child."

Katie was struck by a dizzying sense of discovery. Had her grandmother spoken to her this way long ago, with love and compassion? She saw these emotions mirrored in the lined face and was astonished at what had been hidden so well. Struggling for composure and determined not to reveal all her secret, long-denied feelings, she sank down on the bed, placing her hand in Francine's.

"This is more than you bargained for, isn't it? And Jeremy was convinced you were a little mercenary." Francine smiled. "Fate or the gods or Jesus Christ or whoever it is that guides our destiny has no qualms about thrusting us into situations we never dreamed could exist for us.

"I see your fear, and I share it. No one loved his wife the way Jeremy loved Evelyn. Yet he is a virile young man with such capacity for life. In time, he must bury the past. If you are what forces him to confront reality as he's always done until now, then you will receive a marvelous gift." Bony fingers stroked Katie's hand. "It is a jest of life that we are often required to bear the most unspeakable hurt and grief before the joy beneath is revealed."

Katie dared believe she might be talking about two things at once. There was an openness in her eyes that Katie had rarely seen since coming to Wyoming, a receptive mien. Was Francine drawing close to the time when she might forgive her for whatever caused her banishment?

Francine broke into her confusion. "It is best that you are away for awhile. When you come back, you and Jeremy may both have gained perspective. Don't look so stricken. We will all still be here."

"Are you sure?"

"Of course. By now, you know how stubborn I am. I won't be dying until my affairs are settled. I never imagined Jeremy would be a factor is keeping you here. But now I have to deal with that as one more extenuating circumstance. If you stayed here right now, you would be thinking of nothing but what you need to do in Boston, and you and Jeremy wouldn't have the time to think things through."

Katie pushed away the sudden desire to bury her head in Francine's bosom and sob out all her incomprehension. "Did I sit on your lap when I was little?"

"Only when you suffered some calamity like skinning your knee. Your grandfather wasn't so enraptured with you when you were bloody and crying. Nor was your mother, for that matter. So when the chips were down, you would come running to me and we would end up cuddling in my old rocker. When everything was going your way, you did not have much time for me. You preferred your grandfather and mother who both found your antics highly amusing. I thought they spoiled you, making such a to-do, so I rarely joined that admiration society. You only came to me for serious hugging."

Katie smiled, visualizing Francine as the sobering influence in her grandfather's frivolity. How her mother fit into the picture wasn't clear. "How did my mother die?"

"Of heart failure."

"Was she sick long?"

"No, it was quite sudden."

She checked her watch. "Oh, I must run! My flight's at noon and Jeremy's probably waiting." She hugged her grandmother and kissed her cheek.

"Don't get in trouble while I'm gone."

Francine gave a little snort. "I daresay I should say the same to you."

"Maybe." She gently drew her fingers from her tight grip. "Bye, hon." Despite the persistent threat of tears, she hurried out.

On the way to Sheridan, she and Jeremy talked about the rain clouds over the mountains, Jeremy's obligation that night to attend an open house at Becca's school, about anything but what each longed to talk about - the question between them.

It was only when they stood together in the boarding area beside the commuter plane that Jeremy asked, "Are you running away from me, Katie? Is that what this is all about?"

She was caught unawares at having her private thoughts put into words. "Can you blame me if I am?"

"Will it change anything?"

"I don't know."

"I think you know it won't."

She stood still, caught in the trap of his steady gaze.

The pilot and a stewardess walked from the hangar and boarded the plane.

"I think that's a sign," Jeremy said.

Grateful, she stepped back from him as he kissed her. "Take care, Katie."

While she climbed the steps to board, she knew he thought she was the one who must resolve matters, accepting what neither of them could change.

Katie stared into the encircling black beyond the faint light, her breath coming in painful spasms. Her entire body went rigid with panic as her eyes caught the hazy movement in the darkness. Flinging herself back, she clutched the edge of the library table to keep from falling.

Her throat hurt and she realized she'd been screaming, yet when she focused on the face above her, she saw kindness, concern.

"Are you all right, Mrs. Meade?" the flight attendant asked.

Katie straightened in her seat. "I don't know."

"Shall I bring you water?"

"Yes. Thank you." She took the glass pressed into her hand and drained it, then gave the woman a smile. "I'm okay now. Thanks again."

The woman retreated with a final questioning look and Katie closed her eyes. She felt nauseous and wanted to find the restroom but couldn't bear having all passengers' eyes following her along the narrow aisle. Strangers whispering, speculating about her crazy behavior.

She pressed fingers to her forehead as if she could push back the rising despair. Dazed, she tried to think why the dream had returned when she traveled away from its source. Perhaps she'd drawn closer to the truth at *Radbourne* than she realized. In retreat, she was vulnerable as she hadn't been while she actively sought answers. With abrupt perception, she knew the force would drive her back to *Radbourne*. Her life depended on her return. She realized now that *Radbourne* offered sanctuary. How that was possible, she couldn't yet imagine.

Still, if she didn't heed this warning, she knew the nightmare would chase through her nights with ever greater wrath and she hadn't the strength to fight it. Her thoughts turned to Jeremy with a sense of inevitability.

CHAPTER EIGHT

Katie spent a month in Boston, lunching most days with one or more in her circle of friends. She attended a wedding and went to the theatre and sat alone in the Indian Summer sunshine. She arranged for an indefinite leave of absence from the magazine in exchange for the promise that she'd do a photo profile on Sheridan for a summer issue. She also sublet her condo and visited her gynecologist for a new prescription for the pill.

Exhaustion stalked her every day. Every night, the nightmare yanked her from sleep and left her groggily awake until first light. She tried napping during the day but the dream assaulted her then as well.

It was only during the return flight to Denver in late October that she felt her vitality haltingly returning. Solace filled her as she descended from the commuter plane in Sheridan. Keen anticipation raced along every nerve.

Jeremy waited for her and she hugged him in relief.

"Hello, Katie."

She saw his concern and concluded she must look ghastly in spite of her rising mood.

He said nothing more until he'd driven into the country. "What the devil have you been doing? You look like you haven't eaten or slept since you left here."

"That's pretty much the way it went." She told him about the string of days and nights when the nightmare manipulated her with ever-increasing fury. She chose her words cautiously in an effort not to alarm him further.

Halfway to *Radbourne*, he swung the Accord onto a side road. "Damn it, Katie, it's me you're talking to!" He twisted toward her. "I've only to look at you to see you've been through pure bloody hell. And you sit there talking to me like I'm Becca. Jesus, why didn't you tell me when you called? Why didn't you call me sooner?" His fingers dug into her arms. "I would've been on the next flight. I probably couldn't have kept this thing from hurting you but you wouldn't have been alone."

His fury left her shaken, groping for the control she'd clung to for days now. She was abruptly weeping in great shuddering sobs.

Jeremy drew her close. "Katie, I'm sorry I yelled, but it terrifies me, seeing you so thin and tired...."

She couldn't stopped crying.

"You'll be safe here. You were before, and it'll be the same again." His words and touch had become gentle, soothing as he shifted himself over the console.

She had little awareness of passing minutes as he eased her seat back and pressed himself protectively along the frail length of her, stroking her hair. Never before had she given herself over completely to the terror, and it was a long time before she lay drained, weak in the curve of his body. He caressed the back of her neck, waiting with her for the crisis to pass.

"How have you lived with this all these years?"

Eventually she could answer. "For a long time after I was sent away, I blocked everything. I...was so little I didn't know what was happening to me. Even now, I don't remember a solitary thing about that first year in Boston..."

"Are you still angry with Francine because she won't tell you outright?"

"Not so much. I was letting go of the rage before I left. Then when the dream knocked me on my butt, I realized whatever happened when I was five was truly dreadful, life-altering. After I got that letter, I believed my grandmother sent me away because she was so preoccupied with her own life. Now I think she sent me away to protect me."

"Everyone who's ever dealt with Francine has on occasion, been confused and offended by her motives. But I can't recall a situation when she didn't come around in the end."

The release of long-guarded emotions left Katie slightly disoriented, struggling against returning agitation. She chafed now in the confines of Jeremy's embrace.

He shifted, looking at her a second before he straightened and slid behind the wheel. They continued on to *Radbourne.*

"How's Francine?" Katie asked, trying to dispel the uneasiness she'd caused.

"Some better, actually. We even took her outside one day since it was so warm so she could watch Becca ride. She was wiped out when she got back to bed but claimed the October sunshine was a tonic. Ever since, she's been sitting in a chair for a few hours every afternoon."

"Bless her heart." Would Katie ever stop being taken aback by her evolving love for her grandmother? "And how's Becca?"

"As full of the devil as ever. She talked Pearl into picking her up from school today so she'd be home when you got here."

Katie smiled. "That's my girl." She pictured Becca's campaign with Pearl helpless against her ploys. She turned her gaze toward the hills and glens edging the highway. The landscape now held a comforting familiarity. Was this because of the pull on her in the present, or did some faded memory feed her feeling of belonging?

She considered Jeremy's profile, sensing the question in his mind. Regardless of his careful reserve, she knew the direction of their relationship must soon be discussed..

When he parked in the carriage house, Becca streaked down the lawn, hair and sneakers flying. Jekyll loped beside her. Katie opened her door and Becca leaped into her lap.

"I'm so glad you're home. I was *so* lonely."

Katie smiled at her exuberance." "I missed you too, Becca."

She sat beaming at her while Jeremy removed Katie's bags from the backseat and started up the hill. Katie disentangled herself from Becca's smothery hug and they got out, heading to the house.

Inside, the three of them climbed to Katie's room where Becca pointed out the fresh bouquet on the nightstand. "Francine got a whole bunch of roses this morning and she gave me some too."

She grinned. "She said it's time I have roses all my own. She has about a million in her room." She rolled her eyes.

"Why don't you go tell Francine that Katie will be up in a few minutes," Jeremy suggested.

Becca cocked her head, considering him quizzically a second, then ran out the door.

"Walk," he called after her, then took Katie in his arms. "You okay now?"

"I'm good."

His earlier impatience and detachment had gone, replaced by playful contemplation. He kicked the door shut, then held her face in his hands while his mouth covered hers. His tongue parted her lips and he kissed her deeply, thrilling her, lifting her from the dark place in her soul. She met his tongue with assent that melted the last of her doubt.

Her heart raced when he raised his head, his regard conveying such delight her breath caught. She relaxed against him, completely malleable.

"Katie, the suspense is killing me. Have you decided?"

She met his forthright gaze for a few seconds, then in a voice steady and certain, she said, "Yes." She offered what she'd long denied she could give until now. She had never felt more in control.

He threw back his head and pulled her into a joyful little dance, then stopped, burying his face in her neck. When he considered her again, the hunger in his eyes deepened. "Katie, you'll never regret this. I give you my word."

"But where?" she asked, suddenly overwhelmed by practicalities.

He pressed a finger to her lips. "Remember Francine's cabin?"

"Ah, yes." She cocked an eyebrow.

"It's very romantic."

"How would you know?"

"Francine told me."

"You never took Evelyn there?"

He shook his head. "She wasn't the rustic type. But I have been there many times, alone. It's a great place to recoup and gain perspective."

She slid her arm around his waist, resting her head on his shoulder. "I shouldn't have asked you if you took Evelyn there."

"You have every right to know." They continued there for awhile, neither speaking but caught in their separate thoughts.

Running in the hall hauled them back to the moment and with one long stride, Jeremy flung the door open just as Becca lurched to a stop. "Is Francine ready to see Katie?"

"She said she can't wait another minute." She hurried to stand beside Katie.

"It's time for your lesson with Patrick. Go put on your boots, and I'll walk you to the arena." He winked at Katie as his daughter rushed out again. "Duty calls."

Katie stepped into her bathroom and splashed water on her face, then stared into the mirror. That morning her image in the cheval glass in her Boston bedroom was drawn and white. Now her cheeks glowed with color and the fatigue in her eyes had eased a bit. She granted herself a smile and went to see her grandmother.

"Come in, my dear," Francine sang out. tap

Katie wondered at how right the endearment was now. It seemed an eternity since she'd felt only hostility toward the old woman who sat in a chair by a window.

"I missed you." She kissed her and in a chair facing her.

"You have no idea how bereft I've been in your absence." She laughed a little. "You do know how to make a lady happy, coming back to me."

"I see you've made progress while I was gone."

"You have not. You look like death. Lord, almighty, was Boston as bad as you look?"

"Tell me how you really feel."

"Don't be flippant."

"Actually, the dream was worse than it's ever been. It came every time I fell asleep, the first time on the plane out of Chicago." She paused, absorbing Francine's concern. "I do know now that I belong here for now. I won't be safe until I learn the truth."

Francine touched her hand. "You may have a bit of my good sense after all. Welcome home, honey."

Katie took a deep breath, contemplating her. She struggled to put into words the gratitude she felt. "Thank you. After leaving Boston, I hoped love and acceptance waited for me here. But still, I had my doubts. Now you've put my private fears to rest and I have something to hang onto.

Pleasure shone in the sapphire eyes as she cradled Katie's hand between both of hers. "My dear, you are a treasure."

"I know now why you won't tell me the

truth. Something ungodly happened just before I was sent away. Maybe I caused it."

"The dream in Boston told you that?"

"I suppose so. I know now that you wouldn't send me away just because I'd become inconvenient with both my parents dead."

Francine observed her with placid expectancy. "You truly believed that?"

"Yes, I did."

"No need to spare my feelings." She looked away and let go of Katie's hand.

"I'm sorry if I offend you but I don't know what to do. You'll tell me nothing, so my panic in Boston is the only insight I've gained."

"Nothing in our lives happens without a reason. What happened here twenty years ago changed your path but I cannot imagine you could be a more capable, delightful woman had you remained at *Radbourne*. Perhaps Jessie did more for you than an indulgent mother."

Did Aunt Jessie do more for me than you might have? "All my life I've been waiting out this thing that keeps shoving me back and forth? I must know, yet I dread seeing what's there in the darkness that I can't see." She clutched the twisted fingers.

"My darling, Katie, I wish I could do what you want. I wish I could tell you everything. You say you know why I have kept silent. I will say you are correct about my motives. But I will not risk wounding you further by blurting out the whole story." Her look was beseeching.

"I can't blame you anymore. I only wish it was over." She was helpless against new tears.

"You are so strong. I can't put into words how gratified I am because of that. You belong here as mistress of *Radbourne*. It's time for the changing of the guard."

Katie took the Kleenex she handed her and wiped her face in an attempt to regain some composure.

"This is your heritage," Francine went on. "Do you believe in predestination?"

"Yeah, I do, even if it's hard to accept that we're locked into a life plan we can't change. So we keep railing against destiny."

"Perhaps it is not as arbitrary as that. But nevertheless, I believe fate exerts a powerful influence.

"Did Jeremy get his theories from you?"

Francine smiled faintly. "As a matter of fact, I got more of my theories from him. He is a very spiritual man and he and I have enjoyed many a lively discussion."

"So you're convinced I was destined to come back here?"

"From the moment you were born, you were bound to *Radbourne*. You told me yourself you would have come back even if I had not summoned you. My letter only made it simpler to chart your course."

Katie left her chair and moved to the nearest window. Down on the lawn, Becca and Jekyll chased each other in mad circles. "So you've decided to make me your heir?"

"I still have time before I contact my attorney. Perhaps I'm waiting for you to have a change of heart, for you to *want* what I'm offering, knowing its worth lies within you, not at the bank."

Katie felt disappointment so keen she wanted to continue weeping. The barriers were up again and there were no more words, no way to make Francine understand how she felt. She'd tried so many times.

"When I choose, I will tell you and Jeremy together what I've decided," she said dismissively. Speaking of Jeremy, what are you going to do about him."

"Take your advice."

Francine remained silent, yet satisfaction bordering on triumph made her smile.

With a final peeved glance at Francine's smug face, Katie circled from the window and kissed her cheek. She wanted to make a rude comment about her presumptions but declined and headed downstairs..

After she'd settled Becca in bed after dinner, Katie entered the drawing room where she knew Jeremy waited. From the sofa, he watched her sit beside him. Leaning forward, she pressed her hands to the ache in her lower back.

"You okay?"

"My period."

He considered her with knowing concern. "Shall I get you some ibuprofen?"

"That would be lovely." She squeezed his hand.

Interlacing his fingers with hers, he bent closer to kiss her. "I'll be right back."

Katie hugged herself, savoring their new ease. Her doubt and confusion were even more distant tonight, irrelevant.

He returned with water and the bottle of pain killer. After she swallowed the tablets, he reached for her. Once he arranged pillows under her head, she stretched out, relaxing. Slowly, he slid his hand down to massage her lower belly. "Okay?"

"Umm, I love it." She closed her eyes, drifting. "Without your mother, how'd you get to know women so well?"

He was puzzled. "You think I do?"

"You know you do." She didn't open her eyes.

"I guess Francine got hold of me before it was too late. When I was ten or so, she started writing me letters every week, and we talked on the phone. She claims she had a premonition that I'd be coming to live with her. She said I could come help her breed mares. She made everything sound exciting. Breeding mares sounded cool but also pretty gross and embarrassing. When I did end up moving here, she was very open and matter-of-fact about it all and soon had me bringing the stallions to the mares without blushing. I still love the whole process of producing a foal from breeding to birth."

His gaze drifted to the fire on the hearth. "While Francine taught me about the horses, she also gave me insight into girls and cleared up a lot of the big mysteries. One day in sixth grade, a girl had bled on the back of her skirt. I felt bad for her because some of the boys were pointing and whispering, but I was clueless. Later, I asked Francine what that was all about. After she'd filled in the gaps in my sex education, she said never to disrespect a woman during her period because it's one of God's biggest miracles. I never forgot just how she said that. It made a big impression on me and I became that girl's guardian from afar, making sure none of the boys ever gave her a bad time again. If they had, I was ready for battle."

"My knight." Katie reached up to touch his face. "That was a wonderful thing you did in case no one ever told you."

He laughed. "Actually, Francine praised me extravagantly. As for me, that episode proved that I could talk to her about absolutely everything, and I was amazed at all the things she knew, like how to get a girl to talk to me." His voice was warm now with reminiscence.

"I can't believe that was ever one of your big problems." Reveling in his touch, Katie still didn't look at him.

"Madam, have you no memory of being twelve? As I recall, everything was either intimidating or mortifying. But Francine claimed positive thinking makes all the difference. She said compliments also work wonders, but only if they're sincere. If I complimented a girl's sweater, I had to really like it. At twelve I didn't grasp the finer nuances of what she was telling me."

"That came later obviously." Katie pushed up on her elbows. "You understand that women are born of mystery. Not many men get that, you know. Most find women threatening."

He gave her a smile. "I'd definitely agree that mystery's your magic. You came here with a boatload of secrets and intrigue that've had

Francine and me in a state of astonishment ever since. Becca's tail over tea kettle for you as well."

"If I'd known the effect I'd have on everyone, I'd have come sooner," she mused.

He studied her silently for a time. "You know years back, Francine also told me women are born of mystery. She said it almost exactly the same as you did a minute ago."

Katie felt a tingling of wonder at this new insight into her grandmother's philosophy of life. "She does manage to flabbergast me at times."

"Did this help?" Jeremy asked as his fingers continued tracing slow circles."

"Yes." She tugged him down for a kiss. "Thanks."

He shifted to lie beside her, their separate thoughts pondering the new connection to Francine across years and generations.

"I knew you two were amazing," Jeremy said, "but I had no idea you have ESP."

"Are you serious or teasing me?"

"A little of both, I think, but either way, I love it!" He pressed his lips to her temple.

She felt loved and safe and drowsy. The despair she'd suffered in Boston was far removed tonight.

When Katie woke sometime later, her elbow hit Jeremy square in the chest.

"...W...Whoa...." He'd sat up and was staring at her.

"Sorry. I must've been dreaming. She draped her arms around him. "Becca was talking to me...."

"While you were sleeping?"

"I guess. Have you noticed anything strange going on with her?"

"Like what?"

"Earlier she told me she's going to see her mom soon. She made it sound like you were going to take her."

"What? That's crazy. Why would she say that?"

"Maybe she wants some resolution no matter what."

He disentangled himself from her and got to his feet. When he returned with two glasses of brandy, he handed her one but didn't sit down.

"Jeremy, please don't think I'm interfering, but you have to talk to her. She's way too smart to go on this way for very long."

He glowered down at her. "Just what the hell am I going to say?"

"The truth but in the most gentle way possible. Say her mom can't get well and right now it'd be too sad for Becca to see her. Say nurses and doctors are taking really good care of her mom and when Becca's a little older and can understand better, you'll take her to see her."

Jeremy's hand shook so the brandy sloshed from the glass. "If I told her that, it would absolutely break her heart. And who am I to tell her Evelyn's isn't getting better. Sometimes terminal patients get well."

Katie felt threatened by the same futility that had filled her days before she fled to Boston. Now she set her glass aside and edged forward on the sofa, pressing her hands together. "Jeremy, I don't have the answers. I just know what I saw in Becca tonight. It was like she wanted to shock me so I would pay attention to what she was saying. I knew she was lying and that upset me but even that didn't seem to worry her."

Jeremy emptied his glass and slammed it down on the mantle with such force Katie half expected it to shatter. "I won't be manipulated by my seven-year-old. I know how much she's hurting but I'm the adult. I know what she can handle. I'll talk to her but I won't destroy the illusions that keep her afloat."

"Are they her illusions or yours?"

He gave her a exasperated glance, then came to sit beside her. "I know you want to help, but I've been floundering around in this crap for two years. I have to do what I can to protect Becca."

Katie retrieved her glass and gulped some brandy, watching calamity hurtling toward them with no way to stop it. There was nothing to explain her foreboding, only a raw reaction to the resolve in Becca's eyes, a dangerous overtaxing of a child's patience.

She slipped her hand into his.

"I'm really not an ogre."

"I never thought that...a ghoul maybe." She let her head drop onto his shoulder. "I have an excuse for meddling. I love your little girl."

His lips nuzzled her cheek. "And we've both fallen in love with you."

A tremor drifted through her even as she sat very still, afraid to reveal all she was feeling.

He tipped back his head to survey her.

"You look better. That little catnap must've helped."

"I slept longer before dinner."

He massaged her shoulder. "I knew that. I went to see Francine while you were sleeping. Until she asked me to mail that letter, she made it her business to keep me in the dark about the two of you. Even that day, she told me very little. Now I love hearing her talk about you when you were little. She adores you. I know you're worried about this inheritance business but she'll do the right thing."

"I understand that now." She considered the sinuous dance of the flames. "We're both very loved by that lady. Can you imagine me saying that when I first got here."

"You'd have sooner had her drawn and quartered. And me as well." He took her into his arms.

Slowly she let everything but the two of them filter out of reach.

His kiss was gentle, still tentative. He murmured her name.

Her entire body came alive, straining toward him. Gradually the tenderness gave way to urgency. Nothing, no one, had prepared her for this raw sexual need. Not the three boys, men, she was with before Zachary, certainly not her husband. Trembling, she pulled away a little, her heartbeat hammering against his.

"Katie, my God, I want you...I love you...."

Just the stalwart feel of him reassured her. How could someone this slender be this strong and resolute? She had always prided herself on her self-reliance but at this moment, she gave herself completely to the certainty that he would keep her safe.

Now he held her still while he claimed her mouth anew, this kiss hard, uncompromising. It was a long time before he looked at her again. "Will you go to the cabin with me next week? Becca's going to a birthday party."

Katie hesitated. "Francine's cabin? Won't that cause questions?"

"That's why I talked to Francine tonight. Everyone takes their cues from her."

His breath was hot on her cheek and knuckles brushed soft patterns against her breast. "Katie...I want to make love to you. Will you go with me?"

She knew a final moment of unease, a recognition of the danger, but as she'd known the day she tried running away from him to Boston, the decision was already made. "Yes."

CHAPTER NINE

Katie pulled up her horse and looked back over the vista rolling down toward *Radbourne*. Leaden clouds hung in the west while ruffles of fog lay in the valleys.

She lifted her camera. After two shots, she sat still, letting the quiet and solitude wash over her. A faraway rumble emanated from the clouds steadily building in a great crest above the mountains. Her senses quickened; exhilaration sang along every nerve.

"Do you ever get used to the stillness?" she asked Jeremy.

"No. Sort of makes one want to whisper, doesn't it?"

She laughed and urged Murphy closer to his horse. "Is it going to rain?"

He considered the clouds roiling in ominous banks. "That'd be my guess. Maybe snow too."

"Isn't it kind of late for thunder?"

"Here, hardly anything is out of the question. We've had thunderstorms in January in the middle of a blizzard." He grinned at her. "Maybe we'll get snowed in."

"I'd love that."

The storm system built rapidly now and before they'd ridden another half mile, wind swept down the slopes, lashing the trees. Rain fell in large drops, making the horses jittery. Katie slid her camera into a water tight bag around her neck.

"Want to put on the slickers, or shall we make a run for it?" Jeremy shouted over the wind.

Racing the final distance to the cabin was irresistible. "Let's go!" She clamped her heels to Murphy's sides.

Both horses charged up the trail. Katie's blood pounded and her hair whipped down her back. Oblivious to the thickening rain, she knew only the intoxication of the chase that reminded her of her fox hunting days.

When they reached the cabin, they halted in a small stable fully prepared for the horses that they rubbed down and blanketed, finally leaving them snug in stalls. Outside, Jeremy grabbed Katie's hand and they ran through the downpour. Lightning flashed nearby, followed by huge booms of thunder that made Katie duck.

They were both laughing when they burst into the cabin thoroughly soaked. Jeremy left Katie dripping on a rag rug while he lit the prepared sticks and logs in the stone fireplace. Then he was back, holding her. They kissed, melded by the magic and madness.

They drew apart long enough to pull off their wet clothing, their eyes holding each other as fingers tugged at buttons and zippers. When Katie stood before him nude, he enveloped her in his warmth, his hands caressing, inciting.

Their movements slowed into an erotic dance without music. Despite aching for consummation, each sensed in the other the reluctance to break the spell of discovery, the dimension of newness they could never know again. They remained there in the widening circle of heat from the fire until Jeremy swept her into his arms and carried her to the bed in the corner, laying her on fresh sheets.

He gathered her body to his, trailing kisses from her mouth, over her cheek, across the curve of her neck to her breasts and lower. She returned his hunger with a fervor she'd not known she possessed, hadn't known could exist for any woman.

Rain hammered on the roof while thunder shook the cabin, the fury fueling their reckless pleasure. Moving together with ease and unexpected familiarity, they merged with the primal rhythm, became part of the storm's frenzy. A perfect perception of each other and the violence outside flowed between them until at last, they neared completion.

She moaned with her need and then went still, suspended. He slid one hand along her arm until he entwined his fingers with hers, both trembling. Then they clung together as he followed her over the edge.

When at last they lay quietly, Katie had no wish to find the part of herself apart from Jeremy. She wrapped her arms around him, holding him fast against her as spent passion lulled her toward the welcoming void of sleep.

She came awake awhile later to find Jeremy propped on one elbow, watching her with such tenderness and love, she suddenly felt tears rising.

She tugged him to her, kissing him as her hands explored the planes of his back, his long, muscled thighs. She pressed his shoulders until he lay flat and then scattered kisses over his chest and lean stomach, pleasuring him with her mouth and hands until he groaned, drawing her up to kiss her with renewed need.

It was then that she straddled him, taking him again. Her body's slow rhythm fed his arousal until his restraint broke and he tensed against her.

"Oh, God," he breathed when Katie snuggled along his side, her head nestled into his shoulder.

Evening shadows fell across the bed. Katie glanced at the fireplace where he'd hung their clothes over the backs of chairs. Her gaze circled the room. When they approached the place, she'd expected something of a crude shelter. Again she realized this was more like a charming cottage. But, of course, she mused, her grandmother would never settle for a line shack out of a B western.

Three wide windows offered a majestic view of the Big Horns. Now snow hung in a shroud over the meadow, creating isolation that Katie knew was all too elusive. She longed to stay there.

She turned toward the pull of Jeremy's gaze. His face was open, conveying the same chaos of emotions that circled in her brain – hope, fulfillment, delight, and something she couldn't name. Vulnerability? Fear?

He traced his knuckle along her jaw. "Katie, I love you."

He'd said those words so many times while they made love. She'd said them as well in frank, conscious surrender.

"You do believe that, don't you?" He held her chin steady.

"Yes, my dearest, Jeremy. If you have any doubt about that, you haven't been paying attention all this time I've been here in this bed, making wild, wonderful love with you."

He relaxed, staring at the ceiling a moment before he laughed. "Wow, I had no idea this whole adventure would bring out all my insecurities."

"Are you going to become my darkly jealous lover?"

His eyes reflected her teasing. "Maybe." Easing up on elbows, he looked toward the darkening sky. "But right now, we better head down or they may not see us until spring." He rested his chin in his propped hand. "How am I going to bear not making love to you until we come back?"

"We'll have to come back very soon. Do they sell snowmobiles in Wyoming?"

"What a good idea." He grinned, tapping the end of her nose.

Dressed again in clothes now warm and dry, they walked to the stable through snow. After donning slickers, they were underway down the mountain.

They traveled as fast as the slippery trail allowed and by the time darkness had fallen, they entered the *Radbourne* stable yard. Stable boys came for the horses before they headed to the manor, Jeremy's gloved hand on her back guiding Katie.

When they came to Bordeaux's glen, Jeremy drew her into his arms, his kiss. Clinging to him, she felt strangely sad and alone. Would it always be this way? Stolen joy, always ending.

He soon set her back from him and tucked her hand into the crook of his elbow as they continued through the snow to the rear balcony. They were still taking off their slickers in the utility room when Pearl rushed in.

"Thank God, you're back!" The panic in her plump face sent instant alarm through Katie. "It's Becca." She twisted her hands. "She ran away from the birthday party and went to the nursing home...."

"Where is she now!?" Jeremy demanded, a vein throbbing in his temple.

"In her bedroom."

He and Katie ran into the hall. Katie was unable to think beyond the certainty that Becca had possibly seen her mother. *Please, God, let her be okay.*

They reached Becca's room together. She lay on her side atop of the comforter, wide-awake with Jekyll crowding close beside her, his big, soft eyes never shifting from her. There was no sign of injury, yet something was terribly wrong. Her eyes mirrored a hurt so intense it clearly took every ounce of her strength to withstand it.

Jeremy knelt beside her, brushing the damp hair from her face. "Sweetheart, are you all right?"

She didn't respond, gave no indication she'd heard.

Jeremy glanced up at a tall man Katie didn't recognize. "Katie, this is Dr. Scott Remington. He's an old friend and most everyone's doctor around here."

"Hi, Katie." Scott smiled warmly before he

turned to Jeremy. "We should talk." He nodded toward the hall.

Jeremy and Katie's followed.

"Becca must've been planning this for awhile because she pulled it off without anyone knowing what she was up to." Scott stood with folded arms, his thin face grim. "That party was just a few blocks from the nursing home. She managed to get in there and find Evelyn. A nurse found her there by the bed, freaking out, screaming at her mother, trying to make her talk. Fortunately, the nurse knew who she was and called Pearl who immediately phoned me. I picked up Becca and gave her a sedative before bringing her home.

Jeremy leaned against the wall, one hand holding Katie's in the crook of his arm. "So what the hell's going on with her?"

"Shock. She saw for herself there's nothing left of her mother. No more fantasy, no way to block out the truth. So now she's grieving. It'll take awhile but she's tough. On the subconscious level, she wanted a confrontation. She was ready to risk everything to settle the matter in her mind."

Katie glanced at Jeremy, feeling no victory at the doctor practically echoing her own words of last week.

He stared at the floor, his jaw set. She saw his struggle to accept what his trusted friend had said.

"I wish you'd prepared her for what she had to know," Scott said, "but I can't fault your motives. It's a moot point now so no need to beat yourself up. She needs you, and you have to help her through the rest of it. She'll be fine in the end;

I promise you that."

"What can we do for her?" Katie was so eager to help to help Becca, she couldn't curb her impatience.

"Talk to her, tell her what she needs to hear, that she's safe. It won't be easy reaching her because she's drawn so far into herself. That's her only defense since everything's been torn to hell inside her head. Even if you don't think she hears you, keep talking because some of it'll get through. It will give her grounding to what's safe and certain, and help her find her way back." He put a hand on Jeremy's arm, smiled at Katie, then turned toward the stairs. "I'll be back in the morning. If you need me sooner, call."

Katie moved closer to Jeremy as his shoulders sagged with exhaustion. Tears lay in his eyes. She entwined her fingers with his. "Let's go sit with her."

In the bedroom, they found Cheryl sitting by the window. Her cold eyes settled on Jeremy. "Where were you?"

"Out." He lowered himself to the bed. "Thanks, Cheryl. Katie and I can handle this now."

With a snort, Cheryl charged out. Watching her enraged departure, Jeremy moved to the rocking chair and sat with one leg thrown over the side.

Katie went to Becca and began massaging her back. "Sweetie, we're right here. We won't leave you alone. Your dad and I went riding this afternoon and guess what happened while we were up on the mountain. It started so snow. I wish you could've seen how pretty it was."

Becca sighed and turned on her back, her eyes on Katie for a second before they closed again.

"Yes, you sleep now and don't worry about a thing. I'm going to tell you something very special that I've never told anyone before. I have two guardian angels who talk to me and keep me safe. You, my sweet Becca, have angels of your own who are always near you. But right now when everything's so scary, I'm going to ask my angels to watch over you, They may whisper cool things in your ear. You won't be afraid with them close by."

She straightened, searching Becca's face, seeing that she slept and the unbearable confusion was gone. She stooped to brush her lips over her forehead. "Night, honey."

Becca sighed and threw one arm over Jekyll. Katie spread the comforter over both, catching Jeremy's intent gaze.

"Is that true about your angels?" He held out his hand and she went to sit on his lap, relaxing into the circle of his arms.

"Yes. They started talking to me when I first got to Boston. I was so sick I would've died if they hadn't held onto me and helped me through the sorrow."

"You may be interested to know that angels are plentiful at *Radbourne.* They scared the hell out of me when I moved here. When I told Francine, she said it's an amazing gift being able to communicate with them. She said they'd been talking to her since she was three years old."

"When he came to see her, was my grandfather an angel?"

"No, he was a ghost."

Katie thought *Radbourne's* supernatural bent was another contributing force pulling her back here. "I was just destroyed when Zachary and Ursel died. One night I was feeling so alone and afraid. I'd gone to bed and was floating just before sleep when one of my angels whispered in my ear. "Katie, you're going to be just fine. We're taking care of you so don't worry about a thing.""

When Jeremy made no comment, her mind veered to their time at the cabin. Memory of their passion was an opiate to her troubled spirit. Still, the enormity of cause and effect was all too clear when they returned to find Becca sick and confused.

Pearl tapped on the door, then stepped in without waiting for a response. She hurried to Becca, her features carefully neutral when she discerned the new status between Jeremy and Katie. "I've been sitting with Mrs. Chamberlain. She wants to talk to one of you before she goes to sleep." She leaned over the bed. "The little darling's finally resting. God bless her." She frowned. "If only I'd sensed what she was planning, I wouldn't have let her out of my sight."

"Pearl, let's not go there," Jeremy said. "If anyone's to blame, it's me. Now please go home. You're exhausted."

"Very well, then. Good night." With a little bow, she stepped out.

"Why don't you go see Francine," Jeremy said. "Tell her I'll see her in the morning."

Sudden anger at him and fear for Becca pulled Katie to the window where she stood trying not to cry. He followed and put his arms around her.

"Thanks for caring so much, Katie." He looked into her eyes.

She kissed his cheek. "I won't be long." She turned toward the hall.

"Honey, please go to bed when you're finished with your grandmother. You're so tired and I need to be alone. I'll stay here with Becca."

She forced calm into her voice. "I love you, Jeremy."

He kissed her cheek and she left him, carrying away the certainty that he was pulling away from her, back into the self-deception that had faded in recent days. She acknowledged the futility she'd recognized when she first realized Evelyn's power.

Lamplight fell over Francine's bed when Katie approached. "How is she?" she asked without preamble.

Katie sat on the edge. "According to Scott, it's like her mother has died. She's in the same kind of shock and grief."

"Then she'll be all right." She snatched off her spectacles. "She's dealing with the truth instead of that fairytale Jeremy's been cooking up for her."

"He's still not ready to give that up."

"Not even now? With matters as they are between you two?"

Katie shrugged. "It might be different if this hadn't happened today. As it is, I feel him going back inside the pain and denial."

Her grandmother took her hand. "How I wish it was in my power to help both of you through this. I do know that time always gives us answers, showing the way out of even the worst pain." She replaced her glasses, inspecting Katie over the top. "Jeremy will deal with the truth. I have every faith in that. It's his integrity as a man."

Katie sat still, drawing solace from the insight, letting the quiet grow within her.

"Go to bed now, dear, before you fall over." She gave her a smile. "And do not start feeling guilty."

Katie kissed her. "Thanks for being so wise."

Jeremy awoke to the sound of Becca crying. "Daddy...please hold...me."

"I've got you, sweetie." He strode to the bed, scooped her up and returned to the rocking chair.

"Oh, Daddy, Mommy wouldn't talk to me." The words came in an agonized moan. "She just lay there and wouldn't say anything. Before she went to that place, I scared her sometimes and she'd yell at me and cry. Today, she lay there with her mouth open, staring at the wall. She's not pretty anymore. She has hair all over her face and she smells...." She broke off into sobs.

Jeremy swallowed hard and it was awhile before he could steady his turmoil enough to speak. "Honey, I know how much it hurt you seeing her that way. I wanted to keep you safe from that but I was wrong not to tell you how sick she really is. I'm very sorry."

He wasn't sure Becca heard him because her weeping grew more tortured. She lay curled in a little ball against him. He cried with her, sickened and relieved at the same time to be so out of control.

He continued talking to her, opening his heart, forgetting he was speaking to a child. At last, she was still, exhausted.

Scanning her mournful face, he saw the change, the calm after a terrible storm. Was this the grappling with grief Scott had predicted. If so, she'd clearly come partway through the agony.

Tonight he didn't bother putting her back to bed. The gray-gold light of sunrise was just lighting the bedroom when Katie found them both asleep in the chair.

With daylight, Jeremy's hope for Becca gave way to renewed worry. She appeared little changed from the night before, still and withdrawn. She didn't mention her mother again and seemed oblivious to the gentle encouragement from her dad and Katie.

"There will be ups and downs and lots of false starts, probably for weeks, maybe months," Scott Remington predicted when he arrived. It's a very good sign that she's already let down her guard a little. It's scary returning to reality. It feels much safer looking at the pictures in her head of how she'd like things to be. When the truth doesn't look so threatening, she'll come all the way back."

A tall, spare man with a calm demeanor, Scott remained with them for an hour, his serene demeanor offering sensitivity and hope. Before he left, he managed to coax a weak smile from Becca.

Katie thought he was likely Jeremy's age although his hair was gray. She was quickly aware of the important role he played as the family's doctor.

Jeremy continued sleeping beside Becca's bed at night. He and Katie stayed with her during the day. At the end of the week, Francine had her wheelchair carried down to Becca's room where she spent an hour, earnestly talking to her, mostly about Jekyll and Juniper.

Everyone in the house had been struggling to deal with Becca's lack of further progress out of the her grief and suffering. It had been nearly two weeks when Katie sat beside her bed one afternoon, reading *The Wind In The Willows.*

"Don't read any more."

"Okay." Katie laid the book aside, appraising her.

"Do you have a mother?"

"She died when I was a little girl."

"Littler than me?"

"Yes."

"Do you remember her?"

"No."

Becca thought about that for awhile, then slid further under the comforter, burrowing her head into a pillow.

Katie waited but she said no more and was soon asleep. She wondered what, when she'd come so close, kept Becca from mentioning Evelyn.

Jeremy hardly ate or slept. Fatigue shadowed his features and the haunted aspect deepened in his eyes.

Katie suffered with him, yet was helpless to reach him. Their intimacy was now remote. They spent hours together every day but he was no longer the man she'd come to love. He was back in a world off limits to her.

Patrick came to see Becca most every afternoon. He regaled her about the fabulous autumn weather and the fun he was having riding the young horses up the mountain. He told her that her dad had given permission for Becca to ride with him whenever she liked.

A month ago, she would've been ecstatic at such an opportunity to be free of the arena and riding with Patrick on the mountain she loved so much. Now she could only smile wanly even as she refused to budge.

Scott said Becca should be persuaded to take up her usual routine but nothing interested her. Even when Katie helped her dress in jeans and t-shirt, hoping to entice her to visit Patrick and Juniper even if she didn't want to ride, but again she refused to leave her room and was soon back in bed.

Although she cried at unexpected times, it was the weeping of someone exhausted and bewildered. The tempest of agony that'd swept over her the first night never returned. She continued in her prison of fear and bereavement until she reached the end of her struggle the last week in November.

Jeremy awoke in the rocking chair to a scene very different from what had greeted him for so many painful mornings. Becca, already dressed in jeans and sweater, sat on her bed, swinging her legs, fondling Jekyll's ears.

Jeremy was so startled that he started to get up but sat back, studying her instead.

She cocked her head, grinning. "Daddy, you can sleep in your bed again now."

He relaxed, unsure of what had occurred exactly yet aware of its import. He could think of nothing to say to her.

"Are you happy you don't have to sleep in that rocking chair anymore."

He rubbed his neck. "You can't imagine. Honey, I'm so happy." He moved to sit by her, wrapping one arm around her frailness.

She looked up at him, her eyes bright. "Now I know why you couldn't take me to see my mom."

Jeremy's breath caught in his chest. How many times she'd approached this moment, then retreated without putting her thoughts into words. "Tell me, hon."

"You knew it would be too sad." She jumped off the bed and stood beside Jekyll, hugging his neck as she surveyed her father. "But I had to see."

"I know that."

Her features creased with concentration. "I'm going to remember when I got Jekyll.

Jeremy's mind reached back to Christmas three years ago when Becca discovered the shepherd, newly graduated from his year of service dog training, sitting under the tree with a big red bow around his neck.

"My mom was so pretty and she laughed." Tears trembled at the edge of her eyes. "I'll remember that and it won't hurt so much."

He was amazed at her innocent resolve to find a way through the fear.

"When I'm twelve, I'll go see her again. I won't be so scared then." Her tone was matter-of-fact, almost dismissive. With a sigh, she came to put her arms around her father. Returning her embrace, he buried his face in her hair, giving silent thanks.

Katie, arriving a bit later, saw the change. She sat beside Jeremy and Becca was instantly before her, gazing up at her. "I feel better."

"I can see that." She smiled at Jeremy who winked.

"I can go to school now." Despite her outward bravery, her voice shook.

"Monday will be soon enough for school." Jeremy reached for Katie's hand and kissed it. "In the meantime, Patrick will be delighted to have a riding student again."

Becca's eyes held her old merriment. "May I go tell him after breakfast?"

"Yes you may, but right now, will you go tell Pearl what you want for breakfast."

Becca put her hands on Katie's knees, looking into her face. "What would *you* like for breakfast?"

Touched, Katie kissed the end of her nose. "Let's have French toast," she said, knowing this was Becca's favorite.

"Okay." She consulted her dad. "Should I tell Francine I'm fine again? She was really worried about me." Jeremy nodded and they watched her bounce to the door, disappearint into the hall with a jubilant Jekyll. The dog's renewed animation indicated his awareness of Becca's emotional return.

Jeremy gave Katie a rueful look. Deep

fatigue weighted his shoulders. "I must say, I'm pretty jealous of her resilience."

During the next weeks, Jeremy and Katie continued in their separate orbits, only finding time occasionally to have a drink together in the drawing room and talk. They couldn't recapture the intimacy they'd known before Becca's meltdown. Jeremy was often away from *Radbourne* for hours at a stretch and Katie knew he was with Evelyn.

That reality sat at the back of her mind, leaving her in a challenging limbo where she no longer had a firm perspective on her life to come. She was again lost in uncertainty.

Only Becca was carefree as she'd not been since Katie arrived at *Radbourne*. Her demons defeated, she again behaved like a rambunctious seven-year-old and her nightmares had stopped.

Watching her with such gratitude, Katie wondered if Jeremy would ever find the same resolution. Or if she would., for that matter.

CHAPTER TEN

The first heavy snow came to *Radbourne* the week after Thanksgiving. All the horses were housed in the barns now. The broodmares that had run free on the mountain all summer and fall had been coaxed down to the barns where they were separated from their foals.

The confined weanlings continued their early lessons in the kindness of humans. Every day when stable hands mucked out stalls, they spent time with each youngster. As Patrick instructed, they ran gloved hands over wooly bodies and picked up each hoof, talking quietly all the while. On warm, sunny days, all the horses were turned out into paddocks. Katie and Becca loved watching everyone romping about.

Bordeaux was moved into a large stall connected to his enclosure next to the stream. He could come and go as he pleased but seemed to prefer romping outside to being confined.

The horses bound for winter shows wore heavy blankets and hoods to keep their coats short and glossy. The garb reminded Katie of medieval warhorses draped in their masters' coats of arms.

Jeremy and Katie remained in their indeterminate state, unable to connect with each other as *Radbourne* manor was transformed into a showplace of yuletide goodwill. Three days before Christmas, Francine carried on a tradition begun when she and Boyd Gellis were first married. Friends and employees were invited to a Christmas open house.

Francine held court near the towering, twinkling spruce in the parlor. For three hours in late afternoon, guests filled the house, enjoying bourbon-spiked eggnog and fruitcake laced with rum. It was dark before Jeremy ushered out the last guest.

Katie lingered with Francine. "This was wonderful. What a marvelous tradition."

Jeremy returned from the front door with Becca who inspected Francine magnificently attired in green velvet. "That was a very nice party and you look so pretty tonight."

"Thank you, my dear Becca." She drew her close and kissed her cheek.

Jeremy kissed Francine before sitting beside her.

"You were an exemplary host. Thank you, Jeremy." She clasped his hand.

"My pleasure. You throw a mean cocktail party. Everyone left happy." He winked. "Did you sample your eggnog?"

She smiled musingly. "If only I could have without bringing on a heart attack." Leaning closer, she patted his knee. "In my day, I would have polished off considerable eggnog."

"No doubt." He laughed as Becca came to snuggle in his lap.

"I'm hungry."

He craned his neck to look at her. "You're not a fan of eggnog and fruitcake?"

She wrinkled her nose. "Maybe when I'm

forty."

"What if I take my favorite women to McDonalds?"

"Cool." Becca clapped her hands.

"Let's go for casual and wear jeans." He gently urged her off his lap and rose to summon the wheelchair bearers while Pearl began cleaning up.

Francine still gazed out at the snow and lights, weary but content. Katie stood behind her, one hand on her shoulder, the other arm tight around Becca.

"This is the last open house," Francine said, no sadness in her voice, only wistful pleasure. "I've been doing this for decades. Do you think they realize there won't be any more?"

"Why wouldn't Jeremy keep on with it?"

"Perhaps he will if it's his place to do so."

As soon as the men arrived to carry Francine upstairs, Katie and Becca went up to change. Katie stopped in Becca's bedroom to help her out of her party dress, then continued to her own room. When she opened her door, she gasped at the sight of Jeremy sitting in her armchair.

"Oh, my gosh." She collapsed on the bed in delighted laughter.

"Sorry I scared you." He came to hold her, searching her eyes. "I suppose I've pretty much blasted off the top of your shit list."

The ache of tears stopped her laughter. "Something like that."

His arms tightened and he rested his forehead on hers. "My Katie. Jesus, it hurts when I can't be close to you." He brought up fingertips to wipe her wet face, studying her. "Sweetheart, are you still with me? You've been so wonderful helping Becca, and I adore you for that. I'm so sorry I haven't told you that sooner." He frowned. "I've just been so confused and preoccupied with Becca, I didn't keep my priorities straight for awhile there. Can you ever forgive me? Probably in your shoes, I'd have taken a hike some time back."

"I'm still here and I will be as long as I know you love me." She touched his face, seeking assurance. "After our time at the cabin, I couldn't help but be in for the duration. That's just the way I am. When I give my body and soul, I'm very serious."

"Thank God," he breathed, rocking her tenderly. "You may be interested to know that I took Scott's advice. I'm talking to a therapist."

Elation washed through her. "Oh, I'm so glad, Jeremy."

"Please don't give up on me."

"Not in this lifetime." With a final kiss, she got up to change.

Jeremy followed and when she stood before her closet, she felt his fingers lowering the zipper of her snug black dress. He tugged down the spaghetti straps. "You looked fabulous today." His mouth explored her back. "I better go find Becca before I get us both in trouble," he murmured when her dress slid to the floor, but stayed where he was, watching her pull on jeans and a sweater.

When she sat on the bed to put on boots, he joined her, nuzzling her neck, then pushed her down on the comforter, kissing her until a noise in the hall caused them both to groan. "I think we're busted."

They were on their feet a second before Becca tapped on the door. Katie collected her coat. "McDonalds, here we come."

Christmas night, Katie sat in the parlor with Becca. The tree sparkled in all its tinsel splendor. Becca, dressed for dinner, sat primly in a wingback chair, ankles crossed, looking at a book from her Christmas largess. Jekyll, sprawled by the fire, sporting a purple bow the exact shade of Becca's dress.

The tantalizing aroma of Pearl's roasting goose drifted from the kitchen. Snow that afternoon had once more transformed the ranch. Huge flakes still drifted through the light beyond the windows.

"Do you like goose?" Becca inquired.

"Not especially."

"Daddy and I don't either. It's greasy. We have it because Francine likes it. She's had it every Christmas since she was a baby, I think."

"It's nice of you to let her have what she likes." When Becca didn't answer, Katie's thoughts returned to the scene at hand.

Cheryl was in Chicago visiting a niece. Pearl had been cooking all afternoon and was now upstairs helping Francine dress for dinner in the dining room for the first time since Katie arrived from Boston. Unease edged through Katie. Not even the carols from the CD player eased her feeling of being caught in a surreal scene where all was grandly in order, yet in chaos.

Jeremy was with Evelyn and those at *Radbourne* had waited two hours with no idea when he might join them. With the resignation and good humor that'd visited themselves on Becca in recent weeks, she seemed oblivious to Katie's tension. She was no longer so keen at picking up negative vibes.

Now she jumped out of her chair. "Daddy's home!"

He walked in from the front hall dressed in a gray flannel suit. Katie was caught off guard by his dynamism, the current of sexual energy undiminished by his chronic sadness. Tonight she discerned an easing of his anguish.

He swept Becca into his arms. "Did you think I got lost in the snow."

She shrugged and hung her arm over his shoulder. "We knew you'd want to stay with my mom longer tonight."

He kissed her before putting her down. "Please go tell Pearl I'm home." When she'd disappeared, he pulled Katie to him. "I'm sorry I'm so late, hon. I wasn't with Evelyn all this time. I needed to think so I walked around town for a couple hours. It was nice with the snow and all the lights. I wished you were with me." Stepping back, he took in the curves of her red satin dress. "You look amazing,"

"You're looking pretty amazing yourself." She slid her arms around him. "Do you feel better?"

"Great actually. Merry Christmas, my darling." He arched an eyebrow. "I have a surprise for you and Becca and Francine after dinner. And then one just for you."

"Sounds intriguing."

"You've no idea." His hands explored the contours of her breasts and hips with such delight it might have been the first time he touched her. His eyes held the same passion that coursed through Katie. "We better have dinner before I have you under the Christmas tree." He grinned and they proceeded to the dining room where Francine and Becca were already seated at the festive table.

Katie eased further into the warm curve of Jeremy's body. The snow had stopped and the moon bathed the landscape in pale silvery light. The bells on the horses' harness jingled merrily in the stillness.

Katie's mind played through the magic hours since Jeremy came home. After dinner, he said he had to check on a sick filly. Half an hour later, Katie, Becca and Francine, pushed in her wheelchair by Pearl, were drawn to the front windows by sleigh bells. Jeremy waved from an elegant swan sleigh pulled by two white Arabians.

"Oh, Daddy," Becca yelled, dashing coatless out the front door.

Francine clapped her hands with enjoyment when Jeremy stepped out, bowed and swept his arm toward the sleigh in invitation.

Katie ran out to retrieve Becca, then grabbed wraps from a closet. While she got Becca into warm things, Jeremy came to help Francine into the fur coat she hadn't worn for more than a year. Her laughter as Jeremy wheeled her out and lifted her into the sleigh was young and carefree. Katie could picture her as she must've been as a young girl, ready for any adventure.

They set off into the snowy world. Not wanting to tire Francine, Jeremy headed back after half an hour, but she would have none of that and insisted on a jaunt up the mountain. Despite the snow and freezing temperatures, the sleigh's cowhide lap robes kept them snug and warm.

"Jeremy, my boy, you are superb," Francine declared when he pulled up the horses in the front drive two hours later. "What a lovely Christmas gift. How long have you been working on this project?"

"I unearthed a wreck of a sleigh last spring and sent it back east to be restored. Patrick's been training the team for over a year. He plans to show them in carriage classes."

"What a splendid idea. I can't recall when I've enjoyed myself more." Francine's voice was serene, reflective.

When she and Becca were eventually settled in their beds, Jeremy led Katie to the sleigh still in the driveway. "We're going to take another ride, my love." He handed her in. "Just you and me." The sexual promise in his voice deepened the keen awareness that had lain between them all evening. His cold mouth brushed hers before he took up the reins. Soon enough in the whiteness all around she could see the faint outline of the cabin on the opposite side of the meadow. Her pulse quickened at the memory of the hours they'd spent there in October. A small eternity had passed since then.

Once they reached the stable and blanketed the horses, they tramped to the cabin. Katie noted a path had been shoveled between the two structures so someone had been there sometime earlier tonight.

She stopped, looking toward the mountains where the moon was intermittently covered by retreating clouds. "I want to remember every detail."

Jeremy's arms went around her from behind and he lay his cheek against hers. "No need for that. You'll be here again before the snow's gone."

Would she? She turned to face him, wishing she could read what lay in his eyes but they were hidden by the night. She was afraid to ask if the last of his doubt was gone.

He soon drew her with him inside where a lamp was burning and the room was warm despite the dying fire on the hearth. "Generator," he said in answer to her questioning look.

She could hear the dull sound of a motor coming from somewhere beyond the rear wall.

"Otherwise it's a bit too frigid even with a fire," he added, walking to the fireplace to add logs. When new flames spread orange warmth over the rug, he was back, reaching for Katie.

He fell on his knees to undress her without haste, beginning with her boots, socks, then lacy panties, a sublimely erotic process that left her breathless. She lost all sense of time as she gave herself completely to his love pouring over her in words and kisses and intimate touch. Her body arched toward him in fierce response.

He groaned as his hands went beneath her dress, caressing her skin, unhooking her bra. Their shadows swayed together on the wall in an arousing waltz. She was conscious of every detail, the taste of him, his citrus cologne, the comfort of his arms holding her with such tenderness before he drew her down with him before the flames.

"Love me...."

"Oh, God, yes," he whispered as he put her beneath him.

The following afternoon, Jeremy, Katie and Becca built a snowman below Francine's tower. Several attempts at starting their creation had disintegrated into play with Jekyll and snowball fights but now the lower two-thirds of the body was complete.

"Hey you, over there with the camera," Jeremy called from where he and Becca struggled to heave the head into position, "we could use a little help here."

"I'm not into construction." Katie said, strolling toward them. "I am an artiste." She ducked the snowball Jeremy tossed at her. "Well, I can see I'm not appreciated here." Turning on her heel, she marched toward the rear entrance.

Minutes later, she'd searched closets and the kitchen, and was back with an old fedora, nuts, an apple, a carrot and a paring knife.

"Are you ready to show proper respect for my genius?" She stood before the featureless snowman. "I shall create a masterpiece."

Soon she stepped back to inspect the jolly fellow she'd fashioned, setting the hat on his head at a rakish angle. Finally, she pulled the purple scarf from her throat and tied it in a stylish knot around his fat neck.

Becca clapped her hands, laughing. "You are a genius!"

"Thank you, my dear, and by the way, *you* look fabulous, darling." She stood on tiptoe to kiss the droll gentleman's icy cheek.

Becca giggled and came to stand in front of her. Katie draped her arms over her shoulders as they looked to Jeremy for reaction.

He came to embrace them both. "He has a bit of the Elephant Man about him, don't you think?" He chuckled and leaned in to kiss Katie's cheek.

She looked up to find Francine framed in a window. The discovery that they were being watched unnerved her and she pulled free, murmuring that she wanted to take some pictures.

Walking away, she knew they'd looked like any teasing, laughing family and she was abruptly bent on escape. "I'm getting cold so I'm going in."

Jeremy was quickly beside her. "What happened out there?" he asked when they stood in the rear hall.

She pulled off her gloves, slowly meeting his gaze. "It scares me, I guess. Being so loved."

He enfolded her in his arms. "Honey, please don't be afraid. Believe in me. Just believe in us."

She held tight to him, needing reassurance, wanting to believe. Yet, the doubt remained, dispelling the magic.

Katie and Jeremy returned to the cabin often during the next months; when the snow grew too deep for the horses, they went by snowmobile. It became their refuge, the one place where no other consideration intruded on their love.

Still, the promise of Christmas once more

proved elusive. They could not totally find the completeness and sense of right that held them for those few hours. Katie realized again nothing had changed for Jeremy no matter how much he wanted it. He was still ruled by obligation.

They knew hours of intense happiness followed always by uncertainty. Katie seemed always waiting for a resolution that never came.

Other areas of her life were no less bewildering. Becca brought constant joy, even as Katie's dream and dread hovered close, then retreated Her bond with Francine deepened but the reality of the will couldn't be kept on hold much longer. Now she was more uncertain on that front as well. Her total disinterest in the ranch had evolved into a profound love. But she felt as strongly as ever that Jeremy must be Francine's heir.

Becca's new assurance lent the weeks one positive development. As surely as her night terrors and her constant waiting for calamity had released her, so had her habit of being intimidated by Cheryl. Now she ignored her grandmother, and when that wasn't possible, she faced her, protesting her criticism and bad temper.

For her part, though she glowered and threatened, Cheryl never had real authority over Becca and these days, except for meals, she rarely saw her. Katie had taken over all Becca's care not handled by Jeremy or Pearl.

The once tense, silent meals with Becca on the verge of tears were now lively affairs, filled with talk and laughter. Though, like Jeremy, Becca was studiously polite to Cheryl, she no longer let the woman unsettle her. Soon enough, her high spirits and chatter were too much for Cheryl who began eating all meals in her room.

"Why doesn't Grandma eat with us anymore? Becca inquired one night in April.

"She likes quiet while she eats." Jeremy grinned. "Have you been quiet during dinner lately?"

She giggled. "No." She concentrated on her Brussels sprouts a moment. "Patrick said I can ride in a real horse show next summer. In September, there's one in Billings where I can enter a bunch of classes. May I?"

"Just when did Patrick decide you're ready for the big time?"

"Today he said by September, I'll be ready. May I go, Daddy? Patrick'll take really good care of me."

Jeremy leaned back in his chair. "Honey, you know I wouldn't let you go without me. I'll talk to Patrick. If we decide it's time, Katie and I will both go"

Becca beamed at Katie. "Would you really?"

"But, of course. I love horse shows. Through the years, I've ridden in lots of them."

"Then you can ride in the Billings show too," Becca decided. "Murphy would do great."

"He might," her dad conceded, "but I think Katie might like to blow the competition out of the water on Bohjalian or one of the other stallions Patrick shows." He considered her, a twinkle in his eye.

She smiled, warmed by his confidence in her. "I think we'll have a lovely time."

"Me too!" Becca pressed her hands together under her chin, lost in happy contemplation. "I'll get all the entry stuff from Patrick," she said at last. "He said if I print, I can fill them out myself."

"I guess you gave him no peace until he agreed to that. But remember, I have to talk to him first and September is a long time from now."

"Well, yeah." Becca slid from her chair and went to hug him. "But I'm so happy. Thank you, Daddy."

"You're welcome, sweetie." He kiss her cheek.

Jeremy approved the trip to Billings the next day, and Becca returned from her riding lesson with a handful of entry forms. Jeremy had a dinner business meeting in Sheridan, so Katie and Becca ate without him.

"I want to fill out my entries," Becca announced after her bath.

"I'll be in the library if you need me."

Katie spent more and more time there, drawn by the pull in the back of her mind. The nightmare had receded into total silence. Katie concluded from past experience that the forces were gathering strength. But for what purpose? She had the dim impression that the stage was being set for one final clash of wills.

Tonight when she entered the library, she switched on the table lamp and went to her favorite window seat. She hadn't realized her visits there had become so ritualistic. She presently forced herself to see what she'd seen hundreds of times in the dream. There was no threat now, only an awareness of being where she belonged.

Some of her old handsome children books were stacked on the seat and she picked up one, flipping through it, as always hoping the bright illustrations, verses and rhymes might conjure a memory. The quest had become less driven and she came merely to love the solitary time when she could locate a core of calm within herself.

Now she looked outside. A warm Chinook had blown all week, removing most of the snow banks but tonight it had calmed. The trees stood still and stark in the lamplight. Jeremy's Honda glided along the drive to the carriage house.

He soon joined her, kissing her before he sat down, glancing at the open books. "Does it help coming here?"

"This room is a paradox. I feel safe here now, I suppose because on a subconscious level I remember how much I loved being here with my grandfather. But it's also where something ungodly happened. If I can figure out the contradiction, I'll have solved the puzzle."

He squeezed her hand and brought it to his lips. "I didn't know this room existed for several years after I came to *Radbourne*. The door was always locked. I never gave it much thought because there are lots of locked rooms on the second and third floors. I was a voracious reader but didn't really think that the house might have a library; there were hundreds of books to my liking in bookcases in my bedroom and downstairs.

"One summer Francine sent me to riding camp. When I got back, those double door stood open." He nodded across the room. "I was amazed to find this treasure trove of books. When I asked Francine why it'd been locked before, she said there had been a big hail storm that broke a window and there was water damage on the oak floor. So she'd had it refinished."

Katie pondered the explanation for the chamber being locked for several years. "I think she lied to you."

Before he could answer, Becca arrived with Jekyll. "I got them all finished!" She thrust the papers at her father.

Katie saw the tightening of his jaw. "Why'd you put Katie's name as your mother?" His eyes blazed into Becca's.

She stared at the floor a second, then looked up defiantly. "I thought it'd be okay because Katie's going with us, and my mom can't. Ever."

"Becca, that's beside the point. Katie isn't your mother."

Becca looked at Katie. "I'm sorry, I should have asked you."

"It's okay." Katie smiled and pulled her closer for a hug.

"It's time you were in bed," Jeremy said. "Go on down and I'll be there in a minute." He handed her the forms. "Take these with you and I'll look them over in the morning."

"Will you come say good night?" Becca asked Katie.

"Not tonight, sweetheart. I'll say goodnight now." She kissed her. "Sleep well." When she was gone, she met his troubled eyes.

"Well, I handled that well." He grimaced.

"Jesus, I can be a jerk."

How am I to deal with this? Katie wondered why she hadn't thought of a way, knowing sooner or later, she would be faced with this situation. "Don't apologize. I can't bear hearing how sorry you are."

"You're right. It'd accomplish nothing for me to apologize for something I can't change...." He studied her. "Damn it, Katie." His voice was hoarse and he grasped her shoulders. "I *am* sorry. I despise hurting you this way. But it's wrong to encourage Becca's fantasies."

Katie fought for control. "Don't you think I know that. Jeremy, I've worried about just this sort of thing. How Becca will cope when I leave."

Jeremy sighed. "I thought we were past talking about leaving."

"All love affairs end. You know I'll be leaving."

"I don't believe that."

She saw how genuinely wounded he was. "Let's keep playing it your way," she said at last. "For now."

"I love you, Katie." His smile kindled the gold undertones in his eyes. He held her against him and kissed her again before he walked out without looking back.

CHAPTER ELEVEN

Francine's eightieth birthday arrived in early May. After breakfast, Katie, Becca and Jekyll trouped up to wish her Happy Birthday. Halfway up the staircase, Becca unrolled the picture she'd painted. *"See it's all of Radbourne."*

"She'll love it. It's wonderful."

"I don't know." Becca scowled. "She's grumpy like my grandma sometimes."

"Don't you think you may be grumpy sometimes when you're eighty."

"I guess your bones hurt a lot."

"And remember, her heart is getting weaker. She can't breathe very well. Speaking of which, Scott has prescribed oxygen so that's something new."

Becca stopped, staring at her, fearful. "So she's getting sicker?"

"No, honey." Katie squeezed her shoulder. "The oxygen just makes it easier for her to breathe and helps her heart."

"If her heart hurts, is she sad?"

"There are two ways of talking about the heart. One is about feelings. The other is the organ that pumps Francine's blood. Haven't you studied that in school?"

"I'm only in second grade."

Becca's quick insight always made her seem older. "You're so smart, I forgot. Anyway,

Francine's heart is worn out but her feelings will never change."

"My mom's did."

Katie groped for words. "Actually, I think she still has the same feelings she had before she got sick. They're just locked inside her now."

Becca nodded with a feeble smile.

When they entered Francine's bedroom, Cheryl brushed past them with the breakfast tray. Francine, her eyes like daggers, hurled a magazine at her retreating back. Cheryl took a step back toward the bed. "Don't start with me, you miserable...."

Francine grabbed a pewter pitcher. "Get out! I'll bounce this off your brainless skull!"

Cheryl departed without further comment.

Would Cheryl actually hurt Francine? Though Katie despised the ridiculous woman, this possibility hadn't occurred to her.

Becca stared at the magazine lying beside the door, then giggled. "Why'd she make you so mad?" She sat beside Francine who rubbed Jekyll's ears, her gaze fixed on the top of his head.

She didn't look up for some time.

Becca took in the oxygen line. "Does that hurt your nose?"

The old woman came back to the moment. "It's just a big nuisance. I refused any part of it for years. I would not have it! Imagine not being able to breathe on my own." She sighed. "But then I got so weak and Scott said I was going to fall." She chucked Becca under the chin with a misshapen finger. "So I had to give in. Be sensible, were the words he used. I've always thought myself a sensible woman so I said, fine, bring in that horrid, noisy thing over there." She indicated the humming oxygen condenser some distance from the bed. "And I'll puff oxygen the livelong day and night."

Katie came to sit on Francine's opposite side. "Happy Birthday, sweet thing." She gently touched her face. "Has Cheryl been giving you a worse time than usual?"

"She's always rude and obnoxious. Today and every day. She rushes me through my breakfast like she's paying me instead of vice versa. I do love to linger with my tea and she snatches it right from under my nose. I think I deserve a little consideration on my birthday...." A tear rolled down the crepey skin of her jaw as she implored Katie.

She drew her into a hug. "I'm so sorry."

"Me too." Becca leaned closer. "Look what I brought you."

"Is this not the grandest thing?" She surveyed the painting. "You have captured the spirit of *Radbourne* exactly."

Despite her grandmother's restored good humor, new fury at Cheryl coursed through Katie. Still she realized it was unwise to commiserate with Francine who was already much too agitated.

Francine peered at Becca over her spectacles. "Once Pearl has it framed, we will hang this right there where I can see it every minute of the day." She pointed at a spot between two windows.

Becca stretched one arm around her. "Really?"

"Absolutely. I never say what I don't

mean."

Becca giggled and kissed her. "Thank you for doing that. It makes me feel important."

"You are very important. You always remember that." She tipped up her chin to examine her mouth. "Why, you have nearly all your teeth back. I hadn't noticed that until now. And aren't the nice and straight."

"Daddy says I won't need braces."

"That is very good news."

A knock announced Pearl's arrival with the weekly order of roses in two big buckets. After wishing Francine "Happy Birthday," she began humming softly while she emptied wilted blooms and created fresh bouquets in the vases scattered about the room.

"Don't forget Becca's roses," Francine reminded her. "What color would you like this week?"

"Yellow are my favorite."

"Then yellow you shall have, my dear."

"Thank you. I love my roses." With that, she bestowed another boisterous hug.

"Careful," Katie cautioned.

"Oh, it's quite all right. I cannot recall anyone being injured by hugging.

Becca laughed at the thought, then slid down and dropped her arm over Jekyll.

"Don't miss the bus."

"Okay, 'bye." She gave Francine a little wave, kissed Katie and headed to the door.

Katie placed an extravagantly wrapped package on Francine's lap.

The brilliant blue eyes pondered her with

rueful speculation before she untied the ribbon and lifted the lid from the flat box. "Oh, my dear, you do splendid work." She lifted out the framed portrait of Jeremy and Becca. "I adore it." Tears welled up as she studied it. "Hold it there against the wall. Just a little above the spot for Becca's painting."

Katie moved the photo an inch or two this way and that until Francine was satisfied. She was proud of the picture taken by the drawing room fire. Jeremy sat relaxed in a wingback chair with Becca in the curve of his arm. The warm light brushed their features with a rosy light that somehow intensified Becca's innocence, Jeremy's strength.

"Pearl, if you are going to town today, please have both my gifts framed, then ask Hugh to hang them this afternoon.

Pearl stood beside Katie. "Of course. They're wonderful. I'll come up for them as soon as I finish with the roses."

When she'd left, Katie laid the portrait on a nearby table, then returned to her seat on the bed.

"Jeremy was here early. He knew I would be awake hours before dawn today, restless, filled with doubts."

Katie waited, puzzled.

"I told Jeremy some weeks ago that I would make my decision on my birthday. And so he came before the sun and sat with me, knowing I was still unsure. He came to tell me to follow my heart and dismiss any strictures from the past." Her gaze was straight forward. "I told him I want to see both of you at ten o'clock."

Katie stared at her with old resentment. "I'd have thought you might've given me the same courtesy of informing me in advance instead of just springing this on me."

"I am quite sure I told you I'd let both of you know on my birthday."

Katie pinched the bridge of her nose, trying to clear her head. "I don't think so."

"I doubt you would have been any more receptive if I had sent you weekly bulletins all winter." She spread her hands in a tired gesture

Katie sighed, wanting to offer some rude retort to her grandmother's nastiness. Instead, she gathered her scattered wits, and managed the semblance of calm. "Do you remember your promise to me? The one you made the night I arrived?"

"Certainly." The keen eyes took her measure. "I said if you stayed long enough for me to decide whether to make you my heir, I would tell you why you were sent away."

"But now you have no intention of telling my anything. What a surprise," Katie said, unable to keep the venom from her voice.

"I also said that night that I would tell you only if I thought you were strong enough." She put up a silencing hand. "In the past months, I have learned just how strong you are. I have come to possess immense pride that you are my granddaughter, and I love you more than I can ever express."

Katie pushed down the childish urge to ask if she loved her more than Jeremy. She'd welcomed her grandmother's concern and counsel for months now, but, nevertheless, the actual voicing of what lay between them swept through her in waves of emotion. She barely heard her when she continued.

"When you first came here, I was sorely tempted to hurt you. Your hate was so palpable, I saw you more as an enemy than the ideal I had conjured. With an old woman's fancy, I was groping for my lost granddaughter. I had fashioned someone with no animosity, someone desperate to love me in spite of the past.

"What arrived in my drawing room was the most stunning woman I had seen since your mother was alive. But your hate went through me like a blade, shredding my illusions.

"Because you destroyed what had become a pleasant obsession, I wanted to wound you as well. I wanted to blurt out the truth. But I knew that would be far too dangerous. You had guarded the secret in your subconscious for a lifetime. It I had suddenly stripped away all the layers of forgetfulness, I would have sent you to the edge of insanity. In the end, my love was stronger than my want for revenge.

"With only a little information, you have come so near the truth. If I told you the rest now, I would rob you of the final release you have earned. If you continue on faith, you will free yourself of the specter." Her face softened, her eyes beseeching. "I want that so much for you, so I remain silent."

Her concern defeated Katie's anger. She saw her compassion and was trapped by her resolve as surely as she'd been when she first agreed to stay on at *Radbourne*. Now, however, she realized they were no longer adversaries.

Francine clasped Katie's hand. "Let me have a little nap now. I don't want to be dozing off when you and Jeremy come.

Katie squeezed her fingers, offering acceptance, trust in her wisdom. She longed to tell her she loved her but some small obstacle prevented the words today. She headed to the door, then remembered the earlier scene. "Are you ever afraid of Cheryl?"

Francine's eyes narrowed. "Mercy, no! She is ill bred and it is a mystery how she ever reared Evelyn, the epitome of grace. She is pitiable, but I cannot imagine anyone less fearsome."

Far from reassured, Katie went to the library, searching for the calm she usually found there. Today any serenity eluded her and she was soon drawn to Jeremy's office.

When she'd curled up in his canvas armchair, he leaned back behind the desk, rolling a pen between his fingers as he studied her thoughtfully.

She tried to read his expression but couldn't. All she knew for sure was that he wasn't that concerned about the impending meeting...or Francine's decision.

"Don't be too hard on her if she's changed her will," he said at last. "I'm guessing that's what she's going to tell us."

"She didn't tell you when you talked this morning?"

"Are you kidding? She loves intrigue way too much. Still, I think I know why she's so troubled. It's not easy going against your wishes.

But blood is paramount with her."

"I've said it a hundred times...you're more her blood than I'll ever be."

"Not true and you know it. My bond with Francine is of the heart, and if you stop fighting it, you'll see yours is too. You belong here because you were born here."

She still wondered. Did she really belong here, aside from her relationship with Jeremy? All those years, had she been fated to return? Had predestination drawn her back, giving her no choice?

She was caught in a labyrinth of questions. Seeing her incomprehension, Jeremy rose to massage her shoulders, then sat on the arm of the chair.

"We still have a few minutes and there's something else we need to discuss."

Katie looked up, uneasy.

"Francine and I have been talking for sometime about hiring a fulltime vet, and now Patrick has located a woman who's graduating this spring from Ames, Iowa. We need to decide if we want to bring her here for an interview in the next few weeks."

"Why do I have to decide?" Katie inquired, caught totally off guard.

He chuckled. "Because you may be the new owner of *Radbourne*. And at the very least I want your input." She could just stare at him. "Maybe we can talk about this another time," she finally managed.

"Of course. Sorry. Let's go up." He offered his hand.

She puzzled over his curious calm as they climbed the stairs. Perhaps he was so unconcerned because he expected an inheritance to tie her to *Radbourne*. Did he now welcome that choice because it would free him from resolving matters with her himself?

She tried dismissing this kind of speculation but it persisted as they climbed to the upper tower. Francine sat in a rose brocade armchair, wearing a dressing gown in the same exact shade. The effect created a picture of unquestioned power and vibrancy.

Katie recalled this same chicanery in staging that had greeted her at her first audience with her grandmother. Although quickly enough her outward appearance had proved a mere facade, she had maintained a demeanor of fierce invincibility that first night long enough to draw Katie under her spell.

Now she nodded to two chairs before her own, her smile inscrutable. For several seconds, she sat with hands folded, apparently enjoying the drama. Finally, she opened the folder on her lap. "Katie, I am naming you my heir."

There it was. Katie had tried to prepare herself, yet she still felt the shock thrumming in her brain. She wanted to protest, to scream that her grandmother was making a huge mistake, but she couldn't pull free of the gridlock in her head. As Francine kept talking, she could only sit still, filled with dread.

"Katie, I have searched my heart and found that I must force you to acknowledge your heritage. Nevertheless, I want you to live here only because you want to. Toward that end, I have stipulated that Jeremy will manage *Radbourne* for the rest of his life. He cannot be replaced unless he chooses to be."

She gazed at him, then Katie with no hint of compromise. "You both get what you want. Jeremy, you will continue as the soul of *Radbourne,* and Katie, you may stay or go as you wish."

Katie blew out her breath in a puff that lifted a few strands of her hair as she stared at the ceiling.

Francine indicated her impatience by tapping a finger on the arm of her chair. "I declare you are a peculiar little thing sometimes."

Katie sighed, lowering her gaze.

The snapping blue eyes held a challenge now and Katie knew she'd won. Whether Katie made a new life here or returned to Boston, she would be irrevocably anchored to this ranch, ensnared in its history and Jeremy's hopes for its future.

"Do either of you have any objections?"

Jeremy glanced at Katie, and when she didn't comment, looked back at Francine. "You know I don't."

"And what do you have to say, my dear?"

Katie neared hysterical laughter. "Why would I care to repeat my objections? I've already done that at least three dozen times. And now you've done what you decided to do long before I came back."

"That is not true! I decided nothing before you came home. I had no idea what kind of woman you had become. That was the point of you coming here, so I could see if you were worthy of *Radbourne*. That was clear within a week. I only waited to see the beginning of your love for *Radbourne* because that is what made up my mind."

Katie heard the force of her determination, and was powerless against it. To her immense astonishment, she was abruptly possessed by a sense of security and belonging she could not have fathomed thirty seconds before. The same sentiment had come over her off and on all winter but this was altogether different. Something had shifted in her perspective. Perhaps her grandmother had put a spell on her.

She laughed, shrugging in surrender. "I give up. You're too much for me."

Francine threw up her hands in triumph. Tears sprang to her eyes and she fumbled a handkerchief from the pocket of her dressing gown. "Darling, Katie. You have made me very happy indeed. I only hope you will love *Radbourne* as much as I have all these years." She looked at the door. "Now I wonder why Pearl isn't here with the champagne I ordered to celebrate."

Amazed by the old woman's premature confidence in herself, Katie swallowed the prickly remark that came to mind, granting her the grace of silence.

In the days following Francine's settlement, Katie and Jeremy were surprisingly at ease, mutually comfortable with the outcome. For Katie, the purposeless drifting had given way to pleasant progress toward a still-unveiled destination.

She began a personal campaign to learn all

she could about the day to day operation of the ranch. To that end, she was part of the decision to invite Janel Dickerson, the newly graduated veterinarian to *Radbourne* to be interviewed for employment. The young woman would arrive in two weeks.

Warm days pulled Katie outside and she walked through the pastures with her camera, sometimes sitting on a boulder above the ranch where she could absorb the panorama. She recognized the unfolding life force, a very different energy from other seasons here. Now there was promise everywhere, the greening of grass and trees, the mating songs of meadowlarks and turtledoves. It was nowhere more evident than at the foaling barn.

Hugely pregnant mares lolled in the sunshine of small paddocks outside. New foals capered about or lay flat, soaking up the sun's strength. Inside the barn, there was a climate of constant anticipation that excited Katie during frequent visits.

This morning she'd awakened well before daybreak, eager to go check on any new babies. Now at the barn, she walked along the breezeway, inspecting the newborns when Nick Carter stepped from his office to intercept her. Shaking his head, he pointed through an open doorway and Katie realized she'd been about to disturb a mare giving birth. She followed him back to his office.

"Sorry," he said when he'd shut the door, "but we have to be careful of the ladies' feelings." He nodded toward a window that offered a view of the stall.

"I didn't realize."

"No harm done. How about coffee?"

"Thanks. How many foals now?"

His attention was focused on the mare. "This one makes twenty-seven. About a third of the total." He spoke softly as if the mare might hear him. His leathery features reflected the awe that hadn't lessened in all the years he had tended the broodmares.

Katie was caught up in his wonder. She had no idea how quickly a birth was completed once it began. Within seconds the slippery black foal lay on the straw and its mother nuzzled and licked it roughly, tipping it this way and that, as it struggled to lie upright.

Katie laughed at the antics. "Is it always so fast?"

"If everything's right. Within half an hour, that guy'll be on his feet and able to keep up with his mom."

Katie lingered there, fascinated as Nick continued talking, sharing his reverence for his work. They watched as the mare heaved herself to her feet and continued licking her baby, her tongue offering warmth, stimulation, welding the bond that would link the two for months. It wasn't long before the foal, awkward and ungainly, tried standing on impossibly long legs. Three times he tumbled, but on the fourth attempt, he stood, feet splayed to counter balance his swaying.

"Oh, how wonderful!" Katie focused her camera just as Jeremy entered.

"Looks like another stallion prospect, Jeremy," Nick commented while he studied the new colt.

Jeremy stood beside Katie, his arm going around her waist. "Your buddy Bohjalian is his father." He chuckled, his mood mellow, deeply satisfied. "And grand daddy Bordeaux's magic is as potent as ever."

"Lord, isn't that the truth," Nick agreed. I'm still taken aback every time I see that extreme head Bordeaux's stamped on so many generations of *Radbourne* foals."

Katie noted the foal's bulging forehead, the ears nearly touching at the tips, the sharply tapering muzzle, and huge, wide-set eyes. Now she realized these were among the most desired characteristics of a classic Arab. She smiled, remembering her total ignorance of such details not so long ago.

Jeremy glanced at her but didn't ask why she was smiling. He and Nick continued discussing the foal, and Katie saw their mutual reverence, their pleasure in reaching shared goals.

She acknowledged her longing to be a real part of this quest. The admission within the privacy of her mind amazed her.

Before she could sort out her feelings, Jeremy tightened his arm around her. "I'm going to walk down and look over some of the yearlings. Want to come?"

"I'd love to."

He grinned at her. "Who'd have thought Francine's choice would make you so happy."

"Who's have thought." She linked her arm through his as they walked along the tree-lined drive to the lower meadows. She felt buoyant, unencumbered by her doubt about *Radbourne* that'd shadowed every thought for months.

They came to a railed enclosure holding a small herd of yearlings so refined they might have been cast in the finest porcelain statuary. Jeremy scanned the youngsters crowding the fence for attention.

He pulled out a handful of carrots he'd stuffed in his jacket pocket and began dispensing them while scratching ears and patting necks. "Patrick's putting ten of these kids in advanced halter training so they can be shown this summer. He picked these and now I get to make the final cut. We'll eventually cull them to six that will be trained to saddle and bring us top dollar." His gaze teased her. "...or rather, bring you top dollar ."

Katie was surprised that she laughed. Only last week she'd have reacted badly to his good-natured reference to their future as owner and manager.

"Are you going to stop being the martyr now and admit you've fallen in love with *Radbourne?*"

The question held a dare. It had been some time since she'd accepted her love for this place with all its power and promise and beauty. But she only now remembered that she'd not yet told Jeremy or Francine of the private shift in her loyalty. Her grandmother had pressured her from the start and she'd fought her, run from her, but now there was no reason to run.

"Yes, I do love it!" She tipped back her head and shouted the words.

"Are you sure, sweetheart?" he asked when he stopped laughing at her. "About this? All of it?"

She couldn't decipher his look. "I'm sure, Jeremy." Her conviction still startled her.

With a final searching appraisal, he smiled, his concern dissipating.

Katie lay still, wondering what had awakened her before she saw Jeremy sitting on the edge of her bed.

"Hi, hon." He kissed her cheek. "I'm going to the foaling barn to make sure a baby gets here okay. Want to come with me?"

She pushed back the covers, excited now. "Why are *you* going out?"

"Nick took Pearl to the hospital. Their daughter's having her own baby."

Katie pulled on a coat over her pajamas and followed him. As they walked across the lawn toward the barns, he held her tight against him. "Back when it was just Francine and me, I handled every single foaling. There were no monitors then, and because losing a foal was a disaster, I usually slept in the foaling stalls. Since prehistoric times, mares have foaled in darkness that helped them stay clear of predators. It's relatively rare for a foal to be born in daylight."

Once they reached the foaling barn, they went to Nick's office to appraise a delicate gray mare in the adjoining stall. Her foal was already halfway out. Gripping Jeremy's hand, Katie stood transfixed.

"I loved being out here in the middle of the night watching over the mares." He leaned his chin against the top of her head as he continued observing the horses. "In any case, it gave me a lot of confidence I probably wouldn't have had otherwise when I was thirteen. I had to learn a lot quickly, like when a mare was in trouble I couldn't get her out of. It was often a difficult call because if I waited too long, the foal could die. If I called the vet when it wasn't necessary, it meant a vet call we couldn't afford. Francine and I worked out a protocol of sorts. When I couldn't figure out what to do, I woke her and she came out and made the decision. After hearing her complain for an hour about having to traipse out here, I soon got better at reading the symptoms and more adept at helping the mare deliver even if things were going wrong. I got better at spotting trouble early as well."

"What about now?" Katie asked, still watching through the glass.

"Perfect so far." He pointed. "See, a hoof on either side of the nose? All set up to dive out of the birth canal. Only worry with this one is the mare's so finely built all over, it may be a tight fit. And it's her first foal." He stepped closer the glass, glancing at the clock on the wall.

"Is something wrong?" Katie asked after a few minutes of his intense scrutiny.

"I doubt it but it's taking too long so I'm going to go check her. He took off his jacket and pulled on sterile gloves from a box mounted on the wall. "Could you get the door." He walked to the stall door that she opened. By the time they entered the dim box, the mare had collapsed on the damp straw, stretched prone, her sides heaving. Jeremy drew on a plastic sleeve from another box on the wall, then knelt to push aside the white membrane partially covering the protruding nose and only one leg. "I thought sure I saw two," he said as he lay flat, working at the slender foreleg, maneuvering it back until it disappeared with a few inches of his arm.

Katie knelt beside the horse's head, soothing her while she watched Jeremy's battle. She saw the gentleness in his face, concentration and regret for the pain he was causing. Sweat soon beaded his forehead and soaked his shirt.

The struggle ended abruptly and within seconds, the brown foal slid free, and landed unceremoniously against his chest.

Katie relaxed and reached for her camera.

"Good job!" Jeremy addressed the sopping length of brown hide. "How do you like your life so far?" He peered into the foal's face, then lay back on the straw to let his muscles unwind. Katie took several shots before he looked up at her. "Breeding Arabs is damned glamorous, ain't it?" He winked and got to his feet, stripping off his gloves. "Filly," said as he bent to pull the foal around in front of her mother who sniffed and licked her.

As he walked out of the door, Katie saw he was shaking. "You're freezing." She went into the office for his jacket but he waved it away.

"I'm going to grab a shower." He strode to a door at the rear of the office that Katie now saw was a bathroom.

She waited beside the viewing window, still entranced by the foal's battle to gain her land legs. She lost track of time until Jeremy stood beside her, wrapping her in his arms.

"She's going to be gorgeous. A dappled gray

with all the elegance and grace of her mom. Maybe we should train her in Park and have no one show her but you."

Katie turned within his embrace. "That is an absolutely lovely idea." She searched his eyes. "And it can happen, can't it?"

"Of course."

"She can really be my own?"

"Darling, you own every horse at *Radbourne.*"

"Oh yeah, I forgot. But what I meant was this is such an amazing moment, seeing her born and knowing that one day, we could be in the show ring together. That's life changing." Tears ached in her throat.

He pulled her close. "Ah, Katie, you finally get it. You know why Francine and I have given every bit of our heart and soul to this place and these splendid horses." His swiped the tears from beneath her eyes before cradling her face to kiss her tenderly. "I love you so much."

"I want to name my filly Ashara."

"Where on earth did you come up with that?"

"Remember last fall when you told me to do some research on the Arab. I found lists of Arabic names and that one stayed with me." She shrugged. "I can't remember what it means. How do you knew she's going to be gray?"

"Because she has some white hair in her tail. If it was all black, she'd grow up to be a bay."

"Wow, I wonder if I'll ever learn everything you just rattle off without thinking."

"Trust me, you will."

She laid her head against his shoulder. He smelled faintly of bleach from the freshly washed sweats he'd put on after he showered. She'd never considered bleach to be an aphrodisiac but it seemed to be working for that purpose now. Throwing her arms around him, she covered his mouth with her own.

He crushed her to him, his tongue finding familiar, exquisite nerve endings. Her intense, tremulous response left her wanting more.

"Good Lord," he mumbled, haltingly pulling back, even as he still held her. "Maybe we should head back before we cause an incident when a stable boy wanders in here or Nick comes home." He kissed the end of her nose. "I'll take a rain check. Very soon."

Sighing, she managed a smile. "I'll hold you to it." She nodded toward the horses. "Is it okay to leave them now?"

He stepped to the window. The filly had gained her feet and was suckling. "They're all set." He grabbed his jacket and they departed.

"You just adore this, don't you?" Katie asked as they walked.

He squeezed her hand. "I do. Do you ever stop and think what truly brings you joy, past or present?"

"Not often enough. How about you?"

"The first time Francine let me handle a foaling alone, I floated the the rest of the day. I must've gone to the barn to check on that baby two dozen times that day."

They fell silent. The faint radiance of dawn hung beyond the trees. Katie tried to decide what made her really happy in the past. Ursel's birth was all that came to mind. What was wrong with her? Had nothing about her life with Aunt Jessie or Zachary brought her true joy? From her present vantage, it seemed not. "What else is on your list?"

"The usual things – the first time I rode Bordeaux in a major show and won every class we entered, the day I met Evelyn, our wedding day, Becca's birth, the day I knew I was in love with you."

Francine wasn't feeling well the day her attorney was to bring papers transferring ownership of *Radbourne* so Katie cancelled the appointment. She was no better by the end of the week. Scott was summoned and decided she was only suffering from fatigue again. She slept most of the time and was often disoriented. It seemed now that she'd made her choice, she was having difficulty mustering the strength to make it legal.

CHAPTER TWELVE

Becca spooned up the last of her oatmeal. "Nick's going to let me watch a breeding before I go to school."

Katie stared across the table at her. Jeremy had a breakfast meeting in town so she sat with Becca in the sun porch. She couldn't think of a reply to the announcement so remained silent.

"Daddy wouldn't let me until this year but I've seen it three times now." She propped her chin in one hand, her elbow braced against the table. "Want to come?"

"No, thanks."

"Okay." She slid off her chair. "Daddy says people do what the stallion and mare do." She made a face. "Have you?"

Lord, why did this have to come up now when Jeremy was gone. Katie struggled with her distress. "All married people do. Otherwise there wouldn't be any cool kids like you." She tugged Becca close by the straps of her bibs. "And there wouldn't be any fabulous foals unless mares were bred. But with people it's part of grownup love."

"That's what Daddy says." She still frowned. "How'd you keep from laughing?"

Katie suppressed her smile. "You'll find out when you grow up and fall in love."

Becca gave her a quick kiss and was gone. Outside she and Jekyll raced toward the barn. After a final swallow of coffee, she headed upstairs. When there was no answer to her tap on Francine's door, she let herself in.

Cheryl jerked to her feet on the other side of the bed. "Jesus Christ, why can't you knock!?"

"I knocked." She refrained from asking why Cheryl had been on her hands and knees.

Cheryl flailed her hands about, apparently grasping for an answer to the unasked question. "I didn't hear you, what with wondering if she's ever going to wake up so I can get the hell out of here. I don't know what the devil's wrong with her lately. She sleeps the livelong day."

The old unease had often filled Katie of late and now it had turned to outright alarm. She avoided looking at Francine. "You're free to go. I'll stay until she wakes."

"That'll be half past noon at least!" she snapped, then with a quick look back, fled from the room.

With difficulty, Katie held herself still until the door closed and there was silence in the hall, then she rushed to the bed. Something about the way Francine lay added to her worry. Her grandmother's head was askew on the pillow, her mouth agape, her breathing labored. The oxygen tube had been knocked from her nose and Katie replaced it and straightened her head.

Her grandmother's hair hung in unkempt strings. Katie had never seen her when her hair wasn't freshly washed and styled. After Francine stopped driving herself to town for salon appointments, her stylist came to *Radbourne* twice weekly. Whenever, she didn't feel up to the girl's ministrations, Pearl did what she could or concealed her hair in an elegant turban.

Now Katie went to a highboy and searched through the drawers filled with antique jewelry, expensive lingerie, and dozens of other accessories. She unearthed a red silk scarf and in an awkward process, lifted Francine's head and wrapped her hair, finishing with a chic bow over her right ear. "Perfect." She kissed her cheek and sat beside her.

Observing Francine's sleep, she was intermittently seized by panic when it appeared she wasn't breathing. But each time she put her face close to hers, she felt her faint breath.

Still, there was no attitude of rest or ease. Having been able to examine her grandmother for a time, Katie had the impression she had collapsed during a fierce struggle. A bruise had materialized on one cheek, prompting Katie to fold back the comforter. She gently straightened Francine's head and shoulders, lifted each arm in turn and rolled back the sleeve of her nightgown. She stared at a tiny wound just above her left elbow, a small tear in the discolored skin. Higher up were less angry injection sites.

After she settled the covers back, she scanned the carpet and under the brass bed. At first she saw nothing but when she lay halfway beneath the box springs, she found the plastic syringe with a bent needle that Cheryl had been searching for when Katie surprised her earlier.

Katie grabbed the phone and dialed Scott's home number. "Hi, Scott, have you been prescribing I.V. tranquilizers for my grandmother?"

"No, Katie. I prescribed a mild sedative

last fall but in tablet form. Lately she's been so tired there's been no need."

"Scott, she's been drugged. Can you come?"

"I'm on my way."

Katie slipped an arm under Francine, lifting her up against the pillows to ease her breathing. She took in her pale features, afraid to leave her, yet knowing she must.

She hurried into the hall and down the rear stairs. In the kitchen, she dispatched a startled Pearl to watch Francine, and immediately began her search for Cheryl whom she eventually found in her car in the carriage house ready to leave.

Lowering her window to crane her head out, Cheryl yelled at her for blocking her exit. "What the hell to you want?"

"You're fired. Pack what you need before you go. I'll send the rest later."

"You have no authority."

"I have authority. Don't push me or you'll find yourself in jail." She left the garage and had almost reached the terrace when she heard Cheryl marching along the driveway, shouting expletives.

"Wait right there! I want to speak to you!" she screamed. "Why're you doing this?"

"You know why. To save us both embarrassment, don't force me to elaborate." Katie hurried into the back hall and up the rear stairs with the enraged woman panting behind until she heard her turn down the second floor corridor.

"What on earth has happened?" Pearl demanded when Katie reached Francine's bedroom. "Did Cheryl hit her? Her cheek's turning purple."

Katie searched for any change. "Cheryl's been drugging her among other things."

"Why would she do that when Mrs. Chamberlain's been so good to her?"

"She probably planned to keep her so out of it, she couldn't sign her new will."

Comprehension dawned in Pearl. "What should we do?"

"I've called Scott and Jeremy should be home any minute."

Pearl leaned close to peer at Francine. "I just can't imagine she would allow this."

"She fought. She has a wound on her arm that looks like she knocked out a needle. My guess is that Cheryl hit her then so she could get an injection in. But then I startled her and she dropped the syringe. I found it under the bed."

"It was only to help Jeremy that Mrs. Chamberlain brought her here."

"What possessed her to do that, I'll never know."

They fell silent, caught in their separate anxiety. Presently, they heard Jekyll barking and Pearl went down to let Scott in.

When he strode into the room, he laid a hand on Katie's shoulder before turning to the bed. "Valium I'd say. A blood test will tell for sure." He glanced up. "Do you know who did this?"

While Katie recounted the details, he continued examining Francine's still form. "You do know this is a criminal offense?" He raised his eyes to Katie. "At the very least, Francine's a vulnerable adult. Where's Cheryl now?"

"The nursing home I'd think."

He stroked his chin. "That's pretty weird, isn't it?"

She shrugged. "She's obsessed with Evelyn so I can't imagine anything would keep her away."

He nodded and took a syringe from his bag to draw a blood sample, then listened to Francine's heart. "I can't see that she's in any danger. She only got a small amount this morning so even if she was given considerably more a few hours ago, I'd say she'll come around in an hour or so." He considered Katie again. "One thing's for sure, this can't go on."

"I fired her. As soon as Jeremy gets here, we'll decide what else to do."

"If I have anything to say in the matter, our friend Cheryl's going in for questioning. You should call Bernard Mayhall."

Katie recognized the name of Francine's attorney.

"Unless Jeremy or Francine press charges, I doubt much can be done, but I'd like to put the fear of God in her," he added, preparing to go.

Before he reached the door, it opened and Jeremy stood still, taking in the scene. "What's happened?"

Katie hurried to him, explaining as quickly as she could.

When she finished, he strode to the bed and sat next to Francine. He stroked the bruise with one finger. "How long has Cheryl been doing this?"

"Since Francine made me her heir."

He nodded. "Figures."

Katie took in his genuine shock at Cheryl's duplicity. Why should she be surprised. He was still as deep in denial about his mother-in-law as he was concerning Evelyn.

But now that her grandmother was involved, Katie wouldn't let him carry on unaware any longer. "Scott thinks we should bring charges against her."

To her surprise, he offered no argument. "I'll do that right away." He left the bed and clapped Scott on the back. "Thanks for coming out."

"I'll check back. If you need me sooner, call." He retrieved his bag and left.

Katie hugged Jeremy. "I'm so sorry this had to happen."

He kissed her absently. "I'll go talk to the sheriff. And in case, you've forgotten in all this turmoil, Janel Dickerson is arriving for lunch. We're to interview her after."

"If you're not back when she gets here, I'll make her comfortable."

He smiled. "Thanks. I'll be back as soon as I can." With a parting wink, he was gone.

Pearl left to begin preparing lunch for the prospective veterinarian. As Scott predicted, Francine haltingly came awake within an hour.

Her gaze settled on Katie and several seconds passed before her eyes cleared in recognition, then she looked at the clock on the nightstand. "That loathsome woman's been after me again."

Katie dismissed the compulsion to shake her. "Why didn't you tell me or Jeremy?"

"I was determined not to alarm you. I...I thought I could deal with her, but she was too strong." She gave a small laugh. "Surprising really for such a scrawny little witch." She brought shaky fingers to her bruised face. "I suppose she felt threatened by my will despite knowing Jeremy will always take care of her...."

"I fired her."

Francine took her measure. "I was certain you would if you ever found out. Jeremy will be in a rage over this. Where anything has to do with Evelyn, he hasn't an ounce of his customary good sense."

"He's gone to press charges against her. Abuse of a vulnerable adult."

Francine's look was filled with regret now. "Well, this segment of my life is over. I hired Cheryl with the best of intentions but she was a conniving bitch from the start. I put up with her rudeness for Jeremy's sake but now I doubt we did Becca any favors having her here."

"Your heart was in the right place." Katie gave her a smile. "I love you, my wonderful grandmother. Would you like some breakfast?"

"Lord, no," she grimaced. "My stomach hasn't felt this wretched in the morning since my last hangover."

"We'll wait a little then, but you really should eat something. Pearl's in the kitchen right now, creating an incredible lunch for our new vet prospect so maybe I'll bring you some."

"Don't rush. Now go on with you so I can have a nap before I face your gourmet lunch."

Jeremy got home well before Janel Dickerson arrived. "Cheryl's gone," he said when he and Katie sat in the drawing room. "She was at the nursing home earlier but no one's seen her since. The sheriff assures me it won't take long to find her. When they do, she'll be in jail for a time

"I hope they find her soon. She scares me."

Jeremy squeezed her hand. "I wish I'd been paying more attention to her lately."

"Things didn't go so far that they can't be turned around now. The sooner she's far away from Francine and *Radbourne*, the better."

Pearl arrived to tell them their guest had arrived.

"Thanks, Pearl. What's on the menu?" Jeremy asked.

"Crab Louie."

"Great. Please serve a bottle of Chablis in here before we eat. You may show Miss Dickerson in now."

"Of course." She disappeared, then returned with a beautiful woman.

"I'm Janel. The lovely blonde dressed in a tailored tweed pants ensemble came forward with her hand extended. "So nice to meet you, Mr. Foxworth and you must be Mrs. Meade," she added, turning to Katie.

"We're very pleased that you've agreed to meet with us today, Janel. Please sit." He gestured to the loveseat opposite the sofa where he and Katie sat.

Katie was instantly drawn to Janel, the picture of professional finesse. Her short, casually styled flaxen hair and delicate features would have fit perfectly in any beauty pageant, yet her soft brown eyes held a depth of intelligence that Katie instinctively knew set her well apart from most women. Her fit, compact build suggested she could handle the physical demands of handling horses.

"Radbourne is a beautiful ranch. I'm stunned by the mountains after living in Iowa."

"Where did you grow up?" Jeremy asked.

"In Philadelphia. My father had a small-animal practice there. I spent most of my childhood and teen years helping him and by the time, I graduated from high school, I knew I wanted to study veterinary medicine."

"Why do you want to work at Radbourne?" Katie inquired while Pearl arrived with the wine and a slab of Brie, warm from the oven.

"I love the East but I've always been drawn to the West. I like the idea of fewer people and a less frenzied lifestyle." She accepted a glass of wine with a smile.

They continued there for half an hour, soon talking like they'd known one another for years. By the time they adjourned to the sun porch, both Jeremy and Katie were in agreement that Janel would be an invaluable addition to Radbourne.

Patrick and Nick were invited for dessert because they would both be working closely with the new vet. Within minutes, Janel had captivated them both.

After the two men returned to the barns, Jeremy took Janel on a guided tour of the ranch facilities as well as the cottage she would live in if she wished. While they were out, Katie went to tell Francine about Janel.

"So both you and Jeremy like her?" she asked.

"Yes, very much, and I think you will also. She's very professional, yet friendly and sensitive about what we need her to do here at *Radbourne.*"

Her grandmother mulled this over. "I'm sure you've made an excellent choice." Her eyes drifted to the window, then back. "Where has Cheryl gotten off to?"

"We don't know. She disappeared this morning after she left here and they're still looking for her."

Francine twisted her mouth. "I never dreamed doing that woman a good turn would cause such debacle."

The events of the day had brought questions to Katie's mind she hadn't considered before. "When Jeremy came to live with you, did you adopt him?"

Francine's gentian eyes hardened. "Why would I do that?"

"I would've thought to protect his rights legally."

She waved her hand dismissively. "I've never felt that Jeremy was my son although he is a large part of my heart. He's been my equal partner since he was twelve years old. We had a legal and binding contract to that effect drawn up years and years ago."

Katie thought about this. Since coming to *Radbourne*, she'd thought it odd that Jeremy and Becca addressed her as Francine but now it made perfect sense.

"So does that arrangement meet with your approval?"

Katie laughed at her perplexed expression.

"Absolutely. I just hadn't given any thought to just what Jeremy's legal relationship is to you. As soon as I came here I realized the two of you are far more than employer and employee...." She glanced over her shoulder at the sound of footsteps in the hall.

A tap on the door was followed by the appearance of Scott and Bernard Mayhall. After Scott checked Francine over, they both sat near her bed, a study in physical contrast. A few years older than Jeremy, Scott was tall and elegant, his graying hair emphasizing his lean features. Francine's attorney was short and pudgy with protruding belly.

"What have you done with Cheryl?" Francine inquired.

Scott eyed her uneasily. "She turned up back at the nursing home and was arrested. Seems she's been bribing a a nurse there to get Valium. Cheryl wasn't that nurse's only customer so when an undercover policewoman turned up, the woman was happy to name everyone she'd sold to in hopes of some leniency."

"The loyalty of thieves," Francine mused. "So Cheryl is in jail??"

"Yes," Bernard said. "She phoned my office about an hour ago, looking for bail. For some unfathomable reason, she thinks you or Jeremy will put up the money."

She made no reply, apparently waiting for more information.

"Francine," Scott implored, "you owe her nothing. She did her best to hasten your death."

"Criminal charges are in order," Bernard

said.

She regarded them haughtily. "She did not succeed in doing me much harm, did she? It is true, I owe her nothing, but I owe Jeremy a great deal. I won't add to his grief by keeping her in jail."

"Jeremy's already filed charges," Katie said, sitting beside her grandmother. "At least, let him pay her bail." She sighed. "After what she's done, it's hardly your place."

She mulled this over, then nodded. "Very well. A few more hours in jail may be beneficial."

"Where's Jeremy?" Bernard asked.

"He's showing a new employee around the barns," Katie said.

"If I'm gone before he gets back, have him call me immediately." He abruptly left his chair and approached Francine. "What on earth are you doing, may I ask?"

She had hauled a cumbersome checkbook from a drawer in the nightstand. With movements remarkably steady, decisive, she proceeded to write a check while everyone gaped at her. When she'd signed it with a flourish, she held it out to the attorney. "Now kindly deliver this for me."

"Have you lost your mind?" Katie inquired.

Francine said nothing and placidly returned the checkbook to the drawer.

Bernard regarded her with pursed lips, shaking his head before he folded the check and placed it in his pocket. "I must say, you are the most exasperating woman! I hardly approve of your misplaced compassion."

She wagged her fountain pen at him. "My good man, we have not agreed on many issues during our long and colorful association. Cheryl will do me no more harm. She is a wretched soul but once my will is signed, she will have nothing more to gain by her antics."

Bernard snorted. "I hardly think antics typifies her recent wickedness."

She ignored his continued concern. "I want you here first thing in the morning to make the changes in my will we discussed." She peered at him over her wire rims. "Is nine o'clock convenient?"

"Fine." He shook his head and stepped back.

Scott took his place and lifted Francine's hand. "How do you feel by this time?" he asked when he'd taken her pulse.

"Like a good night's sleep will have me in fine fettle."

"Keep the oxygen in your nose."

She granted him a placid smile. "Yes, of course." Bernard snorted again, rolling his eyes behind his thick glasses.

"We'll see you tomorrow," Scott said and followed the attorney to the door.

Katie walked them down. "Is she really all right?" she asked at the front door.

"It's hard to know with her, what's theatrics and what's real. But her heart's still functioning fairly well and her mind is functioning in top form so I'd say she's doing okay. With rest, I expect she'll be back where she was before this happened. She's hard to keep down so don't worry." He grinned and stepped outside.

Bernard touched the brim of the fedora

he'd donned. "Mrs. Meade, I will no doubt see you in the morning. Goodbye." He followed Scott.

Voices led Katie to the drawing room where she found Jeremy and Janel back from their tour. A bottle of wine cooled in an ice bucket.

"Janel has agreed to become our new vet," Jeremy said when Katie sat beside him.

"Wonderful," she said, accepting the wine he poured for her.

"I've never seen such an amazing horse ranch. And I've been in love with Arabs since I owned one as a 4-H project as a teenager." Janel lifted her glass. "To our new association."

They clinked glasses and Katie relaxed into the warm circle of accomplishment at being part of her first major decision as owner of *Radbourne.* How had she ever believed she wanted no part of this incredible place?

"I need to fly back to Ames for a week to get my SUV and pack up my apartment," Janel informed Katie. "I love the cottage Jeremy showed me earlier so as soon as I get moved in there, I'll be ready to begin work on June 10."

"Great. Would you like to have dinner with us this evening and spend the night?"

She smiled, revealing the perfect teeth that were a big part of her beauty. "I would love to but I'm flying out at six. As you might imagine, I have a lot to do in the coming week. And speaking of that, I must be on my way. I want to thank you both for a lovely afternoon and tell you again how much I appreciate this opportunity." She rose and shook hands. "Don't get up. I'll let myself out. I look forward to seeing you next week."

"Have a good flight. We're delighted you're going to join us," Jeremy said.

"See you soon," Katie added. Once Janel had disappeared, she moved closer to Jeremy. "I really like her."

"Me too." He grinned before kissing her. "And I must say, if I didn't know better, I'd think you'd been in management for years. I'm sure she's relieved that she's going to have such a charming and capable boss."

She laughed.

"Have we heard any more about Cheryl's whereabouts?" he asked after awhile.

She told him about the visit from Scott and Bernard. "Francine sent a check with Bernard to cover her bail."

He straightened and stared at her. "Has she lost her mind?"

"That's what I asked her. You're supposed to call Bernard so you can stop him from paying her bail."

"I'm on it!" He headed to his office.

CHAPTER THIRTEEN

After Jeremy left to call Bernard, Katie gathered the wine and glasses onto the tray and carried everything to the kitchen then climbed the back stairs to see that Becca had gotten herself to the arena for her riding lesson.

She'd just passed the room Cheryl had used before her dismissal when she heard a faint thump. She stood staring at the closed door, her heart thudding. Just then, Jekyll squeezed from behind a large potted plant and trotted off to Becca's room.

So Becca *hadn't* left for the barn. Katie shook off her anxiety and continued toward her room. Halfway there, she stopped, her half-formed dread shoving up, making it hard to breathe. A few seconds ticked by before she started running along the corridor. At the open door of Becca's bedroom, she pressed her back against the wall, listening. She couldn't stop shaking. *Dear, God, Cheryl was inside.*

"...you'll only need your sneakers....Now move! I'll have none of your dawdling...."

"I have to go for my lesson," Becca's voice was calm, curiously devoid of fear. Katie heard Jekyll whining in the bathroom.

"You've never cared to mind me but now there'll be no one to interfere. Not your father, not Pearl, not Katie...You'll learn to obey *me*. Now, get off that bed...."

"I'll let Jekyll out and he'll bite you."

"Then I'll shoot him, drop him in his tracks...."

Katie edged closer the door jamb until she could see the revolver. Cheryl sat in the rocking chair, the gun cradled in her lap. Becca crawled off the bed, stared at her grandmother a moment, then sat on the rug to pull off her riding boots and pull on her sneakers. Finished, she got up and stood in front of Cheryl.

Katie's pulse echoed in her ears as she moved back along the Oriental runner that deadened her footsteps. Once she reached the stairs, she ran for Francine's room.

A startled Pearl watched her lurch through the door.

"Call 911! Then go get Jeremy in his office. Tell him to find Patrick and Nick and Hugh and anyone else to help. Cheryl's got a gun and she's downstairs with Becca." Without waiting for a reply, she retraced her steps.

She realized from the quiet of the second floor that Cheryl had already taken Becca. She freed Jekyll and he flew down the steps ahead of her. In the rear hall, she snapped on his leash. He quieted, trembling as he strained to hear Becca.

Katie had no idea if Cheryl had left the house. She turned to the door and looked out, spotting Cheryl and Becca moving across the lawn to the carriage house. Bordeaux stood silhouetted against the trees near the stream, standing stock still, watching the figures walking past as if he sensed the danger.

Movement behind him alerted Katie to Jeremy, Patrick, Nick and Hugh inching into the thick vegetation. Jeremy's voice cut through the quiet. "Cheryl, let Becca go right now! Don't be an idiot!"

"Stay back!" Cheryl screamed, spinning toward the men, the gun in one hand, the other clutching Becca's arm. "Don't come one step closer or I'll kill her...I swear I will...."

Flashing lights from a sheriff's car caught Katie's eye and she watched it approach from the main road and park along the driveway. An officer remained behind his car but trained a rifle on Cheryl.

This action appeared to rattle her further and she stopped before the carriage house doors, the gun wobbling.

Still holding tight to Jekyll's leash, Katie moved out onto the terrace, her eyes on Jeremy who had used the few seconds Cheryl concentrated on the sheriff to sprint from the trees to the carriage house. She lost sight of him and assumed he had gone inside through a side door.

She descended the terrace steps, praying Jekyll would stay quiet. At the bottom of the stairs, she stopped in the protection of a lilac bush. Becca now stood with Cheryl beside her car. Patrick had moved out of the trees, talking to her, drawing her attention.

Another sheriff's vehicle careened to a stop beside the first one, the revolving lights slashing the two uniformed men with red despite the bright daylight. Frozen in the space of the open garage doors, Cheryl appeared transfixed, staring at the deputies.

Katie concluded Cheryl would likely

abandon caution and ram through the sheriffs' vehicles if she was allowed to get in her car. Katie unhooked Jekyll's leash but motioned for him to stay with her. When Cheryl edged closer the car door, terror for Becca sent Katie in a mad dash across the lawn, the shepherd running beside her.

Cheryl shrieked and fired the revolver. The bullet thudded into a tree trunk behind Katie who dropped to the ground even as she yelled for Jekyll to keep on.

Her eyes locked on Becca, Katie saw sudden joy cross her face and knew she could see Jekyll. A second later, she spotted Jeremy a few feet to the side of Cheryl.

Jekyll launched himself at Cheryl, knocking both her and Becca on their backs. Jeremy was on top of them as well, pushing Becca to one side where she crawled madly toward Katie.

Cheryl still grasped the gun, using both hands now but Jeremy threw his arms around her. Light glinted on the barrel as they rolled on the floor, Jekyll jumping around them, snapping and snarling. Whenever he saw his chance, he darted close enough to bite Cheryl's legs or rip at her clothing.

Becca rushed into Katie's arms and they ran toward the terrace where they sank down on the top step. Katie shook so violently she had trouble holding onto her.

A shot rang out and Becca screamed. Katie twisted around to look back where Cheryl lay limp in Jeremy's arms. He slowly lowered her to the floor where he knelt over her, his hands touching her chest, finding the blood soaking her blouse.

Nick and the others ran to the carriage house. Patrick coaxed Jekyll outside and pointed toward the mansion.

Jekyll ran to Becca, streaking up to steps to collapse beside her, licking her face. Katie still watched the carriage house. The deputies drove closer and parked outside. Horror wrung a moan from her when she saw one of the men cover Cheryl's face with a sheet. Becca's arms convulsed around her neck, her screams now sobs.

Forcing her legs to work, Katie stood and carried Becca inside. She took her to the drawing room where she wrapped her in an afghan.

She began pacing the room with Jekyll keeping pace. She finally noticed Becca had stopped crying. Glancing down, she saw she was staring vacantly at Jekyll.

She continued moving, burrowing her head against Becca to muffle the wail of sirens outside. When the clock on the mantle struck seven, Becca tensed, raising her head. Jeremy rushed toward them, embracing them both.

"Is Grandma dead?" Becca asked.

Katie felt his trembling body and ragged breathing as his tears fell on her arm. She pressed her mouth to his wet cheek while he held her head with one hand.

"She wanted to hurt me." Becca burrowed her face into his neck.

"I know, hon. I'm so sorry that happened." His long fingers stroked her hair while his eyes sought Katie. "You okay?"

She managed a nod.

"Let's take her up to bed now."

In Becca's room, Katie sat on her bed where Jekyll had taken up his usual station, stretched out close to Becca.

Katie's senses were dazed and everything felt surreal. Jeremy sat in the rocking chair pulled close. She had no idea how long they'd been there when Becca touched her arm. "Will you stay with me?" She scooted over to make room for her.

Once Katie lay beside her, she pulled up the comforter. Her face held no trace of her ordeal. Still, Katie was afraid for her. What damage might the terror have done? Would this bring back Becca's nightmares, the fear and guilt.

Katie's exhaustion soon overtook her agitation and she slept. Sometime later, she woke to find herself snuggled against Jeremy's back. Gradually, she realized he was rigidly awake, unlike Becca and Jekyll who both snored.

She reached over him, taking his hand that squeezed hers before he turned over to cradle her in his arms. Within minutes, she was asleep again.

The next morning, Katie secured the final comb in Francine's well-brushed hair. When she had brought her breakfast, she'd answered all her questions. For half an hour now, after learning of Cheryl's treachery, Francine had sat silent, absorbed in private thoughts. She barely touched her food but sipped tea, looking off into some faraway place.

Jeremy had driven to Sheridan very early. Now he came into the room. Francine held out her hands to him. "Darling, I'm so sorry."

He nodded at Katie before sitting close to Francine. "I've made the arrangements. There'll be a graveside memorial service this afternoon. Cheryl was Jewish although I never saw her attend Temple. But in any case, I found a rabbi. I want this over quickly."

"That is only proper." Francine selected her words carefully before she continued. "Jeremy, I did this to you, and I will never forgive myself."

"You were only trying to help me. I wanted Cheryl here even though she brought nothing but grief. Having her here seemed like my penance for Evelyn." His face had taken on a haunted demeanor.

"What did they put on the death certificate?"

"Accidental death. Two deputies witnessed the whole ghastly thing so it was all straight forward."

"Why did she take Becca?"

"My guess is she wanted to get back at me for turning her out. She always knew people's weak spots."

"A wicked woman and I brought her into our home. A bit like inviting a rattlesnake to tea. Dear, Lord!" She leaned her head into one hand before looking back at him, her inspection grave now. "Darling, I'm worried about you. You look ill."

"I'll rest after this service is over."

"How can I help you today?"

He kissed her cheek. "Say a prayer." He touched the bruise. "I was so distracted yesterday, I didn't even see this. I haven't been seeing a lot of things lately."

Francine shook her head. "Don't look so

grim on my account. I am no worse for a few shots of Valium!"

Katie watched the exchange from a window, her heart aching for both of them. She smiled at her grandmother's flare of defiance. Also grinning, Jeremy stood, kissed Francine again, then asked Katie to walk down with him. Halfway down the staircase, he wrapped her in a tender embrace and they stood there drawing strength from each other until he finally tipped up her chin, his fingers gently tracing the hollow of her throat. "Will you go to the burial? I'm asking more for Becca than me." He bent to kiss her. "Actually, I'm asking for me."

Familiar warmth went through Katie and she laughed softly. "Of course, I'll go." She saw him relax a little.

At two o'clock, Katie sat between Becca and Pearl in the graveside tent. Jeremy sat stiffly on the other side of Becca, his face impassive.

Katie glanced around the nearly vacant enclosure.. Cheryl had no family besides Evelyn, Jeremy, Becca and the niece from Chicago who was a no show. She had no friends. Scott and Bernard sat off to the side. Two aides from the nursing home arrived late.

After the rabbi's brief words, the small group walked into the hot sunshine. Becca watched fascinated when the rabbi chanted a final prayer.

The funeral was over. They left the most remote corner of the Chamberlain burial plot, Cheryl's ultimate earthly castigation.

Back at the manor, Katie took Becca up to change into her riding clothes. "What happens to people when they die?" Becca asked when she'd wiggled out of her dress. "Do they rot like dead birds?"

"Anything that dies, rots, but it doesn't matter because their spirit is still alive."

"Where does it go?"

"To a place we can't see but is much nicer than here."

"Like heaven?"

"That's one name for it."

"Just where is heaven?" She sat on the rug to pull on her boots.

At a loss, Katie was grateful to hear Jeremy in the hall. "Some people think spirits become part of our memories."

Becca considered this, still puzzled. "I hope I remember something nice about Grandma someday." She scrambled to her feet as her father entered. "How come no one knows where heaven is?" She stood gazing up at him. "Why haven't they found it yet?"

He cast an imploring look at Katie. Finally, inspiration dawned and he drew Becca to the rocking chair and onto his lap. "I know where heaven is but it's hard to explain. You'll figure it out when you get older. I can tell you about a cool thing that happens when someone dies. Remember when Insata died after her foal was born? And the bigger the foal grew, the more she looked like Insata. I think so much of Insata's spirit was in her foal that she continued living in her baby."

Becca appraised him gravely.

"Part of your grandma still lives in you. She did a lot of bad things and hurt us, but there must've been something good in her because God made her, and that's the part she left in you."

She slowly nodded. "I think I get it. So when Francine dies, some of her will stay in you and me and Katie."

"Right. And a long time from now when you die, the same thing will happen with the people you love the most. No one ever really dies."

She hugged him, then regarded him, grinning. "Thanks for telling me."

"You are welcome. Now off to the arena with you. Should I walk with you?"

She shook her head. "I know God is going to take care of me. And I've got Jekyll."

She slid off his lap and gave Katie a hug before she rushed into the hall, Jekyll on her heels.

Katie curled herself into Jeremy's lap, leaning her head against his. "You're raising a very wise little girl. Have I told you that lately? I wish I'd possessed half her self-confidence when I was her age. I was such a terrified mess."

Jeremy smiled. "You are absolutely amazing now and I adore you."

Bernard Mayhall arrived promptly the next morning to change Francine's will. He returned that afternoon with the documents ready to sign.

Francine sat by a window and read each page with great care before taking up her pen. Finished at last, she leaned back and closed her eyes as if needing to rest after an arduous task.

When she came alert and appraised Jeremy and Katie sitting opposite, a glint of triumph invaded her azure gaze. "I am so happy that is finished. Do you feel the same?"

Jeremy laughed and half rose to kiss her cheek. "I thought we'd settled all that."

She watched him settle back in his chair. "You're right, it's settled."

Katie stood and gathered her grandmother in a warm embrace. "I, for the record, am delighted."

"I am a very blessed old woman to have you two in charge of my beloved *Radbourne*. My heart is at peace. Thank you."

They continued sitting with her for a time until her pretense of strength and control began to crumble and they helped her back into bed. She caught both their hands, holding them in hers, her smile ample indication of her huge satisfaction.

Jeremy and Katie descended the staircase, both feeling practically giddy after the terror and tension of the past days. When they reached the front hall, they stood together, sharing the moment of completion and triumph over the horror of yesterday. The future lay before them filled with the greatest hope and promise.

Jeremy pulled Katie into his arms, grinning at her. "If we go now, we could spend a few hours at the cabin."

Caught off guard, she could only stare at him until she'd digested the notion. "What a lovely idea. Are you sure we should leave?"

"I can think of no better way to spend a gorgeous summer day."

"Me either."

"You tell Pearl where we're going and pack some wine and cheese. I'll go saddle the horses."

He kissed the end of her nose and playfully swatted her bottom as she headed to the kitchen.

Within fifteen minutes, they were riding up the mountain.

When Janel Dickerson returned to begin her job, Katie thought how fortunate the timing had been that she was away when Cheryl went berserk. But as soon as Janel arrived, they learned that she had read all about the situation in the papers. Evidently, the coverage of the story was widespread.

Jeremy and Katie had invited Janel to stop by for a drink after she'd spent her first day back at *Radbourne* moving into her cottage. The three of them sat in the drawing room, drinking bourbon.

"So do you like your new home?" Katie asked.

"Yes, very much. It's just right for me in size, and very charming. There is one thing I forgot to mention last week. I have a dog. A Golden Retriever named Breighton. He's a sweetheart and very well trained. Will he be a problem?"

"Of course not. We love dogs around here. Most of our employees have dogs. With the exception of Jekyll, my daughter's service dog, we can't have them out among the horses or in the barns, but everyone understands that. Most of the employee cottages and houses have fenced yards."

"I understand completely and I apologize for not telling you sooner." She managed a smile. "I think I was more nervous at my interview than I thought I would be."

"You seemed to have it very much together

to me," Katie said.

"Thanks. It's just that I wanted this job so much."

"Well, we're very happy about that because we need you. We're not yet finished breeding visiting mares. And there's the usual vaccinations for the foals and the blood work for the show horses that will be on the circuit before long. We need you to keep on top of all that and make sure Patrick has all the paperwork he needs whenever he leaves for a show." He left the sofa to refill her glass.

"We're going to make the Regionals in Billings a family affair in September. We'll be preparing several horses that Patrick, Katie, Becca and I will be showing. I'd like you to take special care with monitoring the conditioning of those."

"Oh, how fun for you. I'll make sure the horses are fit as it's possible to get them by September."

"Thanks."

"Now I'm off. I want to take Breighton for a jog." She placed her glass on the table before the sofa. "I'll be in barns at eight in the morning."

"I'll meet you there," Jeremy agreed.

"Goodbye," Katie said and they watched her turn into the corridor. "No wonder she's in such amazing shape. She jogs."

Jeremy nuzzled her throat. "I see not one problem with your shape. But it's going to get even better once we start getting the horses up to snuff for the Regionals."

"I'm getting pretty excited about that actually."

"I can't wait to see how great you're going to be."

"How would you know I'll be any good?"

"Dare I think you've forgotten that ride you took on Bohjalian last spring? I'm still stunned at the memory."

She smiled with remembered pleasure. "That was fun. I loved shocking you because you were so sure I'd never seen a horse before, let alone being able to ride one."

A slow grin lit his eyes. "I deserved that. I was quite intimidated by you, if you must know, so I reacted by being mean." He held her hand, idly tracing circles on her palm with his thumb. "I've been known to harbor opinionated misconceptions."

"Did I really intimidate you?"

"Lord, yes. When Francine told me you were coming, I had visions of you pushing me out of the way and taking over *Radbourne*. Then when you arrived, you were this gorgeous person with such self-assurance I felt as inadequate as I did when Francine first brought me here. You totally unnerved me."

"Wow, you could've fooled me." She sat contemplating him, remembering how formidable she'd found him when she first arrived at *Radbourne*. You scared the bejesus out of me."

He shook his head musingly, then pulled her close "Thank heavens, we soon saw past our misapprehension."

She rested there in his arms for awhile. "I'm starting to remember how much fun it was when I was in formal training for horse shows back in the day." She squeezed his hand. "Now I'm going to see how Francine's feeling."

"Give her a hug for me."

Katie found Francine savoring her after dinner tea. She sat close to her. "How's it going tonight?"

She frowned. "I'm a little down. I don't know what's wrong with me. I felt so good when all that business with the will was finished. Now the wind's gone out of my sails." She gave her a bleak look.

"That's probably normal."

Sad eyes slid toward the window. "Becca is at her riding lesson?"

"Yes. She's excited about getting ready for the Regionals."

"I'm glad she has her riding right now. It will get her through the sadness."

"She really doesn't seem to be bothered much by Cheryl's death. I think she picked up on her grandmother's treachery awhile ago. And because she had already come to terms with Evelyn's illness, she seems to be treating this as merely one more change."

"She is a wise little thing."

"Did I tell you I'm going to ride in the Billings show?"

Francine appraised her intently. "Oh, that is grand! *That* makes me happy. I'm just delighted. Since we've always gone about showing with the right state of mind, I believe you will enjoy it."

Her words puzzled her. "What do you mean the right state of mind?"

She actually rolled her eyes. "What the big

outfits do at shows these days is disgraceful, wicked. It's all about money now. Those guys have no conception of what a sublime privilege it is to own Arabians. We have always done what we do because we have a huge love affair with these magnificent horses. We respect them. Treat them in much the same way the sheiks did centuries ago when they lived in their tents. The big breeders treat them horribly, beating and terrorizing them so they'll come into the show ring looking wild and out of control. Only a handful of breeders steer clear of that treatment and train their horses to perform because they love their handlers."

"I had no idea it was that bad."

"It makes me feel ill just thinking about it. Jeremy and I have fought against the abuse over the years but it's still out there, messing up the industry. I despise it!"

Katie felt at a loss, having had no awareness of this sordid side of the business she found herself enmeshed in. "My dear, I can become quite stirred up by this subject but you mustn't let my talk dissuade you from showing and delighting in it. To this day, I can think of nothing I enjoyed more than winning a class with a well-trained Arabian.

"Our standards have always been extremely high at *Radbourne,* and God willing, that will continue with you at the helm. You simply must remember that we don't compromise. When you enter the show ring, make sure everyone is aware that you are there for the pure joy of it, not to increase the value of your horses. When the heart is right about the first, the second comes with no effort."

Katie sat still as she fell silent. She saw the acuity of her convictions in the gold pinpoints of light scintillating in the blue eyes. I'll do my best to follow your example."

Jeremy will support you all the way because he totally shares my opinion.

As spring melded into summer, *Radbourne's* main focus was the Arabian Show in Billings. Becca's riding lessons in the arena had given way to longer schooling sessions in the larger formal riding ring in an adjoining barn.

Katie decided to show Bohjalian in Park, Dressage, and English Pleasure so began training in earnest with Becca. After a couple weeks of simple ring riding to begin conditioning both the horses and riders, Patrick set up a schedule where Katie and Becca rode two hours each morning and afternoon under his tutelage.

Much of this intensive training was aimed at bringing both horses and riders to top physical fitness. After a month, Katie could feel the increased strength in her back and legs, reminiscent of her days in riding school as a teen. Boh's black hide gleamed with health and his muscles grew toned and streamlined. Janel checked the horses twice a week, monitoring their progress and regulating the grain, hay and supplements they were fed, striving for the lean, muscled finish of an athlete.

Boh's stamina and agility amazed Katie when Patrick instructed her to push him into the most advanced maneuvers in Dressage and Park.

He was clearly the best conditioned animal she had ever seen perform.

To prevent boredom with the difficult ring work, twice a week, Patrick joined her and Becca on a leisurely gallop on the mountain. Sometimes, Jeremy rode with them as he had his own training schedule, readying four stallions for conformation and performance classes.

He was also readying several foals for the show. They received their conditioning on treadmills and hot walkers. She was quite amazed when he told her that he planned to have a swimming pool installed in one of the barns during the coming year.

"Nothing puts the polish on a horse like swimming or trotting in warm water," he explained. "And water therapy is unparalleled for healing injuries. If the owner has misgivings about the cost, I'll point out that we will have the only water therapy facility in the region so can garner a lot of income from injured horses brought here for convalescence." He angled an amused look at her. "Do you think I have a chance of convincing the owner?"

She nodded. "Sounds like a sound investment to me."

As the heat increased in July, everyone either rode in the air-conditioned riding rings, or went up the mountain in the cool of early morning or evening. Katie was inspired to be riding again at the top of her ability. Now she wondered why she had stopped riding in Boston for so many years.

When Patrick began hauling horses to

shows in the adjoining states and was away for several days at a time, Katie became Becca's instructor and Jeremy became hers. She found herself in awe of his ability as a rider as well as his rapport with the stallions and foals he prepared to be shown in halter classes.

It thrilled her when he burst into the show ring with a prancing, snorting stallion cavorting beside him on a long lead. It was the ultimate show of controlled power. He was able to get every ounce of athleticism and fire from the spirited animals while maintaining total command over the brute strength. And he accomplished this with none of the cruel practices many other owners employed. As she watched him work each day, she gained understanding of the standards and pride Francine had maintained and passed down to Jeremy.

CHAPTER FOURTEEN

Despite the long hours she spent training Boh and a flashy chestnut mare named Masada that she planned to ride in English Pleasure at the upcoming show, Katie managed to visit Francine for considerable chunks of time. She sensed a huge change in her grandmother.

At times the old woman was alert and talkative but with worrisome regularity, she began lapsing into confusion and seemed to be drifting further away. This new behavior concerned Katie who questioned if she was going to become senile and rob her of the answers she'd come to *Radbourne* initially to learn. She was seized by a new compulsion to learn all she could about her life there as a child before it was too late.

When she visited Francine now, they talked mostly of those lost years before she was sent away. Francine managed to weave together many of the fragmentary impressions and images that circled in the depth of Katie's mind. At times, she talked for long stretches with no prompting, wandering through memories, floating in and out of coherency. Katie listened and tried to sort out what was factual from the fanciful ramblings.

Francine recounted the drought when Katie was four, when most of the horses were sold for lack of grass and hay. Cinabar was Katie's beagle puppy that died when she was three and broke her heart. When her grandmother said she'd loved gingerbread and apple cider, she was at a loss because she disliked both...so many bits and pieces of time lost.

As the fabric of information grew in strength and dimension, Katie was drawn to a familiar place where she was content, protected and she dared believe that Francine had been responsible for this barely remembered period of happiness. Even with all the fun she was having with Jeremy and Becca and the good work they were doing together, she found herself reluctant to be separated from Francine as if she stood between her and the void she still must look into.

Pearl brought dinner trays upstairs most nights so Katie and Becca could eat with Francine. Later, after putting Becca to bed, Katie often returned upstairs where by this time, Francine was usually asleep. Still, Katie drew solace from being near her. She settled into a chair by the window, surveying the grounds lying still in the lamplight below.

It was often well after midnight when she checked on Becca. Deep fatigue drew her to her own bed. Some nights while she was still with Francine, she saw Jeremy walk back from the barns or arrive back from visiting Evelyn.

Tonight, she watched him stop to feed carrots to Bordeaux, then make his way to the terrace. Katie left her chair and hurried down the stairs, meeting him in the rear hall.

He pulled her close with one arm as they headed to their usual rendezvous in the drawing room. He poured bourbon and they sat on the sofa.

"How's she doing?" he asked.

"She comes and goes. I feel her pulling away from us."

He absently massaged her shoulders. "You know we have a big commitment with this show coming up."

She knew what he was getting at. "I know my heart hasn't been in it the last couple weeks. I was so enthused when we first started but now I find it's really hard for me to be away from Francine. I feel like we're running out of time."

He tenderly drew her against him. "Honey, I know how hard this is. I agree that Francine is in a different mindset than I've seen before. And she's certainly not gaining physically. But I've spoken to Scott and he assures me she's going to be here for some time yet. So I truly don't think we're going to lose her any time soon. I hope you can have faith in that and not worry so much."

"I know I have to pull myself together about this, and get my heart back into working the horses." She straightened a little, searching his weary face. "Guess who would be the first to tell me that?"

He grinned. "Our own Francine, the consummate horse breeder."

"And she's absolutely right. My responsibility lies with our horses right now. I promise to pick up the pace."

He touched her face, his fingers circling to the back of her head to draw her closer so he could kiss her, his mouth achingly gentle. "I love you with my heart and soul. You're my partner."

Katie's foal Ashara was also going to the horse show. She and her mother had been brought in from their pasture a month before and now shared a box stall near the training barn.

Katie and Becca had played with her every day since, teaching her to lead and stand square on all four legs without moving. She also learned to be out of sight and hearing of her mother for short periods while remaining calm. Now it was time for her short stint of serious training.

The morning after her latest talk with Jeremy, Katie led her baby into the paddock where he and Patrick worked with two other foals. For the first few minutes, she watched the men put their charges through their paces. To her surprise, the youngsters already behaved much like the adult show horses .

They circled the paddock at an animated trot, stopped and set up square and unruffled, and amazingly stretched out their graceful necks in perfect show form. After an interval when they would be scrutinized by the judge in an actual show, they were trotted out a short distance, then back.

"Now let's see Ashara do this," Jeremy instructed Katie as he handed his foal's lead to Patrick. "I'm the judge."

She urged her into a trot as they'd practiced and set her up before him. Then using the end of her show whip to get her attention, she put it close to her nose and moved it in and out, enticing her to stretch her neck. When she didn't extend her nose as far as the other foals had, Katie bent her knees and moved up and down which made Ashara curious enough to lengthen her neck a bit more.

Jeremy motioned her to trot away which she did with perfect calm. When she was back beside him, he stood looking at her. "That was remarkable. Who showed you how to do that?"

"Becca had the general idea, then I looked up training foals to show at halter on the internet."

"Wow!" Shaking his head, he went back to working the foal he collected from Patrick.

All was in readiness for the horse show that would last three days. Two Radbourne vans were loaded with the show horses. Patrick was hauling eight stallions that would show in both halter and performance classes. Two grandsons of Bordeaux would vie for a Regional Championship enroute to the Nationals.

The second van to be driven by Jeremy carried five foals and their mothers, Masada and Bohjalian and Juniper. Patrick and two grooms and three stable boys had left the ranch at noon since it was less than a two hour drive to the show grounds.

The other loaded van sat idling in the driveway. Pearl arrived from a dry cleaners in Sheridan where all the formal show clothing had been taken two weeks ago. Some mix-up had caused the order to be finished only an hour before. She parked beside the van and transferred everything into the dressing room at the back of the trailer where the other luggage had already been stowed along with all the show tack and cartons of shampoo, hoof polish and the various equipment needed to groom the horses to perfection.

Katie stood in the carefully packed

compartment with the list Patrick had given her to ensure nothing vital was forgotten. When she'd taken inventory of the clothing, she was about to leave when Jeremy appeared in the hall.

"All set?" he asked.

"Yes." She stepped closer and lifted her face for his kiss. "All we have left to do is go tell Francine goodbye."

He drew her close. "I told Becca to meet us in her room." He patted Katie's backside before they turned down the steps.

When they'd gone upstairs, they found Becca sitting close to Francine on the bed, the two deep in conversation. Jekyll sat close by.

Francine watched them enter. "Becca's just been telling me all the details of your adventure." Her gaze ranged over both of them. "Are the horses calm and ready?"

"Bordeaux's Folly is a little testy but he'll come around. His brother Jester is dozing as usual."

"Which is going to win the trophy?"

Jeremy lowered himself into a chair. "Good question. I prefer Folly's hot edge but as soon as they hit the ring, they both crank it up."

Francine wagged a finger at him. "Since you and Folly get along so well, be sure *you* show him."

"That's how it'll be. Patrick has no personal stake in it so he can win just as easy with Jester."

Francine shifted her eyes to Katie and reached for her hand. "I wish I could see your debut. I know you will be magnificent."

"You can watch the video," Jeremy reminded her, referring to the film that one of the groom's recorded of every class *Radbourne* horses competed in.

"I'll be waiting for that with bated breath." She smiled and surveyed them all with obvious satisfaction.

"I'm making my debut too," Becca said.

"Yes, you are and from what Katie's been telling me, you are going to be superb as well." She lifted her arms to hug her. "Bring me some ribbons."

Becca beamed. "I will. I've worked really hard." She slid off the bed and laid her arm over Jekyll's neck. "I hope you won't be lonely while we're gone."

"I'll be just fine. You all have fun. Remember that's why we do this."

Becca stood regarding her quizzically. "We want everyone to see our beautiful horses."

"Yes, but if it's not fun, it's not worth it."

"I always have fun riding Juniper," Becca declared.

Jeremy stood up and went to Francine. "You take care of yourself." He bent to kiss her, then looked at her intently for a moment. "Scott will be checking on you."

Francine scowled at him. "That's not necessary!"

"I know but he's doing it for the rest of us so we don't have to worry about you."

Her annoyance melted under his smile. "Very well, then, I wouldn't want you to be distracted on my account." She turned her attention to Katie who stood beside Jeremy. "Darling, be as amazing as I know you can be. I am so proud and grateful!"

"See you Sunday. I love you."

"And I you." She watched the three of them take their leave with Jekyll leading the way.

Katie had researched the show and learned of its importance in the *Radbourne* breeding program. It was one of several shows in which horses were awarded points that would eventually determine National Champions. A win at a regional show was a coup in its own right.

Katie was surprised by the measure of her pride as the van rolled across the bridge on the way to the main road. Totally relaxed, Becca settled with Jekyll on the rear seat and both were soon asleep.

When they reached the show grounds, Katie noted the facilities were rather rustic when compared to what she was accustomed to in the East. They found Patrick and the others parked near their assigned stalls. The stallions had already been settled in.

Patrick and the hired men proceeded to unload the rest, then began the first step in the grooming process, shampooing everyone. The stallions were led off to a barn equipped with cement compartments with spray nozzles and drains. Jeremy and Katie went to work giving baths to the rest.

After they were shampooed, the adult horses' manes and tails were conditioned, braided and secured with vet wrap, an all-purpose stretchy material that was originally manufactured to wrap wounds and sprains. "I remember this stuff from my riding school days," Katie said as she bound Masada's tail in hot pink.

"After all these years, I think it has nearly as many uses as duct tape," Jeremy said with a grin.

By the time all the horses had been returned to their stalls wearing red sheets with the white *Radbourne* logo to keep them as clean as possible during the night, Katie was bone weary.

Becca who'd done as much work as her size and attention allowed, came to put her hand in Katie's. "I'm really hungry."

"Then I think I should take my favorite ladies to dinner," Jeremy said, ruffling her hair. "Let me see if Patrick and the others want to join us after they've done the feeding. He walked toward the barn and was back shortly. "Patrick's coming but the rest want to eat at a bar."

Half an hour later, the four of them sat in a Mexican restaurant near their motel. Enjoying the privileges of a certified service dog, Jekyll lay at Becca's feet.

Katie sipped her margarita, hoping bedtime wasn't far off.

"What time do we have to get up?" Becca asked, stirring her Shirley Temple.

"Early," her father answered, "and that's why we're going to bed early."

"Thank heavens," Katie agreed.

"I hope my crew has enough sense to make it an early night at the bar," Patrick mused.

"I remember those days when I didn't have any sense," Jeremy said. "Nothing quite as awful as trying to show with a hangover. Not to mention, I had to do my own grooming back in the day.

Fortunately, it didn't take me long to smarten up."

"Did you win when you were drunk?" Becca wanted to know, getting a laugh from Katie and Patrick.

He gave her a droll look. "I did but I suffered mightily for my folly."

"What's folly?"

"Madness. Craziness."

"Bordeaux's not crazy."

He shook his head at her quick association. "Maybe he felt a little crazy when he saw Folly's grandmother," he allowed. He reached for Katie's hand. "Girls have that effect on guys sometimes."

Becca grinned. "Yeah, I guess." She drained her glass and sat still. "What if I get scared tomorrow and can't show Juniper?"

"You won't," Jeremy said. "You're too well prepared."

"I might," she insisted.

"Listen, Becca," Patrick said from across the table, "I'm the one who trained both you and Juniper so I know what you both can do. Juniper could go through an English Pleasure class with his eyes shut, so at the very worst, all you have to do is stay in the saddle. But I also know what a gutsy little rider you are and once you see the other kids in that class, all you'll want to do is beat them. And we'll be with you in the morning. I'll give you some final pointers before you go in the ring."

She sighed but then brightened. "I may be a little nervous but I can do it."

"Yes, you can," Jeremy said, "and most everyone gets a little nervous which is okay. It makes you a little sharper."

She nodded and appeared to relax as their food was served.

They were all exhausted after a long day and were back at the motel by nine. Katie was pleased to discover she and Jeremy, Becca and Jekyll were booked in one double room.

She and Becca shared a bed with Jekyll stretched out between them. Jeremy had the luxury of an entire bed to himself. Katie was so tired, it didn't matter; she was asleep in minutes.

She was the first one up the next morning. After she showered, she headed to the barn, leaving Jeremy to deal with Becca. She left them a note that she would meet them for breakfast in half an hour.

The halter classes for foals were first on the show roster so she went to see how well Ashara had come through the night without getting dirty. She removed her sheet and inspected her from head to toe, happy to see she was still clean. After she buckled the sheet back on, she mucked out the stall and moved on to examine the other horses that would be shown at halter that morning.

Only one of Jeremy's gray colts had gotten a large manure stain across his pale rump. She hurried to the van to collect aerosol shampoo, rags and a clean sheet, then fetched a bucket of warm water before she returned to the stall. Working quickly, she sprayed the spot with shampoo and lathered it. When the stain was gone, she poured clean rinse water over it, and rubbed it dry with a towel before replacing the soiled sheet with a clean one.

Checking her watch, she saw it was time to go to the restaurant and soon joined Jeremy and Becca perusing a menu. She kissed them both and slid into the booth. Jekyll sat decorously, wearing his official vest.

"When does the first foal class start?" Becca asked.

"Eight for open class so we'll all be in that one. Patrick will show a fourth."

Katie told him she'd cleaned up the gray. They all ate oatmeal, then Jeremy left to check the barns to see that the grooms and stable boys were on schedule with their work.

Katie and Becca went to change into their pinstriped riding suits in the van dressing room. By seven-thirty they were both ready. Katie pinned Becca's hair down so it would fit neatly under her black bowler, then donned her own hat. They stood side by side before the wide mirror. She had braided her own hair and pinned it in a knot at the back of her head.

The door opened and Jeremy came to stand behind them. "Wow. You two look gorgeous!"

Becca giggled and Katie high-fived her. "We look good, girl."

They stepped outside while Jeremy changed into his black riding suit and bowler. When he reappeared, Katie's heart caught at his lithe grace in the tailored ensemble. They headed to the show barn where Patrick had also changed. He and the stable boys had already arrived with the four foals that all wore elaborate halters inlaid with silver. Jekyll sat quietly, watching the proceedings.

The grooms tended to the final details,

applying polish to the tiny hooves, black on black, clear on white. After each claimed their foal, their hides were wiped down one last time.

Numbers were pinned on their backs, then Jeremy led them a short distance from the gate where he set up his black colt. Becca followed suit with a delicate gray filly, imitating her father's actions precisely. Katie saw no sign of last night's jitters.

Within minutes, they were part of the procession of foals entering the ring at a high-stepping trot. Becca ran between Jeremy and Patrick with Katie some distant back so she could watch Becca who was one of only two youngsters in the class. Katie smiled at her aplomb when all the foals lined up. Becca carefully set up the elegant baby and when she was asked to trot her out, she clearly put her heart and soul into showing off her action. Katie was quite sure the judge studied the pair with a few seconds extra interest as they made their way back to their place.

All the *Radbourne* foals made the cut for the top six. Patrick was in first with Jeremy second. In the initial lineup, Katie was in last place. After motioning them all around the ring again, the judge switched Katie to fifth, then paced along the row. To her amazement, he suddenly moved Becca into first ahead of Jeremy.

She nearly shouted with happiness as she watched Becca take her blue ribbon, remaining amazingly serene. It was when they left the ring that the spectators sent up a cheer. Jeremy and Patrick whooped. Katie put two fingers in her mouth and managed the piercing whistle Aunt

Jessie had taught her as a girl. This brought an amused look from Jeremy and Patrick.

They all mobbed Becca outside the gate. Patrick grabbed her hands, dancing her around in a little jig. "Way to go, my number one student!"

Katie couldn't decide who was happiest for her as they waited for the next class. This time Becca was showing a bigger chestnut colt that wasn't as well matched to her diminutive size but didn't seem more than she could handle. Even though she was still stunned by her win, she recovered quickly and went into the ring with her customary intrepid flair.

This time, Jeremy took the class with a son of Boh, a nearly perfect black colt, and Patrick took second. Neither Katie or Becca placed.

In the fillies class, Katie placed first with Ashara. Jeremy came in second. By the end of the foals' competition, Jeremy and Patrick took Grand Champion and Reserve with their two colts. Ashara took the Grand for the fillies.

Katie was at first amazed at the seemingly easy success of the *Radbourne* entries and the nonchalance with which Jeremy and Patrick collected their ribbons and trophies. Gradually she understood how long they'd been doing this and how accustomed they had become to the superiority of the Arabians they handled. The competition also apparently realized what they were up against and reacted with a mixture of admiration and reluctant acceptance.

As the halter classes continued all morning, all four of them had little time to rest or collect their thoughts. Katie saw for herself the efficiency of *Radbourne's* support staff. The grooms and stable boys never failed to deliver the correct horses to the ring gate before each class. The manes and tails had been combed out in rippling waves that accented the finely-sculptured Arabs.

By lunch time when the conformation classes were finished, Bordeaux's two grandsons were bound for the Nationals as was Masada. Becca won a third with Juniper in the geldings class.

Later that afternoon, Becca sat on Juniper outside the ring where her Junior English Pleasure class was about the begin. Patrick stood beside her, his arms resting on either side of the saddle. "I've warmed up Juniper. He's ready to do his best for you. Just relax and ride like you do every day."

She nodded, her gloomy gaze steady on his. "I don't know if I can."

"I know you can. Look what you did in halter this morning."

"Well, yeah..." The flat line of her mouth slowly twisted into a grin and she threw her arms around him. "I won a blue ribbon." Remembered pleasure danced in her eyes. "Thanks, Patrick. You're the best teacher ever." She spotted Jeremy and Katie waiting nearby and gave them an excited wave before she fell into line with the other riders entering the ring.

Katie and Jeremy joined Patrick at the rail to watch the class. As had happened that morning, once Becca was caught up in her role as contestant, her agitation fell away and she rode with the finesse of someone much older.

Jeremy put his arm around Katie, giving her a little hug as he caught her eye. "Isn't she something?"

"She's her father's daughter," she agreed. When the class was eventually culled down to the final lineup, Becca was in first place.

She faultlessly put Juniper through the final maneuvers before the judge and was handed the blue ribbon that she waved gleefully as she trotted from the ring. "You were fabulous," Katie said when Jeremy lifted her from the saddle.

"And you'll be riding for the English Pleasure Championship later on," Patrick reminded her.

"But may I watch the other classes for awhile?" she asked as she took off her hat and glanced longingly at the spectator bleachers behind them.

"We'll watch with you." Jeremy guided her and Katie to an empty spot and motioned Jekyll from where he lay beside the ring fence. He walked sedately to the bleacher where he stretched out at Becca's feet.

They were all tired and Becca soon fell asleep with her head in Jeremy's lap. Katie envied her.

Becca won a Reserve Championship in her English Pleasure class, capping off her triumphant debut in the show ring. By the time, she'd collected her lavender rosette and trophy, she was so tired they skipped dinner in the restaurant. They called for pizza and were all in bed by eight o'clock.

Katie fell asleep so quickly she had no time to reflect on their remarkable day or her part in it. She was again the first one awake the next morning.

The roster of adult performance classes started at eight with English Pleasure – Stallions. Katie, Becca and Jekyll sat in the bleachers to watch Jeremy and Patrick compete on Bordeaux's grandsons. Folly barely edged out Jester to win the class.

A couple hours later, Katie rode Masada to a blue ribbon in her English Pleasure class. Soon after that, she and Jeremy competed for the Championship and to her considerable astonishment, she won with Jeremy taking Reserve.

That afternoon, Becca and Jekyll sat in the stands while her dad, Katie and Patrick rode in Dressage and Park. By the end of the day, Katie and Boh had the Championship in both Park and Dressage while Jeremy won the Reserve in Dressage, and Patrick the Reserve in Park.

Because of the crowd reaction to Boh's winning Park performance, Katie was invited to present an exhibition performance on Sunday, the closing event of the show. As the master of ceremonies announced her and Boh, they swept into the ring with all the flair they could muster.

After one time around, Katie collected Boh, then as he moved out at a faster trot. She remembered their other exhibition back at *Radbourne* when she'd wanted to shock Jeremy into seeing her as worthy to claim her birthright.

Now as she cued Boh to pick up the pace and show what he could do, she was thrilled by his response. He lifted and extended his legs, settling into the over the top, rocking gait that set Park apart from other performance classes. She heard the spectators send up a roar of admiration.

As she circled and passed before the crowd again, she made out the calls and whistles from Jeremy and Patrick and the employees. She glanced at the stands where Becca was jumping up and down, screaming.

A thrill of accomplishment passed through her. In the last three days, she had proven to the world that she deserved to own *Radbourne Arabians*. If other breeders had already dismissed her as a figurehead, she had now disproved the theory.

She presently pushed Boh into a smooth canter, then as she started to bring her ride to a close, she gathered him into an extremely slow trot that exaggerated his radical action. As the crowd once again burst into applause and cheers, she increased his pace to make one last circuit before she pulled up and doffed her hat in a bow. The spectators who weren't already on their feet, rose in a standing ovation.

After the announcer finished praising her performance, he called for Jeremy to join her. When he and Becca had jogged out to stand beside Boh, they were both introduced. A short tribute to *Radbourne Arabians* followed, ending with best wishes to Francine.

When they had left the show ring, Katie leaned against Jeremy, shaking with emotion. He stopped to hold her while Becca grabbed her around the legs and Patrick patted her on the back.

Jeremy took her face in his hands. "How cool was that, sweetheart?"

Tears wandered down her cheeks as she gave him a tremulous smile. "It was...was just so lovely."

He grinned and kissed her . "Actually, it was the most mind-boggling thing I've ever seen. I am so incredibly proud of you."

Katie reached for Becca who'd been waiting patiently for her attention. She reached down to swing her up in her arms. "What'd you think of that?"

Becca considered her soberly even as mischief twinkled in her eyes. "I thought it was so wonderful. I don't think I can *ever* ride like you."

"I think you already do."

She frowned. "I can't ride Boh."

"I think you should try that one of these days."

Becca slowly grinned. "Maybe."

Jeremy turned to lift her into his arms for a kiss before he put her down. "While the guys load the vans, I want you ladies to accompany me on a little tour of the grounds." He winked. "It's time to schmooze with the competition."

Taking their hands, he led the way down the breezeway in the first barn with Jekyll ambling behind. Exhibitors were in various stages of preparing to leave the show. Some were eager to drop everything and lead out their best horses for Jeremy and Katie's approval.

Others were enjoying some after show alcohol which they were happy to share. At one barn, someone unearthed a can of coke for Becca and asked her about Jekyll and his service dog vest.

"He just takes care of me," she explained.

"Why do you need him to do that."

"Well, you never know." She shrugged. "My grandma tried to kill me awhile back."

Katie leapt forward and grabbed her hand as they hurried toward the next barn.

"Well, she asked...," Becca explained.

"I know," Jeremy agreed as they neared another owner's stalls.

After two drinks, he refused more alcohol in preparation for driving home. They continued for half an hour before heading back.

Katie was relieved to see that both horses and equipment were already loaded. She and Becca changed before settling in for the ride home

Once they'd hit the Interstate and she heard Becca and Jekyll snoring softly, she found a pillow and lay down with her head next to Jeremy's leg. He gently massaged her back, lulling her to sleep.

CHAPTER FIFTEEN

Katie, Jeremy and Becca gathered in Francine's bedroom the afternoon after they returned from Billings. Katie put the show tape in her VCR.

They hadn't told her much about their success so it would be a surprise. She sat propped on pillows, her lined face filled with anticipation. She laughed softly and clapped as the Regionals' logo appeared. "I'm so excited," she declared, hugging Becca against her with both arms.

"You're going to love it," Becca whispered as the film opened with the initial foal class.

Katie leaned close to her grandmother, her heart accelerating with pride as she watched Becca collect her blue ribbon. Jeremy dropped his arm around her shoulders and sat next to her on the bed.

The film had been expertly edited so the emphasis was always on the *Radbourne* horses and the awarding of ribbons and trophies. Each time a prize was given, Francine clapped and shouted with pleasure.

"Oh, be still my heart," she said dramatically as she watched Bordeaux's Folly dominate the stallion class for the Regional Championship. She reached up to pat Jeremy's cheek. "My darling, how splendid."

Grinning, he bent closer to kiss her cheek. "We do what we can, my dear."

Francine delighted in every victory, squeezing Becca tighter with each one. By the end when *Radbourne Arabians* was recognized for historical excellence and she heard the personal good wishes for her continued good fortune, she wept, tears coursing down the furrows of her face..

She made no attempt to control her emotional reaction even when Patrick and Janel arrived with a small trunk of trophies and ribbons to show her before they delivered everything to the huge tack room in the main barn. Since the early years when Jeremy and Bordeaux followed the Eastern show circuit to establish *Radbourne* as a premier Arabian breeding operation, major trophies and ribbons were displayed in the chamber along with dozens of enlarged photos and pedigrees of their most famous halter and performance horses. The room was of great interest to prospective buyers who visited the ranch and toured the barns.

Patrick opened the trunk on the floor and Becca hopped off the bed to take her awards and the other most important ones to the bed for Francine's inspection. Patrick carried Folly's Regional trophy to her himself along with Jester's Reserve Cup.

Francine held the trophy in both hands, lifting her gaze to Jeremy. "Thank you for this."

He laughed. "Don't thank me, thank Bordeaux."

"Indeed." She hefted the trophy back into Patrick's hand. "I am truly delighted with all of you. You cannot fathom how much I appreciate your hard work. Patrick kissed her forehead. "You're a magnificent employer. I adore working for you.

"I'm no longer your employer," she countered, reaching for Katie's hand with a smile.

"Katie has shown us all that she's more than capable of filling your shoes." Patrick gave Katie a little hug.

She could not recall ever feeling so proud and fulfilled. She let herself bask in the goodwill. As she watched Patrick and Janel leave with the trunk, she dared consider the amazing state of her life. In her wildest imagination, she couldn't have foreseen the sea change that had occurred. She smiled down at her grandmother. "You are extraordinary. I am very blessed because of you."

"You've claimed your birthright. I really didn't have a lot to do with it other than asking you to come here so you could see what it was I wanted for you."

"It took me awhile before I could get out of my own way."

"It's hard to imagine, I know, but there have been times in my own life when I was so stubborn I caused myself and others way too much grief," she teased. "So you come by that trait through no fault of your own."

Katie gave her a very straight look, a bit taken aback by her words. This was probably the closest she would ever come to an apology from the old woman for her arbitrary stand when Katie first came to *Radbourne.*

Becca's eighth birthday arrived in mid-September, shortly after she'd settled back into the routine of school and daily lessons with Patrick. Jeremy and Katie hosted a party for five of Becca's friends on Saturday afternoon.

Because Becca had regaled her class about her adventures at the horse show, they were all intrigued by her life with horses and she decided to let them all ride while they were at the ranch for her party. Patrick selected five gentle geldings that he brought into the arena with Juniper.

Jeremy and Katie joined him when the guests arrived and they sorted out the kids according to their experience with horses. The two who'd ridden before were put on mounts bareback and Patrick conducted a mini class that included Becca.

The three who'd never been near a horse before were also put up on the remaining mounts that Jeremy and Katie led in circles in a nearby paddock. Angie the gutsiest of the novices proved a quick study and after fifteen minutes she was allowed in the arena.

After the better part of an hour, the riding ended and Becca showed her friends how to brush the geldings and return them to their stalls. They found this portion of the proceedings as exciting as the rest.

While the group walked back to the house for cake, Katie mused that they could offer riding lessons at *Radbourne*. When she mentioned this to Jeremy, he shot her annoyed look.

"We could do that," he agreed, "if anyone had the time or desire."

"You have a point," she said as they ushered everyone into the sun porch.

After they'd eaten, the guests gave Becca, the gifts they had brought – books and games and movies. Once Jeremy had left to drive them home, Katie and Becca still sat in the solarium.

"That was so fun," Becca said, coming to hug Katie. "It turned out just the way I wanted. They really liked the horses. Anthony said they would. He's really smart about things, especially people. He knows what they love the most."

Katie smiled at the wistful look in her eyes. How soon that whole new chapter would be upon them – Becca and boys...dating. The idea filled her with delight. It was going to be so exciting to watch this intrepid, gregarious child meet each new challenge of growing up. She pushed a strand of her hair behind her ear and kissed her. "You are going to have such a lovely life, Becca, girl."

She craned her neck to look up at Katie. "You think so?"

"I know so." She rested her chin against her hair, looking toward the golden light from the sunset coming through the windows. "Remember after the horse show when I said we should see what we can do about you riding Boh?"

She stared at her. "Yes, but I don't think I could handle him yet. He'd be too much for me."

Katie straightened, returning her direct gaze. "You're so smart and you're absolutely right. But your dad and I have been talking to Patrick and he thinks you're ready to go up a level in your riding lessons. So when your dad gets back, we have a surprise for you."

She jumped down and wrapped her arms around Jekyll. "Did you hear that?" she inquired into his nearest ear. "Well then, we better feed you before Daddy gets home."

Katie watched them head to the kitchen, letting her thoughts play back through the afternoon. Perhaps Becca would start giving riding classes, she mused. That would be novel, an eight-year-old training the new crop of show people.

Her mind abruptly veered to her old nightmare that had faded during the summer. She couldn't really remember the last time it had assailed her nights. She was reassured by this total silence. Yet, she concluded from past experience that forces were gathering strength. For what purpose? She had the dim impression that the stage was being set for one final clash of wills.

Eventually she resolved not to borrow trouble. The hiatus from terror had allowed her to have a lovely summer to realize her goals and settle into her new vital role at the ranch. Still she'd always known there would come a time when she was forced to unravel the mystery and defeat it. But for the time being, she would let the matter ride and concentrate on all the blessings of her life now.

Becca and Jekyll soon returned. Becca sat at the table, grinning. "I'm ready. I can't wait."

"Well, as it happens, here's your dad." She watched Jeremy drive up outside. "Let's go meet him." She grabbed Becca's hand and they rushed out the door.

"Where's my birthday present?" She caught her dad's hand and skipped between them as they walked down over the lawn.

When they'd crossed the bridge and continued toward the barns, she suddenly stopped and stood looking between them. "Is it a horse? Are you giving me another horse?"

"You'll see in a minute, hon." Jeremy tugged her forward again..

"Oh, boy. I *hope* it's a horse. Or a filly...." She fell silent as they walked along the breezeway of the first barn, soon stopping beside Patrick who leaned on a stall door."It *is* a horse!" She ran to look.

"Let me introduce you to Cassandra," Patrick said and pushed open the door to lead out a dappled gray mare, small in stature with the most delicate bone structure.

A beat or two of silence went by while Becca stood staring at her. Finally, she went closer and patted her as the mare bent her neck to nibble the carrot she'd pulled from her pocket.

"How'd you know to bring a carrot?" Patrick asked, raising an eyebrow.

Becca giggled. "Well, Katie was talking about Park and we decided Boh was too much for me." She spread her hands. "So I just thought...."

"You were right."

She continued gazing at her gift. "She's so lovely."

"Happy Birthday from all of us," Jeremy said, lifting her onto the mare. "Francine too."

"Thank you, Daddy. I love her already."

"You're welcome, sweet thing."

She reached out to put her arm around Katie, drawing her close. "I don't think we'll ever be as good as you and Boh. But maybe we will...." She kissed her dramatically.

"You give it your best shot," Katie told her.

Patrick came to get his hug of thanks.

"Cassie's been in dressage and park training for three years." He wagged his finger at her. "So you're going to have to work really hard to keep up with her."

"You know I will," she agreed as Jeremy put her on her feet. She rested her head against Cassie and told her good night before Patrick returned her to the stall.

"Now let's go to dinner and celebrate a little more," Jeremy said, leading the way out of the barn.

"May I go tell Francine thank you," Becca asked, running to grab his hand.

"She's probably asleep," said Katie. "You can go see her first thing in the morning.

"Okay, let's have pizza!"

"What a good idea," Patrick said, catching up with them.

Radbourne once more fell under the spell of changing seasons and horses were transitioned into winter housing as the displays of color in the trees gave way to the somber hues of winter. Patrick traveled often with many of the same group of show horses that had excelled at the Regionals. While he was away, Katie filled in as Becca's riding instructor.

Cassandra and Becca turned out to be an inspired pairing of talent. Within a few weeks in the arena, they excelled at intricate dressage drills that not only challenged Becca but delighted her as she mastered ever greater levels of difficulty. Sometimes Katie rode Boh to demonstrate an exercise Becca found hard to execute. She loved these sessions in the arena when she was in perfect harmony with the extraordinary black stallion. She often found herself briefly wishing she could join Patrick on the show circuit even though she was content at *Radbourne* as she'd never been in her life except perhaps during those long-ago years when she was a child at the ranch.

Francine remained stable during the onset of winter although she complained that all the white beyond her windows depressed her and she longed for the green of spring. One evening in November, after she had finished with Becca in the arena, Katie climbed toward Jeremy's office to discuss the *Radbourne* books he'd been working on all afternoon. On impulse, she stopped to visit her grandmother.

The old woman contemplated her. "Do you ever get blue this time of year?"

Katie sat beside her and grasped her hand. "Not lately. While I was in Boston, I was in despair a good deal of the time. Now that I'm not, I realize I was quite impaired but didn't realize it." She studied Francine, noting the edge of melancholy. "You are down aren't you?"

"There doesn't seem much purpose in my life now. In the past year I've been so busy growing to know you again and discovering how much I love you. Now that you've settled in and are happy to be here, I feel rather lost."

Katie made a mental note to ask Scott if Francine was on an antidepressant or should be.

"Do you still have your nightmares?"

"Not for a long time now."

A smile eased the tension in the lined face. "I'm so glad to hear that. Perhaps they've gone for good."

"I don't think I'm that lucky. I have this feeling, premonition really that the forces are gathering strength for some kind of denouement." She smiled. "Sounds morbid but that's my impression."

"Dear me." Francine looked down at her hands clasped in her lap, saying no more.

"Jeremy's waiting," Katie said, leaning closer. "Try to rest and I'll check on you later." She kissed her and headed out.

She'd promised Jeremy that she would join him to go over the accounts before he delivered them to the accountant the next day. When she reached his office, he leaned back in his chair and she went to sit on his lap, curling into his warmth.

"Hi, honey." He took her in his arms and kissed her deeply. It was some minutes before he sat back, grinning at her.

"Wow, I thought I came up here to look at the books."

"Me too." He pulled her close and kissed her again with the same ardor, stroking the flat of his thumb across her face, her cheekbones, following the length of her neck to the soft base of her throat, then further down. "Maybe we should go to the cabin later...." He lifted his head and studied her with a raised eyebrow.

"Maybe," she agreed. It was awhile more before she moved to a nearby chair. "I just saw Francine. She's pretty down."

He sat back, turning a pencil in his fingers. "Should I call Scott?"

"There's probably no rush but I'd like to

know if she's on medication for depression."

"Just to be safe, I'll call him when we're finished here." He turned his computer screen so she could see it, then began going through the figures of the spread sheets.

"Can we wait a minute. I want to ask you something first."

"Ask away."

I've been thinking we should have a little dinner party," she said.

"Really? When should we do this?"

"Maybe when Patrick gets back or on Thanksgiving. Maybe combine the two."

"And whom do you plan to invite?"

"Just a few people. Perhaps Scott and Patrick and Janel. Maybe Janel's met someone she'd like to invite."

"With the hours she'd been working, I doubt she's had time for that."

"Then, a party is even a better idea."

"I say, let's go for it."

"We can all go visit with Francine for a few minutes, then have drinks and dinner. Becca could stay up for dinner."

"Sounds like fun." He nodded at the screen. "Now if we're leaving later...."

"Okay, I'm concentrating."

Held in a bubble of anticipation of a few hours alone together, they gave full attention to the spread sheets.

The dinner party was set for Thanksgiving evening and Katie gave instructions that everyone should dress up a bit. She and Becca set a festive table in the dining room and Pearl was preparing a standing rib roast to be served at eight o'clock.

When Scott, Patrick, Janel and her female friend Vi arrived, Jeremy served drinks in the drawing room before the group filed up to Francine's room accompanied by Becca and Jekyll sporting his usual holiday bow. As soon as everyone had spoken to Francine and Vi was introduced, Pearl arrived with hot canapes fresh from the oven.

"Katie, my dear, this is a lovely idea," Francine declared when Jeremy served her a small plate of hors d'oeuvre and some of the club soda Becca was drinking. "May I wish all of you a blessed Thanksgiving." She raised her glass and everyone came forward to tap it with theirs.

Her eyes fell on Vi, an attractive though extremely thin young woman with lively brown eyes and a tumble of dark curls about her shoulders.

"And what do you do?" she asked.

Vi stepped closer to take her outstretched hand. "I'm a student at the community college. Right now, I'm studying to be a chef."

"Splendid. And eat all you can of the wonderful food you prepare. You're much too frail."

She laughed. "Well, I'm also training for a marathon so that may explain why I don't have much fat on my bones." She turned to include Janel. "Indeed that's how we met because Janel's also a runner."

"Not of marathons," Janel said, bending gracefully to speak to Francine. "I'm so happy to see you again."

She granted her a smile. "I hear you are doing a splendid job as our veterinarian."

"Thank you so much. I love working here."

"Excellent. Now, Patrick," she continued as the women moved away and he stood in their place, "tell me about your success at the shows from which you've just returned."

He kissed her cheek. "We had excellent luck."

"I'm sure luck had nothing to do with it."

"Well, in any case, our horses did extremely well. In a day or two, I'll come tell you just how well."

"Thank you, dear. I shall look forward to that."

Becca sat close to Francine, sharing her plate of canapes. "Daddy's going to take a video of Cassie and me doing dressage so you can see us."

"I'll love to see it. I understand you're both progressing well."

She nodded and began regaling Patrick about her lessons with Katie while he was gone.

The evening proceeded with dinner. Afterwards, Katie took Becca up to bed. In her pajamas, Becca snuggled under the comforter. "That was fun. Do you like Vi?"

"I think she's very nice. It's good that Janel found a friend."

"I think so too. How far is a marathon?"

"A little over twenty-six miles."

"Wow. I don't think I could ride Juniper that far. How can Vi run all that way?"

"She has to train for a long time, running every day."

"That's really cool. I think Janel likes Scott.

Like maybe she wants to go out on a date with him."

Katie thought about that. "You might be right about that," she agreed when she remembered the two talking together off and on all evening.

Becca reached up her arms to hug Katie. "I love you. Night."

When Katie's cheek touched Becca's. she pulled back, looking at her closely. "You're hot, baby. Do you feel okay?"

"I'm tired." Her eyes fluttered shut.

"Goodnight, sweetie."

Katie rejoined the others in the drawing room. She musingly took note of Scott and Janel sitting close together on the loveseat. Leave it to Becca to pick up on what did seem to be a spark between them.

Jeremy came to take her hand. "Would you like another drink?"

"No thanks." She followed him to the sofa where they settled beside Vi.

Patrick sat on the arm, listening to Vi talking about growing up in Malibu.

"Were you a beach babe?" he asked.

She laughed. "Pretty much. Hanging out at the beach with my friends was my life. But I have great parents and somehow they managed to get through my cluelessness and instill some ambition. When I was ready to go to college, I was focused and wanted a career in psychiatry so I got my Master's at Pepperdine. In January, I'm entering the PHD program at MIT."

"I thought you were in chef's school."

"Oh, that's just for fun and I can fall back on

it if I run short of money before I get my psychiatry degree."

"So then, we can all come to you for therapy?" Patrick asked.

"No, I'll actually be doing research. I want to explore some of the new theories about autism."

Katie considered her with fresh interest. "That sounds like a very worthwhile field."

She nodded. "I have a younger brother with autism. Watching him grow up was just one long heartache." She tossed back half the Scotch in her glass. "I suppose that's why I was never at home in my teens. It was either school or the beach. But by the time I graduated, I was obsessed with helping kids like Harry. It was straight to Pepperdine for me."

"What are you doing here?" Jeremy asked.

She put down her glass and straightened her dress. "I needed a break before I start at MIT which is going to be extremely intense if all the experts I've talked with are correct. A good percentage of Clinical Psychology students in the PHD program never get through the first year." She leaned back and draped her arm along the top of the sofa. "I have a beloved aunt in Sheridan who's always been partial to me. When I told her my plans and how I always wanted to be a chef, she said the college here has a short program that's well regarded. She ended up inviting me to come visit and recharge my batteries before I hit the big leagues."

Pearl came into the room and bent to speak in Katie's ear. "Becca's asking for you."

"Excuse me. I'll be right back."

When she got upstairs, Becca was in the bathroom, standing at the sink.

"What's wrong, hon?" Katie rushed to her.

Becca turned around, holding a towel to her face. The front of her pajama top was splattered with blood. A large spot of it seeped into the towel. "What's wrong with me?" she whimpered.

Katie pulled the towel back a little but quickly replaced it when she saw the stream of blood coming from her nose. "You're having a nosebleed. Have you had them before?"

She violently shook her head.

"Come lie down. It'll stop in a minute." She settled her back in bed and brought a dry washcloth to staunch the flow. She still sat beside her when Pearl appeared.

"Is she okay?"

"She's fine. Please stay with her while I go get Jeremy." She gave Becca's arm a reassuring squeeze, then returned downstairs.

Outside the drawing room, she caught Jeremy's eye and he quickly joined her, then bounded up the stairs.

She stepped inside and explained to the others what was happening. "I think we'll have to say good night now."

Everyone hurried to collect wraps and walk to the front door. Scott hesitated as the others prepared to leave. He bid them farewell, then came to where Katie waited by the stairs. "Maybe I should go check her." .

"I'm so glad you're here. She's having a bad nosebleed and she's really hot."

"Bring some ice," he instructed and jogged up

the steps.

She went to the kitchen to fill a bowl from the ice maker and collect some ziplock bags, then climbed the back stairs.

Scott had discarded his coat and dinner jacket and examined Becca. He wrapped a small bag of ice in a cloth and placed it on the bridge of her nose, tilting her head back with pillows. "That should help." He consulted his patient. "How do you feel?"

"Sick...and hot...." She pushed the comforter off

"I want you to swallow some Tylenol. That'll make you feel better. Does anything hurt?"

"My bones hurt."

He looked at her sharply. "Tell me what that feels like."

"Like my legs hurt inside...And my head aches."

"This will make all that feel better too," he promised, handing her the Tylenol and water Jeremy had collected from the bathroom.

They sat with her until the nosebleed stopped and the painkiller kicked in. By then, she'd fallen asleep.

Jeremy stayed with her while Katie saw Scott to the front door.

"It's just a flu bug," he said on the way downstairs.

"But she's had the vaccine."

He frowned. "As we know, it doesn't always work." He gave her a little hug. "Don't worry. If she's not better in the morning, call me but I'm sure she'll be fine."

"Thanks."

"Thank you for a lovely evening." He winked and walked out into the snow.

Katie felt chilled. She wrapped her arms around herself as she made her way back upstairs. For some reason she couldn't pinpoint, she was way more worried than she should be if Becca only had the flu.

After a miserable night of more nosebleeds and increased pain, Becca was no better by morning. Scott arrived at six to examine her again, and to stop the latest uncontrollable nose bleed. "I think she should be admitted to the hospital so we can run some tests to see what's going on," he decided half an hour later. "At the very least she needs some blood transfusions."

Becca turned frightened eyes to Katie, then her father. "I want to stay here...." Tears spilled down her cheek.

"Sweetheart, we'll go with you." Jeremy gathered her to him. "We'll stay with you. Scott needs you in the hospital so he can find out why you're sick. Okay?"

She buried her face against him, her breathing shaky. When she looked up again, she was still crying but managed to nod.

"You're very brave." Scott squeezed her hand.

She reached for Katie who enfolded her in her arms. "I'll pack some things for you to take."

The transfer to the ER was accomplished within the hour. When Becca began to tremble violently on the steel table, a nurse named Betsy wrapped heated blankets around her. She lay shaking, her teeth chattering.

An I.V. was started and Scott came to draw blood. Katie and Jeremy stood on either side of Becca, holding her hands. Her eyes grew huge with worry when she saw the tray holding the syringe and needle.

"I won't hurt you," Scott said as he tied the strip of rubber around her arm. He quickly slid the needle into her vein, then released the tourniquet.

Her eyes never wavered as she watched her blood fill the first vial, then several more before he withdrew the needle and applied a band-aid.

"You're amazing, sweetie," he said. "I'll be back." He gave her a smile before striding into the hall.

"No one ever took my blood before." Becca looked at Katie. "Why'd he do that?"

"He'll take it to the lab and the people who work there, the technicians, will study it and figure out why you're sick."

"Oh." Her teeth had stopped chattering and she burrowed farther beneath the warm blankets, her eyes dropping shut.

Katie and Jeremy pulled chairs close to the table. They lost track of time that was only interrupted by the occasional person looking in from the hall. Becca slept on.

When Katie thought she couldn't wait another minute, Scott returned with the nurse Betsy.

"Come with me, you two. I'll go over the blood work with you." He led the way to an office down the hall.

After motioning them toward two chairs, he

perched on a stool and sorted through the stack of papers in his hand Worry marked his lean features now as he looked from one to the other. "Her white cell count is off the charts which indicates infection. And her platelets are down so that explains the nose bleeds."

They just stared at him. "So?" Katie prodded.

He twisted his mouth. "I must tell you that I'm concerned about leukemia."

"Leukemia?" Jeremy instinctively grabbed Katie's hand.

"Don't panic! We won't know until I check a couple other things. But when I saw her this morning with another gushing nosebleed, an alarm went off."

"So how do you find out?" Jeremy asked. "Test her bone marrow?"

Scott nodded. "And the sooner the better."

Katie felt tears clogging her throat. "But that's so painful."

Scott stood up and drew her into a quick hug. "I'll give her a local anesthetic and a little sedation so it won't be so bad. Why don't you go tell her what's going to happen, then Betsy will tell you were to wash up and change into scrubs. I'll see you and Becca in surgery."

Katie felt stunned and from the looks of Jeremy, she knew he wasn't doing any better. After Scott disappeared, she went to him and for a frozen sequence of seconds, they silently held each other.

When they returned to the ER, Becca was awake and crying. Betsy leaned over her and had evidently been telling her what was next. With a sob, she reached for Jeremy. "Oh, Daddy, I'm so afraid...."

He took her in his arms again, cradling her against him. "I'm right here with you."

She moaned and he tenderly lay her back down.

Katie thought her heart would break when she looked into her small, pale face, tears flowing unchecked. She braced her elbows on the table so she could get closer. "Sweetie, Scott's going to find out what's wrong with you. He thinks there's something wrong with your blood. That's why your nose has been bleeding. But he won't know for sure until he looks at your bone marrow...."

Becca looked at her puzzled. "That stuff that's inside bones?"

"That's right. He has to put a needle into your hip bone and draw some out. Then he can give you medicine so you'll feel better...."

"Anthony's sister had to do that. They took out her marrow...she told Anthony that it hurt really bad...." New tears escaped and she looked helplessly at Jeremy.

"My darling Becca, Scott told us that he's going to give you something so you won't feel much pain...and we'll be right there with you."

She drew a quavery breath. "Okay...I'm ready...."

"I'm so proud to have such a courageous little girl." Jeremy's long fingers spanned her cheek.

"You are extraordinarily fearless. But we knew that already, didn't we?" Katie gave her a wink.

She managed to smile. "Yes, we did."

They both hugged her again before another

nurse came to show them where to go to put on sterile clothing.

That afternoon they learned from Becca's bone marrow biopsy that she had ALL - acute lymphocytic leukemia. According to Scott, the sudden and intense onset of her symptoms was typical of the disease. The initial fever and out-of-control bleeding were what made him immediately suspect leukemia.

Katie recalled the foreboding that had overwhelmed her. All she wanted to do was weep for Becca and Jeremy. How ironic that this happened just when Becca was flying high with her showing success and further training.

Katie fervently prayed that she would recover quickly. She couldn't bear the thought of the sorrow that would swamp Becca if she was away from the horses for long.

But according to Scott, there were reasons for hope. Children with ALL generally have a far better outlook than adults. More than ninety-five percent gain remission.

That evening, Scott broached the subject of Becca's proposed treatment. He sat with Jeremy and Katie in the hospital cafeteria. Another nurse stayed with Becca who was sleeping most of the time now that the nosebleeds had been arrested.

"Induction therapy is the first phase of treatment and is best done in a hospital under the care of an oncologist," Scott explained. "I think we should send her to Billings for treatment which basically means chemotherapy to get her into remission."

Katie immediately started to cry. "Why can't she stay here? I've even heard of people doing chemo as outpatients."

Scott considered her kindly. "That is an option in some cases but our Becca is a very sick little girl right now. And her immune system is so compromised she needs to be in a controlled environment to prevent any kind of infection."

Jeremy slid his chair closer to Katie's and put his arm around her. "We have to trust Scott."

"I know that." She struggled to regain some control. "When will she go?" She lifted her gaze to Scott.

"I'll send her by ambulance tomorrow. You two can drive up at the same time if you want. Incidentally, Jekyll can't be with her in the hospital. I wish he could be to help keep Becca's spirits up."

Jeremy nodded.

Scott leaned toward them. "I can't begin to tell you how sorry I am this happened. I have no answers for you as to how she got it. It's not inherited. Ethnicity plays a role. Whites and hispanics are more likely to get it than blacks."

Jeremy snorted. "So much for that theory. My black blood didn't have any effect."

Scott threw up his hands in a shrug.

"What in the world are you talking about?"

They looked at Katie.

"My mother was black," Jeremy said. "I guess we never got to that. She came from the West Indies."

She smiled. "So that's where you get your striking olive complexion."

"That's it." He reached up to cradle her chin

to turn her face so he could look into her eyes. "Sorry I didn't tell you before. It's never been something I thought much about. Does it matter to you?"

"Of course not. But I do wish it had somehow kept Becca from getting sick."

"Me too." He rested his head on hers. "Why don't you go home and get some sleep. I'll stay here and maybe you can relieve me about four so I can go take a shower and pack. Then we'll be ready to leave whenever the ambulance goes."

"You've got to get some sleep."

"I'll sack out on the couch in Becca's room."

"How are we going to get through this?"

He straightened in his chair. "We just will. Because we have to."

"What if we lose her?"

"We won't. There is no way we'll ever let that happen."

"No, we won't," she agreed. "She's just gutsy enough to beat this. What prompted you to get her a service dog? I never thought to ask about that?:

His face darkened. "We had several threats of kidnapping. Needless to say, we were terrified...no we were terrorized. Jekyll seemed the best answer since we couldn't very well strap a big gun on Becca's hip or hire the Secret Service." He gave her a weak smile.

"Who would want to take her?"

He shrugged. "Any number of people I should imagine. Those who want a chunk of Francine's money, now your money. Some irate breeder who can never quite beat *Radbourne* horses..." He spread his hands. "I don't know who but I can tell you, the thought of someone stealing my daughter scares the hell out of me."

A shiver moved up Katie's spine. She was reminded anew just what it meant to own the ranch and its vast assets.

"Jekyll has helped a lot in relieving my stress over it but when I least expect it, the reality of our life rears its ugly head."

He pulled her head against his chest. "Good night, my love. You should go so we can get some sleep."

"I love you."

CHAPTER SIXTEEN

The next morning, Katie turned from her bathroom mirror and went to inventory her bags and parka that lay on her bed beside Jekyll who'd spent the night stretched out beside her. She picked up his leash from the pile. He cocked his head, looking at her.

"Let's go." She gathered her things as he dashed to the door. Out in the hall, she stacked everything against the wall then went to Francine's room with Jekyll jumpine around, apparently thinking they were going to find Becca.

Though it was only a few minutes past five, her grandmother was awake and watched their entrance. "How are you, dear?"

"Very tired and worried." She sat in a chair pulled close, idly rubbing Jekyll's ears.

"How's Becca?"

"When I left the hospital last night, she was sleeping."

"That poor darling...." The words faded into weeping.

Katie waited, wanting nothing so much as to join her. "She has leukemia," she said at last, putting her arms around the frail, shaking shoulders.

Francine straightened her back. "What is Scott doing for her?" She wiped distractedly at her face.

"She's getting transfusions to replace the blood she lost. Scott's transferring her to Billings later this morning for chemo. "Jeremy and I are driving up."

Francine's gaze wavered, gradually shifting to stare outside. "Will she need blood and such?"

"Probably...but I don't think you could donate...."

Her head spun back toward Katie. "Not me...you goofy girl." She raised one finger. "But I know someone..."

"Who's that?"

Her eyes were suddenly flat, devoid of the usual keen edge in the blue that let her rule her world. "I forget."

A sick feeling went through Katie. These lapses of thought were happening more and more often.

She kissed her, called to Jekyll and walked quickly into the hall. She was losing the woman she'd grown to love and depend on for no nonsense advice and comfort. Her chest cramped with building tears as she hurried to collect her bags.

Outside she walked with Jekyll to Patrick's cottage. She'd already asked if he would keep Jekyll while she and Jeremy were away. She knocked on the door that was quickly opened.

"Ah, Katie, are you off then?"

"I'm on my way." She handed him Jekyll's leash. "I didn't bring his food. Pearl can bring some over if you give her a call."

"Don't worry, Katie. I'll take good care of him." He hugged her. "I'll keep all of you in my thoughts and prayers.   Call me if I can do anything."

"Thanks."

Three hours later, Jeremy followed the ambulance into the Billings hospital parking lot. Once he and Katie were inside, they were banished to a waiting area while Becca was admitted. They were informed that due to the danger of infection, from that point on, every precaution would be taken to provide Becca a sterile environment. They were shown into a room where they changed into sterile scrubs, masks and gloves.

At last, they could see her. She lay still and pale, her eyes following them as they stepped to the bed. "How do you feel?" Jeremy asked, holding her tiny hand in his gloved ones.

She didn't answer but yawned and drifted back to sleep. Already the chemo medication dripped into her arm. Scott had told them that in a day or two, a central venous catheter would be surgically implanted in her chest. Once it was in place, she would receive all medication by that route.

During the next few days, Jeremy and Katie settled into the unnerving routine of waiting. They waited beside Becca who slept except for short periods when she was alert enough to talk a bit. They waited in the room furnished for families of oncology patients.

They went downstairs to a shop and bought paperbacks but neither could concentrate. After three days, they decided Katie should go home to be with Francine while Jeremy stayed on at the hospital.

Katie was nearing Sheridan the next evening when she was overcome by despair and immediately thought she'd made a mistake leaving Jeremy in Billings. She should have stayed with him, continued to lend him what help and strength she could.

She was suddenly weeping as she hadn't done in months. Sadness and confusion overwhelmed her and she had to pull into a rest stop in an effort to regain some control. She sat there sobbing until she had no more tears. As she tried to think, she gradually realized she had no idea why such sadness had overtaken her. She usually didn't fall apart like this.

By the time they'd departed for Billings, both she and Jeremy had overcome their initial terror at Becca's illness. Dr. Cusack, the oncologist, had assured them that the odds for full recovery were very high. He said Becca should be in remission after a month of chemo and then it would be a matter of maintenance treatment. He expressed hope that she might be home by Christmas.

Indeed, when Jeremy kissed Katie goodbye in the parking lot and she'd driven toward the Interstate, she had been in high spirits, daring to believe Becca was going to be okay and they would all soon be back to their cherished life at Radbourne. Now she began to understand that what she was experiencing wasn't the normal reaction to shock and intense worry.

This was the crippling emotion that had attacked her thousands of times. It had always presented itself in the nightmare, never out of the blue like this. So she hadn't at first recognized what was happening.

She gripped the steering wheel in an effort to stay calm but that was impossible. Waves of dread and horror washed over her. *God, help me....*

She looked through the windshield at the thickening winter twilight. She had to get home. To lose all control out here in the cold could be the end of her.

She gathered her inner strength, determined to continue without drawing attention. Every nerve was in rigid alert as she drove through the snowy countryside to *Radbourne.* At last, she parked in the carriage house and made her way to the rear entrance of the manor.

Thankfully, the house was still. Pearl was likely upstairs with Francine.

Katie hurried along the hall, then started up the staircase. She'd reached the first landing when an icy blast blindsided her. shock jammed her brain and she grabbed the railing to keep from being shoved backwards down the stairs.

Staggered by utter weakness and trauma, she let herself collapse onto the nearest step and hugged both arms around the newel post. Sweat wet her skin, instantly soaking her underwear, sweater and jeans. Despite a wave of suffocating heat, cold knifed through every bone and muscle and her head hit the pole with each spasm of her shaking. Nausea flooded her throat.

Appalled that she was going to throw up on

the Oriental runner, she managed to yank off her drenched sweater and use it to catch the vomit surging from her. At last there was nothing more to come up and she rested her head against the post while she sucked huge gulps of air into her lungs.

Something roused her after a time and she looked up the stairs at something white, diaphanous. It was like living tissue caught there in space, its outer surface undulating. She could only stare.

Over the years she'd learned to override horror so she could function, albeit poorly. Dimly aware she must get to her room before Pearl found her there on the stairs, totally undone, she crawled the final distance and collapsed outside the door. When she looked back along the hall, she watched the white mass slowly dissipate until it was no longer there. Marshalling the last of her resilience, she dragged herself through the doorway, then lay gasping on the floor, hugging the soggy bundle of her sweater.

The cold held her motionless there. Concentrating all her attention, she shoved her leg against the door until she thought it was shut. This final expenditure of energy sent her plummeting into blackness.

Darkness hung beyond the windows when she roused, still dripping with perspiration, yet so chilled, she shuddered. She tried to decide what she must do to help herself without alerting the house to her peril. No one else could help her, not yet anyway and the last thing she wanted to do was have Francine or Pearl phone Jeremy, calling him back when he needed to stay with Becca.

She wondered why the force of the past had chosen this time to attack her again. It didn't take long for her to realize it had lain in wait until she was most vulnerable. She had dared to hope she was totally free from it but a vague foreboding had lain buried in her mind all along. She'd known this final onslaught was inevitable just as she knew this was no drill, the violence of the attack on the staircase told her this was the final showdown.

She set about gathering her inner resources, readying. After resting awhile more, she awkwardly gained her feet, swaying with the effort to stand upright. She was still freezing and when she spotted the thermostat, she moved toward it and was suddenly hurled forward, her nose colliding with the wall. Blood spurted, falling over her clothes and the rug. She pushed the lever before staggering to the shower. Eventually, she made it beneath the spray, bracing herself against the wall so she didn't collapse while she adjusted the water.

She stayed there until the heat penetrated her stiff and chilled muscles, leaving her reeling with exhaustion when she finally stepped out to dry herself. A flannel nightgown felt like heaven now that she was warm and dry. She scooped her bloody heap of clothing into a hamper, slipped her feet into wool slippers and stepped into the hall. As quickly as she could manage, she made her way to Francine's room.

Pearl rose from a chair, studying Katie with alarm. Her hand floated to her mouth as she took in her battered face. "What on earth...."

Katie waved her away. "I'm fine. I fell....Could you please bring me something to eat? Soup would be fine. And tell Patrick to send Jekyll home."

"Of course. I'll be right back."

Katie approached her grandmother who appeared to be sleeping soundly but soon opened her eyes.

"My dear. What are you doing here?"

"Becca's okay, just getting the chemo. So I came back to see how you're doing." She collapsed onto a chair.

She didn't reply for a long interval. "I'm not much good to anyone...."

"Oh, but you are, darling. You're good for me." She thought Francine had lost weight, was more fragile than before.

She patted Katie's arm. "You're sweet to say so...." Once again she looked toward the window seeming to forget she wasn't alone.

Katie was swamped by vertigo and had to grab the arms of the chair to remain upright. She was grateful when Pearl came in with a tray holding two bowls of soup. Maybe some food would revive her.

"I brought some for Francine. She's hardly eaten a thing all day." She situated the tray between them on the mattress.

"Thanks." Katie picked up a spoon and began eating while Pearl circled to the other side of the bed where she tried to prevail on Francine to eat.

Waving a bony hand in dismissal, she refused even to turn her head.

"Is it all right if I go home now?" Pearl asked.

"Of course. I'll stay with her." She noted how tired the housekeeper was, her face haggard with fatigue. Why hadn't she and Jeremy arranged for extra help while they were away?

"Thank you. Just call if you need me."

"I will. But go rest now."

A few minutes after she left, she heard Jekyll coming up the stairs. He dashed into the room and came to rest his head in Katie's lap.

"Hey, big guy. I'm so happy to see you." She rested her cheek against his head. He lay down on her feet, his warmth comforting.

Awhile later, Katie was surprised to see that her bowl was empty. She did feel a bit stronger. She studied Francine who had dozed off. How odd it was that she hadn't even noticed her banged up face.

With another burst of resolve, she switched the bowls on the tray and ate the second one with a pile of saltines. She drained her glass of milk before she carried the tray to a table beside the door.

She felt ready to drop and was unnerved by the thought of returning to her own room. Without further thought, she went back to the bed and crawled in beside Francine.

Though her grandmother was sound asleep, Katie was comforted by her presence, as if Francine stood between Katie and the dreaded place. She wasn't quite as afraid here even as the menace drew her into its core.

Why was it so much stronger again? This question was the last thing in her brain before she dozed off. She didn't sleep well or for long. Horrific images crammed her mind. The old dream floated just beyond her consciousness but so close that it repeatedly jolted her awake. In this way, she kept the threat at bay. To give in to her exhaustion was to risk having the nightmare overtake her entirely.

Fully awake long before dawn, she ached from head to foot and felt disoriented, detached. Out of bed, she found some aspirin in Francine's bathroom. After swallowing them, she inspected her reflection in the mirror. She looked like someone had landed several punches to her nose and face. Dark bruises were already purple.

She turned off the bathroom light and went to lie down again. The room was dimly lit by a lamp next to the door and the faint cherry blossom tinge of sunrise.

Some time later, Francine woke and lay staring at her. "Well, this is a surprise, waking up to your beautiful face." She continued studying her. "Well, perhaps not as pretty as usual. What happened to you?"

Sensing that she was back from the twilight of last night, Katie decided to be honest. "When I got home yesterday, whatever's been haunting me all these years attacked me on the stairs."

Her grandmother clutched her hand. "Oh, darling...."

"While I continued on up to my bedroom, I saw something, a ghost I guess but it was hard to see just *what* it was. Just a gauzy mass, almost transparent, ethereal and then it faded into nothing." She was astonished that this fantastic account didn't unsettle Francine in the least. But then she had her own history with ghosts. "Once I got to my room, something blindsided me, knocking me into the wall and that's how I got banged up...."

"So you think this ghost assaulted you?"

She thought back to the events of last evening. "No," she said at last. "I don't think what I saw in the hall had anything to do with what's attacking me. I think there're two different forces."

Her grandmother nodded. "I believe you're correct about that. It is my guess that someone has come from the other side to protect you."

Katie could only gape at her while she tried to grasp the bizarre notion.

"Whoever has come back is here to keep you safe. You have some mighty influence on your side now."

"I've known far back in my mind for months now that this buried memory of mine has been gaining power, lying in wait for some final denouement. I think I'm going to finally see what happened the night before you sent me away. What you've guarded so zealously ever since I came back." She waited for a reaction.

"It's time. It sounds to me like matters are unfolding as they must. And now you will be protected. Someone has come to help you." She fell silent, the serenity in her demeanor indicating an acceptance that Katie wished she could match.

But her faith was still not as fervent as Francine's or Jeremy's. Intense and growing terror still held her captive.

For several nights following her perplexing exchange with her grandmother, Katie remained a prisoner between two forces. She continued to sleep in Francine's bed because she was too unnerved to return to her own. Rest eluded her and she began walking through the house, finding strange consolation in the stillness of dark hallways. Jekyll was remarkably wise and patient as he watched over her. Sensing how troubled she was, he stayed close wherever she went.

She was drawn to the library where she moved within streams of moonlight from the tall windows. She turned on the desk lamp and sat in her grandfather's chair, staring at the pistol. Perhaps if she gave over her entire being to decoding the mystery, it would reveal its secrets. Dawn often found her sitting there with Jekyll, no closer to the truth.

She knew her struggle to keep the past at bay would end soon. Inevitability had replaced her dread. She had slept only an hour or two at a time since she'd left Jeremy in Billings.

Her battle was lost during a raging blizzard when the wind howled about the walls of *Radbourne Manor* and snow piled up in mind-boggling depths. Katie had called Patrick, Nick and Janel several times earlier to reassure herself of the horses' safety. She was told that every animal was indoors. Pearl was unable to get home so settled into a bedroom close to Francine's.

She'd talked to Jeremy, longing to tell him what was happening to her but she didn't want him to feel guilty because he couldn't be with her. He was already torn between his need to stay with Becca and his worry about Francine.

The night the blizzard hit, she reassured him that all was well at *Radbourne* and the horses were safe. "Give Becca hugs for me."

"I do that a lot. Are you okay, sweetheart?

You sound a little sad."

"I am with all the worry over Becca and Francine. But my grandmother has actually taken a turn for the better. When I got home, she was in a fog and hardly knew I was here but the last few days, she's been totally lucid."

"Well, that's wonderful. Give my best to her and the others."

"I will and Pearl said to tell you that everyone's praying for you and Becca."

"Thank them for me. I've got to get back now. Goodnight, love."

When they'd hung up, Katie replaced the kitchen phone and sat at the table. How she missed Jeremy's steadfast common sense that kept her grounded. Without him, she felt like she might literally fall apart.

But at least tonight, she felt weary enough that she dared hope for a good night's sleep. She soon climbed the stairs and once more, settled in bed next to her grandmother who was already asleep. She was caught up in a state of waiting. Finally, her need to know was greater than her terror of remembering. She was ready.

She was helpless tonight against her exhaustion. She knew the danger but was unable to remain near the surface as she'd done for too many nights. Rapidly she descended into deep sleep.

Much later, she came abruptly awake. Was it her own strangled gasps or the fierce wind outside that woke her?

She sat up. Her nightgown was drenched and blood thudded in her ears. Out of bed, she ran, fleeing the nightmare, guided only by dim nightlights along the corridor and the hazy presence of Jekyll barking nearby. Compulsion dragged her toward the library door standing ajar ahead.

She staggered, grabbing the jamb, staring into the deserted chamber, paralyzed by something ferocious and threatening. When the fury shoved her into lamplight washing over the table, she stood staring at the glass case where the pistol lay exposed. Someone had turned the key and the lid lay flat on the polished wood.

She touched the cold metal of the barrel, her brain swirling with noise and pictures like a thousand shrieking reflections in a fun house mirror. As she was hurled through the babble, she saw her hand curling around the pistol stock, lifting the gun. She was doing something forbidden, yet so enticing. Her muscles trembled with the dead weight. She smiled, savoring her rebellion.

As she gripped the pistol with both hands, her thumbs found the hammer and drew it back like she'd watched Grandpa do. It was so hard to do, she had to try three times with the barrel dipping wildly before she heard a click. She stared at the gun in triumph.

"Katherine, where are you?...where have you gotten to, you naughty girl?...come here, at once!..."

*Oh, gosh, Mummy was coming. Mummy always spoiled her fun....*She jumped, twisting toward a horrible screech beyond the light. Mummy was screaming at her again. Mummy wasn't pretty tonight. She was so angry and ugly. Katherine hated her to be so angry at her...she only wanted to spend a little while with Grandpa...but if Mummy found her, she never let her stay....*Where* *was Grandpa?* He could always make Mummy laugh and then she wasn't angry anymore. He would tell Mummy he would carry her back to her bed....But with a toss of her head, she never let him but took Katie back downstairs herself...

Her arms were so tired she couldn't hold the gun anymore. Maybe if she put it back, Mummy would stop shrieking. But when she tried to lift it toward the box, an awful noise knocked her down and the gun fell away somewhere.

She sat there crying, gaping at Mummy lying on the floor with a big red hole in the middle of her chest. Blood, gallons and gallons of blood ran into a big puddle around Mummy.

Katie began screaming, searching the darkness for Grandpa. She crawled closer to Mummy and tried to climb into her lap but when she saw the sticky red all over her nightgown, she jerked away

Sobbing, she thought Mummy might drown if she didn't lift her head but hard as she tried, she couldn't move. She clasped both hands over her mouth, stifling her cries. In the sudden hush, she heard Grandpa coming back. What would he do when he saw what she'd done?

His hands touched her and he lifted her up. putting her on the edge of the table and she hugged him desperately, breathing in the calming smell of peppermint. She finally dared look up into his face, expecting him to be terribly angry at her. Instead she saw kindness and a quiet that stilled her horror.

"My darling, Katie, you're safe now. You will always be safe, my little love. No reason to ever be afraid again. No more sadness for my Katie." His eyes held flecks of gold light. "Now I must get back. I'll leave you in your grandmother's loving arms."

New tears overtook Katie as she watched him, a tall striking man, walking from lamplight into the darkness. A huge puzzle sat in her brain while the present shifted into focus. Startled, she saw Francine in her wheelchair. Jekyll stared into the dark, whining as he moved his head back and forth, listening intently.

"Come, my child," her grandmother said, beckoning. "You have faced it and now you're free."

Katie was on her knees then, clinging to her, sobbing. *Yes, she knew she was safe but would she ever stop crying?*

It was a long time before she considered Francine again, bewildered. "I saw my grandfather."

"Of course, you did. He was the ghost you saw hanging around."

Katie marveled at this. "Wow."

"Indeed."

"My mother found me with the pistol in my hands...."

"Your grandfather was very proud of that revolver and had showed it to a friend that night while you were in the library with them. Later, assuming you were asleep on a window seat, he didn't lock the case before he walked his friend out. Evidently you were never asleep but had been watching them handle the gun. When they left, you picked it up. It had always fascinated you to no end.

"You still held it when Christine came upstairs. I was just behind her in the hall when I heard her scream your name and then the shot."

Even after twenty years, Francine's features still contorted at the memory. Katie's heart cramped as she saw the full impact of what she'd done. Sobs overtook her and she covered her face with her hands. "I'm so sorry...."

Her grandmother's bony fingers touched her arm. "I see now how little and innocent you were."

"You lost your only daughter, your hope for *Radbourne*. I understand why you hated me so much...." She stole a glance at her. "I saw blood on the floor, so much blood."

"It soaked into the oak floor and eventually, I had all the boards replaced. The night it happened, I couldn't face it so after the police left, I locked the door and didn't open it again for years. Until an opportunity finally came when Jeremy was away." She stopped, groping for the right words. "This sounds crazy and perhaps I was crazy but even though the entire floor was completely changed out, I still thought I could see the stain. I was afraid others could see it as well so I had the Aubusson rug installed.

Katie struggled to understand. "Why all the secrecy? It was an accident."

Her face clouded. "I told myself I was protecting you, not wanting you hurt by rumor and speculation. In truth, I was very selfish, so immersed in my shock and grief, I refused to see yours. It's a monstrous thing to admit but I could no longer see you as my precious granddaughter. You had become an abomination, something evil, of the devil."

She reached out again to Katie who's weeping

had become a high keening. "It was I who was evil, not to see how lost and traumatized you were." She faltered into silence again, staring into someplace Katie couldn't see. "Your grandfather and I were so in love we rarely had a cross word between us. Neither of us would have ever talked of leaving the other but that night, my Boyd said if I sent you away, he was going also....." Tears brimmed at the memory.

New pain sliced through Katie.

"I was determined to have my way...of course....And much later when he fell asleep, I phoned Jessie and told her to take the next flight out. In the meantime, I put you in that old cabin in the yard and had one of the stable boys keep an eye on you. When Jessie flew in the next day, I delivered you to her." She wiped at her face with the heels of her hands. "My husband didn't leave me but he didn't speak to me for over a year."

She became quiet again, folding her hands in her lap as her tears continued flowing unrestricted. "So you had every reason to despise me. I am despicable." She glanced up. "*I* am the abomination. I was in such agony after Christine died and Boyd and I were still estranged. I had a breakdown and ended up in the psych ward. While I was there, a lot of doctors talked to me. One said I am a malignant narcissist, someone who gives no importance to anyone but myself. I told him to go to hell and they finally let me come home but I still refused to acknowledge what I'd done. I never spoke your name again until you came back. When the torture of losing my daughter faded over the years, I started to feel shame but by then Jessie had died and I thought it was too late to find you. That's when I realized I never stopped loving you."

Katie had recovered some of her balance. She tried to get in touch with the rage that had filled her for so long but found she couldn't. That kind of perilous emotion was beyond her grasp now. She had found resolution and hope at *Radbourne* and could no longer look back.

"I don't think I loved you during all those years while I was gone. I couldn't because I was in too much pain. But since I've been back, I've found a love for you that fills my heart and heals the rest."

Tears swam in the azure pools of the ancient eyes but she said nothing.

"How I wish I could remember my mother. I think it's life changing to lose a mother, especially so young. It does irreparable damage. My God, how I suffered the loss of her...."

"Jessie wrote me, told me how ill you were. She was afraid she might lose you. She begged me to come. And still I didn't go to you. I burned her letters."

Katie recalled Jeremy's surprise at her arrival from Boston. "So you were so thorough wiping out evidence, I suppose after awhile no one knew I'd ever existed." She was shocked that voicing this didn't send her into another crying jag.

Francine's gaze grew distant. "In time, the talk died down. Sooner or later, people tire of rehashing tragedy. It actually came as a surprise to see what little space I and my concerns took up in others' lives. Boyd never recovered. He was never well again. I thank God he started talking to me again.

But he never stopped blaming himself."

Further hurt touched Katie. Had she caused that too? Grandfather's early death? *No! No! She'd been a child, innocent.* Somehow she had now let go of the guilt she'd carried East with her.

"I must have my bed," Francine said, her adrenaline-fueled energy deserting her.

Katie pushed her wheelchair back down the hall. "How in the world did you get yourself to the library?"

"Omnipotence is an amazing thing."

"You'll probably be a wreck for a month."

She waved a trivializing hand. "Desperate situations call for desperate solutions...or something to that effect. When Boyd called on me to help him, I had no choice but to get myself down there."

"You're irredeemable."

"No doubt."

Katie glanced at her watch. It was nearly five in the morning. "Wait here and I'll get Pearl." She walked on to knock on her door.

When she appeared, Pearl was already dressed.

"You're up early," said Katie

"Yes, I think I finally got rested. I slept so well after the wind went down."

"I need your help with Francine. She decided to go to the library."

"My stars, that woman is a caution."

Within minutes, Francine was settled in bed and Katie lay down beside her.

They continued talking for a time. Her grandmother answered questions, supplied facts, filled in more details. After an hour or so, Pearl brought breakfast and Francine's medications.

After some food, Katie was totally relaxed and ready to sleep after the siege of the night. She could not remember feeling such a profound sense of well-being. Or perhaps it was a total lack of anxiety. Even as her thoughts drifted to Jeremy and Becca, she felt no dread. Her world had righted itself completely.

CHAPTER SEVENTEEN

Katie slept for twelve hours, not waking until the next night. It was the sound of snow removal equipment outside that finally roused her from her nearly comatose state. She turned her head toward Francine who smiled.

"I thought maybe your grandfather took you with him to the other side."

Katie slowly recalled all that had happened. She smiled when she caught sight of the clock on the bedside table. "I think my brain had to recharge."

"I wouldn't doubt it. I am actually astounded that you came through all this so well. I doubt many could. You may remember when you first arrived here, demanding I tell you what happened. I told you then that I wouldn't because the truth would destroy you."

"I remember."

"How do you think you would have handled it, if I had blurted out the entire ghastly tale at that time?"

Katie recalled her rage and frustration at her grandmother's reticence. Now she understood what she had done to protect her. "Not well."

"You would likely have ended up in a mental ward."

Katie knew the truth of what she said. "I'm

the first to agree you were right. It could well have destroyed me."

"I couldn't have dealt with that...not when I had you back with me after so long. I knew you had to have time to gather your strength and let go of your anger. I had been through that same transition myself right after I sent you to Jessie. I was so enraged, I couldn't function. It took years to let go of that kind of fury and regain my perspective so I could deal with your return. I didn't write you until I had my power back."

"You were so wise to withstand my reckless disregard for my safety."

"You had to deal with the threat for far too long but I doubt you knew just how perilous your nightmare was. As in all things, age is the only thing that brings wisdom and patience. When I was your age, I'd have dealt with this exactly like you. They'd have had to lock me in the cellar to keep me from throwing caution to the wind."

Katie laughed. "I guess I come by my daring nature through you."

"I knew that when you were three and was reminded of it again within five minutes of seeing you as an adult. I saw myself so clearly in you and knew I must keep you where you belong."

"I'm so grateful you did."

"You are the treasure of my heart, my dearest Katie. Now, once you've had some dinner and gotten your wits about you, you must phone Jeremy. He has called half a dozen times today, worried that he hasn't heard from you." She pressed a finger to her lips. "I didn't tell him a thing, not wanting to steal your thunder."

Katie considered her musingly.

It took most of the following week to remove enough of the five feet of snow from *Radbourne* grounds, paddocks and fields so the ranch could function with some normalcy again. Once all was in order, Katie packed to go to Billings.

The afternoon she was to leave, she stopped to tell Francine goodbye.

Her grandmother looked up, her eyes narrowing. "Oh, where are you off to?" Her gaze took in her parka and gloves. "Is it cold out?"

Katie's heart lurched. "Well, yeah, we just had five feet of snow."

"Did we?" She gave her a blank look.

Apparently, Francine's return to lucidity was over and she was sliding back into her fog.

"Yes. Now I must run. I want to get to the hospital before dinner time."

Francine continued studying her without comprehension. "Is Jeremy ill?"

"Jeremy's fine. I'm just going to visit him and Becca. I'll be back soon. Pearl will be staying with you. Bye now, sweetie." She kissed her and hurried to the door, trying to dismiss her renewed concern. Just when she'd thought she had nothing to worry about for awhile, now this.

But she couldn't stand the thought of being away from Jeremy and Becca one more day. She needed to be with them.

She hurried across the grounds to the carriage house and got into the Accord, resolved to phone Scott and Pearl later to be sure they were aware of Francine's latest decline. Pleased to see someone had topped off the gas tank and washed the windows, she backed out and turned down the driveway.

While she continued to the Interstate, she set aside her disquiet, knowing that her grandmother was in no danger and would be well taken care of until she returned. After so much trauma and finally walking through the horrific nightmare, she was filled now with pure joy at being delivered. She and Jeremy had talked for hours by phone as she told him every detail of her miraculous encounter with the supernatural.

Though she was well aware of his insights into the spiritual realm, she was somewhat taken aback at his calm acceptance of all she told him. Now she had firsthand knowledge of his profound spirituality.

When she got to the hospital, she quickly dressed in sterile clothing and hurried on to Becca's room. Her lighthearted anticipation was instantly swept aside by the bleak scene before her. She went to Jeremy who stood back from the cluster of doctors and nurses hovering over Becca, so quiet and white in the bed.

Seeing her, Jeremy pulled her close.

"What's happening?"

"She's not doing so great." He nodded at the medical group. "The doctor will talk to us when he's finished." He kissed her cheek before laying his head against hers, returning his attention to Becca.

Shortly, Dr. Cusack left the others, motioning for Jeremy and Katie to follow. He led them into a conference room.

"Becca isn't responding to the chemo the way I'd hoped. Her blood and bone marrow haven't changed since we began treatment. We're over three weeks in and I hoped we'd attain remission by Christmas." He frowned "It's just not happening."

"So now what?" Jeremy inquired.

"We'll start again with more aggressive drugs." He leaned closer. "But I must tell you, this concerns me greatly. When we can get a patient into remission within four or five weeks after starting chemo, the prognosis is good. Longer than that, and the chances of a cure go down."

Katie gripped Jeremy's hand so hard he freed his fingers from hers, then held her hand in both of his. They both waited for the doctor to continue.

"We're going to fight this with every resource we have and I think we'll prevail in the end because we have several chemo drugs to try. But as a precaution, I want to pursue the possibility of a bone marrow transplant. Locate a viable donor so we'll have that option to fall back on."

"Can I be a donor?" Jeremy asked.

"There's a good chance you're a match. Parents often are. Where is Becca's mother?"

Jeremy briefly explained her circumstances and Dr. Cusack told them she too might be a possible donor.

"Any siblings?" he asked then.

"Becca's an only child."

"Well then, let's get some blood from you, Jeremy and if you're not a match, I'll check the National Donor Registry. The odds go down once we get out of the immediate family but sometimes we get lucky. I'll also speak to Dr. Remington in Sheridan and see what he can turn up."

"Thanks so much," Katie said as they all rose to leave.

"I would definitely keep the faith at this point," Dr. Cusack recommended as he showed them to the door, then asked them to go with him to the lab. "We might as well, check your blood as well," he said, guiding Katie along the hall with a hand on her shoulder.

After their blood was drawn and they'd pulled on new sterile scrubs, Jeremy led her back to Becca's room where they sat on a couch against the far wall. Katie settled within Jeremy's loose embrace. As they savored being so close together, his fingers threaded through her hair, steadying her head so he could study her. "I've missed you so much. I literally ached to be with you the night you had to walk through your nightmare. I could feel how terrified you were."

"Until my grandfather came...to help me." She smiled and touched his hand still holding her head.

"It all came down to cause and effect. Your grandfather caused the death of your mother so it was his karma to get you through the memory that damaged you so profoundly. That's another reason you had to return to *Radbourne* before you could find your resolution."

"There are no coincidences."

He grinned. "Exactly." He settled back and continued holding her.

"Do you think Becca's in real trouble?"

"Dr. Cusack made it sound pretty grim but he

also seems to think it won't be that hard to find a donor match. A marrow transplant will definitely put her into remission."

Katie let his words wash through her mind, easing the agitation that had lain there since Dr. Cusack had filled them in. "I'm concerned about Francine."

"What now?"

"She's losing ground again. She's confused and just not tracking. It was a shock because when I was attacked that night...." She threw up her hands in frustration. "I still don't know what to call it. I saw a ghost in the hall...that's all I can think to call it." She looked at Jeremy for inspiration. "It was white and looked like a moving membrane.

"That would be a ghost."

"Okay, that was there the night I got home from here. And there was some other force that just knocked me flat as I was climbing the stairs. I finally got to my room and once I went inside, it shoved me and I smacked my nose into the wall." She pointed at the discoloration she knew still marked the cartilage...."

Jeremy kissed her injury, his eyes troubled.

"You're an expert on the supernatural so what does one call that kind of...thing...."

"An entity perhaps, or energy...or force maybe...a manifestation of evil." He grinned at her. "That's the best I can do...."

"Why did it become something evil and threatening?"

"There are all sorts of evil spirits on the other side, unsettled beings searching for some kind of peace or resolution, or intent on doing harm."

"For revenge?"

"Maybe."

"Well, anyway, what I was going to tell you is when all that started, Francine picked up on what I was dealing with. She became my protector and wouldn't let me out of her sight. I slept in her bed for several nights and it was like she was on guard. I finally ended up in the library and that's when the whole memory of that night just played out in my brain. I know I was in great danger because my grandfather came to protect me. I was in another reality the whole time. When I came back, I found Francine sitting there beside the library table in her wheelchair."

Jeremy stared at her, his brow furrowed.

"I know...I thought Pearl had brought her but I soon learned that Pearl slept through the night...I told you she stayed over because of the blizzard...."

He nodded, tracing a finger along her jaw.

"So when I wheeled her back along the hall from the library Francine told me my grandfather had called her to come help so she had to go...."

A smile playing at the corner of his mouth. "That's our Francine. Resourceful."

"The point of telling you all this is that she just totally rallied when I needed her help. Nothing frail about her that night. But this afternoon before I left, she'd completely regressed again."

He took her hand and pressed it to his lips, his eyes gentle on her. "I'm so sorry *I* couldn't be with you. I'm glad you weren't alone."

"My grandmother showed me just how much she loves me."

Smiling, he kissed her palm. "I've known that

for a long time, my darling."

"I think I should go home in the morning and see how she is."

He nodded. "Yes, you must." He looked so sad she thought he might cry. "I just miss you so much when we're apart."

"I know." She wrapped him close.

"By tomorrow, we should have the results of our blood tests. If neither of us is a match, you can have Scott start looking for a donor."

Talk of Becca's need for a donor sent apprehension through her once more but she refused to give in to it.

"Now I'd like to have dinner with you. Let me escort you to the cafeteria." He stood and tucked her hand into his elbow to lead her into the hall.

Not only was Jeremy not a donor match for Becca, neither was Katie. As she began the drive to *Radbourne* the next day, she carried a new foreboding with her. If it came down to a bone marrow transplant being the only option to save Becca and no match could be found...." The thought trailed into a deep ache of fear settling in her chest. To distract herself from the depressing direction of her thoughts, she turned on a Mozart concerto.

As soon as she reached *Radbourne,* she phoned Scott who'd already been briefed by Dr. Cusack. He told her the plan of action to canvas the area for a donor match He had contacted the media, such as it was in Sheridan, to spread the word. He was coming to *Radbourne* that afternoon to take blood from everyone there

"The worldwide organ donor database is already searching," he said. "There's another factor that complicates the situation for Becca, according to Dr. Cusack. Becca has a very unique genetic makeup. Jeremy has West Indian roots; Evelyn Foxworth's ancestors where Russian Jews. That combination is extremely rare so it's going to be tough. We have to just beat the bushes everywhere we can and hope we hit a match."

Again, the low odds pounded in Katie's brain. How could the prognosis have gone from positive to dismal in a matter of days?

"So I'll see you about one," Scott said. "You might want to warn everyone that I'm coming."

"I will. See you then."

She hung up and glanced at a clock. Already past ten. She started up the staircase with Jekyll.

Pearl was with Francine so Katie dispatched her to the barns to inform the employees of the blood draw, then gave her attention to Francine.

Her eyes that usually held a depth of curiosity inspected Katie dully and she didn't speak,

"How are you?" Katie asked but still got no response.

After a minute or two, Katie decided to tell her what had happened since she'd left her the day before. When she finished, her grandmother continued looking at her silently but some knowing emotion eventually slid into her gaze. "I cannot give her my marrow...."

"Why not?" Katie asked. "I think Scott will want to check to see if you might be a match."

She slowly moved her head from side to side.

"Becca isn't...re...lated to me...."

"There's still a chance you could be a match."

She shook her head with a little more vehemence. "...Lena... could," she managed after a long struggle to speak, "...or Ce...It... the cabin ...."

"Who's Lena?" Katie asked once she had faded into silence.

With some effort, she lifted her chin to look at her, then shook her head again. "The cabin... look...."

Katie waited but she didn't rouse again and soon fell asleep.

Puzzling over who Lena might be, Katie descended the stairs to prepare for Scott's arrival.

No viable donor match was found at *Radbourne* or in all of Wyoming. The search continued worldwide as Christmas came and went with no one having the least wish to celebrate.

Friends and neighbors came to the manor Christmas Eve to deliver gifts of food that accumulated on the kitchen counter until it would hold no more. Katie summoned a team of stable boys to distribute the dishes among the employees.

When all the casseroles and desserts were gone, she carried a cup of hot chocolate spiked with peppermint schnapps into the drawing room. She'd barely settled on the sofa with Jekyll curled at her feet before she heard Pearl and other voices in the hall.

Patrick and Janel appeared. "We come bearing booze," Patrick said, brandishing a bottle of brandy.

Katie lifted her mug. "I'm already imbibing.

Let me bring some more hot chocolate and you can join me."

Janel removed her coat and laid it aside. "No, no, I'll get it."

"None for me," Patrick said. "I'll have my brandy straight." He crossed to the bar in a mahogany cabinet under the window. "We thought you could use some company." He brought his glass and sat next to her.

"I'm so glad." She turned toward him. "Big change from last Christmas."

"It's hard to get my brain around it. After Becca did so spectacularly well at Billings, she showed an amazing talent for Park...I'm quite lost without my star pupil."

She called up a smile. "You're not the only one...who's lost without her...."

Janel returned with a mug of cocoa and he leapt up to add brandy, then proposed a toast. "To our Becca's speedy return!"

They clicked glasses and sat again.

Katie hadn't eaten all day and now she felt the effect of the schnapps and was grateful for the momentary lift in her mood. "I've been so busy, I haven't seen much of either of you. What's been happening?"

Janel sipped her drink, a merry light seeping into her eyes. "Well, Scott's schedule's been very full as well with all that's been happening with Becca and Francine." She smiled and Katie could see her happiness. "But we've found time to spend together as well."

Katie studied her. "Are you dating?"

"Yes, if you call seeing each other for an hour

or two at a time at his house or mine late at night..." She ducked her head. "It's not like that," she said in response to Patrick's raised eyebrow at the color in her cheeks. "Not yet...."

He squeezed her knee. "Good for you."

"He's a lovely man."

"I agree and not bad looking either," Katie concurred.

Patrick listened to their exchange with a grin. "And to think when you first came here, I thought I might have a chance to date you. I could offer more than an hour in the wee hours...."

Janel playfully swung a pillow at him. "Well, you should've made your move sooner."

He raised his glass to her. "Dr. Remington had better watch his step or I'll be forced to step in." He set down his glass and looked at his watch. "Let me take you two lovely ladies to dinner."

"It's Christmas Eve." Katie was disappointed. "Nothing will be open. But that was a wonderful idea."

Patrick stood up. "Well, the next best thing to taking you to dinner is having me cook you dinner. Come with me." He led the way to the kitchen.

Katie suggested they call Scott to see if he could join them. He gave his regrets but promised to meet Janel at her house later.

Katie and Janel watched Patrick select a pan and eggs along with an assortment of greens and herbs. In short order, he served a salad and omelets by candlelight in the solarium.

Katie found a bottle of Chablis in the refrigerator. "I'm so happy to be sharing Christmas Eve with good friends."

"Hear, hear." Patrick raised his glass and they drank another toast.

When her unexpected guests went home sometime after nine, Katie sent Pearl home, then settled in the one comfortable chair in the kitchen and phoned Jeremy. She could tell right away how depressed he was.

"Honey, I wish I was with you tonight."

He sighed. "Me too. You have no idea how much."

"How's Becca?"

"The same as when you asked me that this morning."

"Dumb question. But it's just so hard not being able to at least see her...."

"She still has to be in the sterile environment so it's quite a project getting suited up to go in there. And she's usually asleep so I don't spend as much time with her as I have been. It just makes my heart bleed to see her so sick. I'm spending a lot of time talking to God."

"Me too."

"I believe in predestination but I cannot grasp how Becca's getting sick fits into that."

"I'm sure we'll find out before this is over." She could picture his smile.

"If I don't lose my faith first." He was silent for a minute or two. "Wasn't that a cheery thing to say?" he finally added. "Sorry."

"You won't. I've never known anyone who has a better handle on what God's up to."

"Maybe but it's getting pretty murky right now."

"I know, sweetheart."

"On a lighter note, how's our friend Jekyll?"

"Much better. He's still keeping an eye out for Becca but he's transferred some of his care giving to me so he no longer looks like his heart is breaking. I never knew dogs can get depressed just like people. The medication Janel prescribed is working. We're fortunate to have found a vet right out of school. She has training in a lot of state-of-the-art procedures and medications."

"She is amazing," Jeremy agreed, his voice flat.

"Jeremy, I keep forgetting something. When I told Francine about the search for a donor, she said Lena could be one. Do you have any idea who she was talking about?"

"Not a clue."

"She mentioned another name...or the first couple letters but then she lost her train of thought before I could get even that..."

"Wait a minute. You're saying she knew what you were talking about when you told her about Becca needing a donor?"

"She seemed to. Said she couldn't be a donor but Lena could"

"I have no idea what she was talking about. My guess is, it's just more of her confusion...."

"I don't think so," she broke in. "Her mind's been coming in and out all month. When she's here, she's as sharp as ever. But she lapses into bewilderment much faster now than she did at first."

"My point exactly. I don't think we can put any credence in anything she says at this point."

"I'm going up now to see how she's feeling."

"Tell her she's in my thoughts and prayers."

"I will. Goodnight, Jeremy. I love you."

When she got upstairs, she followed Jekyll into the dim bedroom and went to look down at her grandmother. The oxygen condenser sighed in the corner, filling the quiet like a heartbeat.

Francine looked small and helpless within the arrangement of pillows. Apprehension spread through Katie as she observed her. She looked even more diminished tonight.

As though drawn from sleep by Katie's absorbed inspection, she opened her eyes and reached a frail hand to stroke the side of Jekyll's big head pushed close to her. "Ah, you are a good dog...." She stared at something past Katie's shoulder, her look indecipherable while she continued petting Jekyll.

Katie sat close but Francine gave no indication that she knew she was there. Most of half an hour passed this way. Katie expected her to sleep again but abruptly, she turned her face back, searching her eyes. "...is Becca here...?"

"No, hon, she's still in Billings. Jeremy's with her at the hospital. They're still searching for a bone marrow donor for her...."

Francine uncertainly moved her hand from Jekyll's head to grip her hand. "...in the cabin...somewhere...there ...a...." She trailed off, her face taut in concentration. "...a bottle...or vase.." She shook her head in frustration. "I can...not...remember..."

They both sat very still. Becca was afraid to prod her for fear she would stop completely. Her brain raced with questions but she didn't speak, waiting.

Her grandmother suddenly looked at her again. "...maybe a box...could it...be a basket....?" Her searching gaze probed Katie's face.

"I...I don't know," she said softly.

"It was so long ago... I...think...not...." She lapsed into silence again, then once more seemed to gather herself to sit straighter and took a deep, tremulous breath. "Go into the cabin...and look...for...."

Halting there, she looked helplessly at Katie. "I can't...can't..." She was suddenly shaking, agitated.

Katie inclined toward her, every fiber of her being alert, struggling to hear, to unravel what she was saying. Then inspiration came out of nowhere and she opened a drawer in a bedside table, retrieving pen and notebook.

"Here, maybe you can write what you're trying to say." She put the tablet on a phone book, then situated it in front of her grandmother and slid her spectacles on for her.

Francine took the pen with surprising focus even as her hand trembled and she gave Katie a dubious glance. After some thought, she lifted the pen.

"I'll just let you collect your thoughts," Katie said. She motioned Jekyll to follow her to the nearest window where she sat in an armchair to look out over the grounds brilliant with moonlight tonight. Hope wove itself through her scattered emotions. Could her grandmother possibly know something or someone who could help Becca? She glanced back and saw that she had fallen asleep, her head lying back against her pillows.

Katie looked again out the window. Ah well, Francine had done the best. She may well have remembered something but couldn't articulate it.

Katie glanced at her again. Something startling in Francine's features drew her quickly back to her. A chill passed along her shoulders even though the room was warm. With a whine, Jekyll unfolded himself and trotted toward the bed.

Francine's head was tilted to one side. Katie straightened it and removed her spectacles, suddenly gripped by confusion. She lifted the gnarled fingers to put them beneath the covers, then froze, still trying to see what was wrong.

Her grandmother took a ragged breath that was much louder than it should have been. The blue eyes flew open, finding Katie as she gasped again....

The veined hands gripped in hers were chilled Katie stroked her forehead, so cold. And finally she saw Francine wasn't breathing anymore. As she searched for the reason, she saw something - tiny, hazy mass shoot from the still body and she was compelled to watch as it flew across the room and disappeared into the wall. She stared at the place it had been. *Dear, God, her grandmother's soul had just taken flight....* Jekyll threw back his head and howled, the sound a wavering, haunting spiral that sent a chill up Katie's spine.

With a sob, she collapsed on the bed, gathering the thin body in her arms, rocking her gently. "Oh, Grandma, I love you so much." Laying her back on the pillows, she sat still, absently petting Jekyll who shoved his nose frantically at Francine's leg. "She's okay, big guy." She pointed to the floor and he quickly lay down beside the bed.

Katie looked at the clock. Ten minutes after four. Too early to start making calls so she pulled a chair close and settled beside her grandmother. This was the last time she would be able to sit with her like this.

Shock had faded to tender contemplation. She let her mind drift through the months since she had come to *Radbourne* again, hating Francine with a rage she thought she'd never let go. Now her heart brimmed with love for her.

She would miss her terribly, yet felt no great regret that she was gone. She wished the proud lady she'd come to know and adore might have stayed with them for a long, long time. But she didn't begrudge a peaceful end for the sad woman she'd become in recent weeks who struggled to keep her balance against illness and senility..

Gratitude filled her to know that Francine had escaped the remainder of her decline into confusion and pain. She had gone gently with her dignity intact, still living at *Radbourne*, her beloved home. No one could ask for a greater blessing.

Katie was thankful that she was here this night. But new tears rose in her throat when she thought of Jeremy. If only he could have been with Francine as well. She dreaded telling him but couldn't postpone it any longer.

As she straightened the comforter over her grandmother, she noticed the notebook and pen that she'd given her earlier. She picked it up and glanced at the blank page, then brought it closer.

There was something very faint written there. She sat down to inspect it more closely in the lamplight. DE VE RNLA KE....cab...in....She stared at the scrawled letters, newly annoyed that it meant nothing to her. She'd have to think more about it later. Stuffing the paper in her pocket, she went downstairs to the kitchen where she fed Jekyll and let him outside.

She called Pearl first and told her to send Patrick to the manor. Then she dialed the hospital in Billings.

When Jeremy finally answered, he sounded like he'd just woken up.

"Jeremy...." Her calm instantly dissolved and she was sobbing. "It's...Francine...."

"Darling, what is it? What's happened? Is Francine...?"

"She's...dead...."

"Oh, no!"

The agony in his voice wrenched at her.

The rest of the day passed in a disjointed string of hours. Pearl arrived and told her which funeral home to call, then Patrick and Janel and Scott were there as well. After Scott examined Francine and her body was removed by ambulance, Katie sat in the kitchen with Janel and Patrick.

She turned to Patrick. "Jeremy has to come home so we need you to go to Billings, to the hospital. You'll serve as Becca's advocate until he can get back there. Can you do that?"

"Of course. I'll speak to Nick and he can see that my horses are kept in condition while I'm gone. As soon as that's arranged, I'm free for as long as I'm needed."

"Great. You can go talk to Nick and get packed. I'll have your credentials for the hospital ready by the time you get back. Then you can leave for Billings. Jeremy will come home as soon as you get there."

"I'm on my way. Let me just say how sorry I am about your grandmother. She was an amazing lady and I'll miss her a lot." He kissed her cheek and was gone.

"What can I do?" Janel asked.

Katie shook her head, unable to think for a moment. "Go help Patrick, I guess. Maybe you can help exercise his horses."

"Okay. I'll check with you later, hon."

Katie made her way to Jeremy's office to type up the papers for Patrick to take with him.

CHAPTER EIGHTEEN

Katie sat with Jeremy in the drawing room after dinner the night following Francine's funeral. "Do you think she would've approved?"

He nodded, staring at the glass of bourbon resting on the arm of the sofa, turning it within his fingers. "Yes," he said, glancing up. "A thousand at her funeral. I imagine that impressed her. She loved it when people admired what she accomplished. Despite being so flamboyant, she could be intimidated at times and very humble."

"That came as a big surprise when I first saw that side of her," Katie agreed. "For awhile, I truly believed she would bulldoze through any obstacle to get what she wanted...but I finally realized she could give grace as well. She did with me in any case."

Jeremy's mood grew pensive. He looked into the fire, his grief tangible. "I so hoped you would finally find that in her. She didn't make it easy for you." He grimaced. "I was afraid she might offend you to the point where you would leave before you saw what a decent person she really was."

"It was tempting." She smiled. "I actually thought I'd stay in Boston when I went back. But by then, I was quite intrigued by where you and I might be headed. And then when the nightmare assaulted me all the time I was away, I had no choice but to come back."

"Thank, God, for destiny," Jeremy said, taking her hand and kissing it, his eyes tender on hers.

They continued there quietly, allowing the stillness and being together to relax and restore them after the emotional roller coaster of recent days. They had both strived to lay Francine to rest with the dignity and respect her esteemed life warranted and they were successful. But the effort left them exhausted and profoundly sad.

The fire had died down and Jeremy went to add logs and refill his glass. Watching him, Katie hated to break the spell of renewal but it was time. She drew the folded paper from the pocket of her suit jacket. When Jeremy sat beside her again, she smoothed out the paper and handed it to him.

"What do you make of this?"

He scrutinized the scribbling, then looked up. "What is it?"

"The night she died, she was trying again to tell me something. Like I told you when she mentioned the name Lena. She was really agitated and desperate to make me understand but she couldn't get the words out. I thought it might help if she wrote it down so I gave her this paper. I went to sit by the window so I wouldn't make her more upset. She died a few minutes after. Later, I found what she'd written."

Jeremy studied the letters again, his face tense. "And why do you think this is important? Remind me again."

"The first time I told her about Becca needing a donor, she said Lena could be one. I mean, she didn't just say it outright like that but after a struggle, that's what she finally got out. And she mentioned a cabin that day. And then the night she died, she wrote the word cabin on that paper. I mean I think that's what it says."

Jeremy looked at the paper in his hand. "I guess but this looks like some kind of code...."

"I don't know if it's a code but she was trying to tell us something."

"Like what?"

"I don't know. I think the word cabin is important because she mentioned it twice before she wrote it...." She leaned past him to point out the word. "The first time she mentioned it, she also said some other words...vase was one and box, I think. I can't remember the others. But I'm thinking she could've been talking about something hidden in a cabin that we need to find."

He sat still, looking at her for a long time. "So why was she telling you this stuff?"

"It started when I told her Becca needs a donor so I think she was telling me something that would help her."

Puzzlement worked in his eyes, then cleared a bit as
he studied her again. "But what cabin?"

She shrugged. "We have two to choose from. Which meant more to Francine?"

He considered that. "I don't think she ever went inside the one Tyson Chamberlain built. Not in all the years I lived here. But the one on the mountain, that meant the world to her."

"So if she was going to put something away that might need to be found someday, you think that's where she would put it?"

"I have no clue. The whole idea seems pretty

unbelievable to me."

"Or maybe just eccentric," Katie ventured.

He slowly nodded. "There's that. If Francine managed to leave us some important information when she was on her deathbed, I guess the least we can do is try to figure it out." He gave her an amused look. "Otherwise, she'll haunt us."

They sat thinking about what they were undertaking. "If I had more energy, I'd say we should start the search tonight," Katie said presently.

"We'll begin as soon as it's light. There's no electricity in Tyson's first home," he added in response to her questioning glance.

"No heat either, I suppose."

"Nope." He reached down to pull her up and they made their way up the stairs to his bedroom where Katie had slept in the warm, protective circle of his arms since he returned from Billings. A drowsy Jekyll followed.

Katie and Jeremy decided to begin their search with the ancient cabin built by Tyson Chamberlain in 1872. Stable boys were dispatched with snow blowers shortly after sunrise to clear a path to the single door.

The temperature hovered near zero so Katie and Jeremy dressed in snowmobile suits and insulated boots before they ventured inside the building. They carried a selection of flashlights and the boys were sent to bring in floodlights to illuminate the cramped and dusty interior.

Initially, Katie was overwhelmed by the century-old accumulation of rot and decay.

Fortunately, the roof had been repaired often enough that no water damage was evident but the place was fairly clogged with cobwebs, dead insects, and deep dust that had settled over every surface. They stood still taking it all in before they dared consider how best to proceed.

The original furniture was still there – a wooden table and bed with the remnants of some sort of stuffed mattress, a few rustic chairs whose seats had mostly fallen away. Katie turned her attention to the shallow shelves lining all of the walls. They contained some archaic cooking pans and gadgets the purpose of which they could only guess at.

When she spotted some small crocks nearly covered with a mix of old papers and pieces of clothing, her heart leapt a little. A crock could serve as a vase. But upon closer examination, she found them empty save for the usual dust.

Jeremy rummaged through a battered trunk in a corner but located nothing helpful. He used a step ladder the boys had brought in to search the spaces beneath the eaves with a flashlight but after going around the entire perimeter of the room, turned up nothing.

They kept on like this throughout the morning. leaving nothing unexamined. Once they had searched every square inch of the place, they started over, and went through it all again. They had inspected every niche and hole in the logs that formed the walls, hunting for indentations that might have something hidden within. Nothing there. They tore apart the mattress and inspected the bed underneath.

They went through every nook and cranny of the archaic cook stove, including the stove pipe that they dragged outside and knocked free of build up cinders and soot. As they stood back inside, their eyes roving over the entire building and its contents, they concluded nothing had been secreted there.

"Let's blow this joint," Jeremy said, catching Katie to him in a hug. "Onward and upward."

They went to the kitchen to eat Pearl's soup and sandwiches, then phoned Patrick to see how Becca was.

"Still no real change," he reported. "The new chemo drug still hasn't impacted the cancer. Dr. Cusack is going to try another if there's still nothing by the end of next week."

Jeremy told him about their effort to learn if Francine had actually left them some kind of helpful information. "After this morning, it doesn't look very promising but we're going to go up the mountain this afternoon and see if that cabin turns up anything."

"Well, good luck. Wish I was there to help you look."

"Me too, but you just keep close tab on Becca."

"I am. Whenever she wakes, she asks for both of you and Jekyll, of course."

"Give her our love. Talk to you later, Patrick."

Hanging up, he looked at Katie and Pearl. "The chemo still hasn't affected the cancer."

"Half an hour ago, I didn't think I could keep going," Katie said, laying her head on his shoulder. "But hearing that, I can't wait to get up the mountain."

They thanked Pearl for lunch. "I'll pick you up in five, Jeremy said before hurrying into the back hall."

"Take care up there," Pearl cautioned, filling a thermos with steaming coffee that she handed to Katie.

"We will. Thanks." She heard the snow mobile outside and turned to go.

When she'd stowed the thermos, she climbed on behind Jeremy and they were on their way up the mountain.

Upon reaching the cabin, they found the porch and front door drifted over. Jeremy led the way to the back that was accessible. Once inside, he built a fire before they set to work.

As she perused the familiar chamber, Katie's mind skirted back to the many interludes she had spent there with Jeremy, her heart quickening. Now she tried to be objective as she took in the furnishings, the small table and chairs in one corner, comfortable easy chairs before the fire, the bed she now realized was a wooden box in another corner, made cozy and inviting by a thick mattress and piled pillows and comforters and throws.

Jeremy had immediately approached that corner and began stripping off the bedding that he piled on the chairs before the fireplace. Katie considered helping him but decided to begin her search at the rear of the room. She began a thorough hunt through the free-standing pantry that held all the kitchen pots that had evidently been used back in the day when Francine cooked over the fireplace. She moved from there to some other cupboards and shelves on the back wall that held canned goods of various ages and condition.

After a time, she walked back to the fireplace to warm her hands. Jeremy was nowhere in sight and she was about to look through a window to see if he'd stepped outside for some reason when she heard knocking from the bed. Bending down, she saw him stretched out, prying at something on the far wall beneath the bed frame.

"Did you find something?"

He glanced at her over his shoulder. "Maybe. Come here and I'll show you."

She flattened herself on the floor and slid closer until she could see the expanse of plastered wall illuminated by his flashlight. This cabin had been built with considerably more skill and better materials than the one at the ranch headquarters. This one was a frame building.

As she looked beyond Jeremy, she could clearly see the outline of a small door that had been cut directly into the wall. But there was no pull attached so Jeremy was attempting to push the flat end of a large screwdriver into the crack along one side. He pounded on the handle with his other hand.

Katie moved closer and grabbed the flashlight to light up the darkness. After a couple more smacks to the handle, the screwdriver penetrated the edge. Jeremy maneuvered it further until something gave way behind and he could push it around the edge of the makeshift door.

Katie tried without success to quiet her suddenly frenzied brain. She was possessed by a huge surge of exhilaration.

"This is it," Jeremy breathed as he reached into the opening, grasping something with both hands. "This is it, Katie!"

She could hear him through her reeling thoughts but couldn't make sense of what he was saying. Then she saw that he'd pulled out a box with some sort of inlaid image on the lid and her breath caught. "That's what Francine was trying to tell me about."

"Yes, it is," Jeremy agreed with certainty.

"How can you be sure?" she asked when they had struggled out from under the bed.

"Francine's been my guide ever since we got here." Jeremy sank into a chair with the box on his lap.

Katie perched on the arm beside him, studying the design. "Marquetry," she said, touching the picture that appeared to be a vintage farm scene.

"Same idea as parquetry?" Jeremy ventured, tracing the lines.

"Exactly. What did Francine tell you?"

He grinned. at her. "She was directing me as soon as I came in. That's why I started with the bed."

Gripping the box, he drew a long, shaky breath. "This has to be important."

"Let's look and see." Impatience pulsed through Katie.

He lifted the lid and they both stared inside. His fingers found a long envelope and lifted it out. Smudged and yellowed with age, it had nothing written on the outside. When he turned it over, the flap fell open and he withdrew a sheet with a short paragraph penned in perfect cursive.

Katie bent closer to decipher the faded ink. Jeremy brought it closer and read it aloud.

If you are reading this, I have died. I vowed never to divulge my secret until my death. Because I cannot see into the future despite my ESP, I assume what I have spent a great deal of my life hiding will come as quite a surprise. I hope you will find it within your heart to accept what I wrought. I never could.

The first step in discovering what I must reveal is to visit Nealie Rourke in Denver. She lives at 1022 Mulberry Ave. She will tell you everything you need to know.

Katie met Jeremy's confounded gaze and neither could speak.

"Damn," he said at last, "what in the name of God could she be talking about?"

Katie didn't know what she'd expected to find when they unraveled Francine's message but it wasn't this additional mystery.

"What could this letter possibly have to do with Becca needing a donor?"

"Apparently, we have to fly to Denver to find out."

He slowly put the letter back into the envelope and slid it into his pocket. "Leave it to Francine."

"When they arrived back at the manor, they booked a one o'clock flight to Denver before filling in the others on the results of their cabin searches.

After an early dinner and a glass of bourbon, they went to bed, too exhausted to face more challenges until morning.

It was shortly after two o'clock the next day when their taxi pulled up at 1022 Mulberry Ave. in Denver. Katie craned her neck to take in the three-story Victorian. It reminded her of nothing so much as an oversized doll house. It appeared well-maintained with no peeling paint or loose shingles. Indeed the amazing mix of colors used to paint and trim the edifice suggested recent application. She would've expected the mix of green, burgundy, mauve and pale blue to create a garish impression but instead, it was very charming.

Jeremy's arm lay across Katie's shoulders as they both studied the house. "Shall we?" he murmured, as he opened the taxi door.

Katie looked for signs of life behind the leaded glass windows. Relief touched her when she saw the glow of some sort of light in one room near the front entrance. So far, so good.

They proceeded along the sidewalk to steps angling up to a circular porch that wound around the first story. They reached a purple door sporting a gigantic evergreen wreath tied with an equally large hot pink bow. Katie pressed a doorbell. A resonant gong-like sound reverberated into the heart of the house.

Shortly a black maid in a pink uniform opened the door. "Ah," she said, peering at them through a screen door she quickly pushed open. "We've been expecting you. Do come in." She stepped back, gesturing them into a huge white foyer. "Nealie's waiting upstairs." She nodded toward a staircase to their left.

Katie and Jeremy exchanged a questioning

glance. A gracious dining area could be seen some distant along a wide corridor that converged with the entrance hall. Whoever Nealie turned out to be, her home was a Victorian show place.

The maid stood to one side, giving no indication that she was going to guide them so they started up the steps that ended in an expansive landing on the second floor.

"Come in, I'm here," a raspy female voice called. They saw a jaunty little woman with snowy white hair piled atop her head, seated at an elaborate desk just inside a broad, open doorway. When they stepped nearer, she beckoned excitedly. "Come, come." Artificial logs glowed in a white stone fireplace.

Eyes of brilliant green watched their entrance into a great, round bedroom appointed with an enormous bed and palladian windows elaborately dressed with lace curtains circling two walls. Various elegant tables and chairs created an inviting sitting area affording a spectacular view of a lake stretching toward a distant horizon."

"I am Nealie O'Rourke. I know my dear friend Francine has passed on so I've been expecting someone to soon contact me." Her green eyes held a strange depth of knowing that confused Katie even more than she already was. "Please make yourselves comfortable so we can have a talk." She indicated a wooden couch upholstered with lace. "I should imagine you have a great many questions."

They sat. "We actually don't have any idea why we're here," Jeremy said.

She granted them a warm smile. She was

ancient but her impish face had a bright, eager expression. "If I tell you that I come from a long line of seers perhaps that will help you a bit. I know both of you are receptive to the spiritual so that will make things easier for you." She stopped to evaluate them a moment. "Have you had your lunch? Hettie can serve something here if you like."

Katie shook her head. "I think we're both too excited to eat right now."

Jeremy nodded. "Perhaps you can just fill us in on what's going on...."

The tiny woman nodded and settled back among the pillows overflowing from her sturdy chair, and lifted her small antique boots onto a footstool with a crewel-work cushion. She wore a high-necked lace blouse and cameo and a long black skirt, looking as Victorian as her grand house. "But first, perhaps, you can tell me who you are."

"Oh, of course." Katie was appalled that they hadn't done that first thing. "I'm Katie, Francine Chamberlain's granddaughter and this is Jeremy, the manager of *Radbourne Arabians.*" She considered Nealie. "I'm sure you know about *Radbourne?*"

"Certainly. No one could ever know Francine without knowing of her beloved *Radbourne.* Okay then, let me say how happy I am to meet you both. I didn't know who would show up at my house because I haven't been in touch with Francine for forty years." She suddenly leapt up and came to the couch, holding out her animated hands. "Let me take your coats. My manners have deserted me."

"I left our taxi in the street," Jeremy said when they had surrendered their wraps.

"Well, for goodness sake, you can tell it to go. I will see that you get wherever you need to go."

Jeremy rushed off down the stairs and Katie returned to her seat.

"What a lovely man, you have there, dear," Nealie remarked. "His father was a wonderful friend of mine and I knew Jeremy until he went to live with Francine. We lost his mother much too soon." Her eyes narrowed slightly. "But there're still a few obstacles you must put right between you." She gave her a rapturous smile before waving her hand in dismissal. "We can talk about that another time if you like."

Jeremy appeared and sank down beside Katie.

The jolly little woman was quiet for a few moments, then launched into her account. "I can't recall ever being without my Sight. Both my granny in Ireland and my ma had it and it goes back for centuries in the O'Rourkes. I've had my shingle out since I was twelve. Charles Foxworth was my neighbor as well as Francine Chamberlain."

Katie absorbed the reaffirmation of this information that her grandmother had told her. "Why was Francine living in Denver?"

"Spreading her wings a bit, I'd say. Her family evidently had great plans for her but she was quite rebellious and wished to spend some time on her own before she took up her life on the ranch. She'd already graduated from Wellesley and Charles was headed to Harvard. In any case, they fancied themselves in love. Turned out, of course, they weren't destined to be together but their parting was complicated by Francine's pregnancy."

Jeremy and Katie could do little but stare at

her silently.

Nealie nodded. "I know it is a shock. It was for them as well, particularly when Francine bore twin daughters. Both were very young and neither was altruistic enough to put their lives on hold and raise their daughters. They came to me for advice. I quickly became disenchanted with their self-serving attitude and told them to get a hold of themselves and take up their responsibility for their girls. But they would have none of it. They were planning to go East together and implored me to find a good home for Lena and Celia."

A shiver passed through Katie and she gripped the hand Jeremy offered. To hear the name Francine had spoken, had said could be a donor for Becca left her clamoring for solid ground among the fragmented images swirling through her brain.

"I became quite enraged with both of them and accused them of treating their babies like unwanted puppies that needed a home. But nothing I said dissuaded them. All they wanted was for me to clear the way for them to get on with their lives and in the end, I did as they said. I found caring people who loved the twins as their own. Charles and Francine went on their merry way to Massachusetts but the ordeal of the whole episode split them apart and as you know, they ended up marrying others. They did remain good friends and that's why you were sent to Francine when your father died," she added, addressing Jeremy.

He nodded without speaking, clearly unable to take in the enormity of what she had told them so far. "So I have two half-sisters?" he finally asked.

"Yes, you do. Before she went off on her

happy lark with Charles, Francine seemed to have second thoughts. I hoped she would change her mind and decide to raise the twins herself but in the end, she just made me swear that if I ever moved from this house, I would send her my address. I never had the slightest desire to leave my beautiful home so nearly half a century went by with me not once hearing from her. I knew that I would be contacted by someone when she died."

She gripped the arms of her chair with elegant, remarkably young-looking hands that had clearly seen little exposure to the sun. Her gaze held the disquieting green glow that was her most distinguishing feature. Her body abruptly jerked even while she continued to observe them. "Francine's death hit me like a physical blow. A little like being hit by lightning I expect, just a shock of energy that knocked me to my knees. I blacked out for a short time and came to lying there before the fireplace. I'm usually not affected with such force unless a death is violent but I had the same response as I felt when the Kennedys died. Perhaps in Francine's case, it was because I've been in a state of anticipation for so long. And since her passing, I've known you were coming. I had Hettie prepare the guest rooms." She smiled benevolently, picking up a small bell on her desk.

"I'm positively famished and you must be as well. I'll just have Hettie bring a tea tray." She tinkled the bell and soon the maid appeared at the top of the stairs.

Nealie dispatched her, then returned her attention to Jeremy. "You have a daughter who's in danger. She is very ill. Is that why you've come here?"

His tense shoulders relaxed and he inclined toward her. "Yes. She has leukemia and needs a bone marrow transplant. We've been unable to find a donor."

She nodded vigorously. "Yes, yes, the mix in her heritage is wrong...."

Still unaccustomed to her knowledge, they mutely absorbed her words.

"Francine told me just before she died that Lena could be a donor...." Katie said.

"And that's when you found my address?"

"That's right," Jeremy said.

Nealie moved closer, curiosity in her look. "Where did she put it?"

"Under the bed in a cabin she had built on the mountain above *Radbourne*."

"Oh, how inspired." She rolled her eyes. "Well, it's good that you both have a spiritual connection so you managed to unravel her clues despite their lack of finesse."

Hettie arrived with a tray holding a tea pot, cups, small sandwiches and cookies. Setting it on a table, she poured and served them plates of food.

Having learned that they were precisely where they were meant to be, Katie and Jeremy had relaxed and put their trust in the odd little woman who was clearly going to help them further. Now that some of their frantic bewilderment had resolved itself, they were both ravenous and ate the offered food with complete abandon.

Nealie watched them with delight while she delicately sipped her tea and nibbled on a cookie. What is your daughter's name?"

"Becca."

"She has a humorous dog who keeps close watch over her."

Katie nodded. "Jekyll, her service dog. We left him with our housekeeper."

"He's grieving, not understanding why she's not with him."

"Yes, he's totally devoted to her."

A companionable silence settled around them as they continued to eat and drink tea. Nealie seemed in no hurry to continue but after awhile, she rang the little bell again and Hettie came for the plundered tray.

"I gather that Francine was of the opinion that her twin daughters might be suitable donors for Becca."

"Yes." Jeremy said. "Do you know where they live?"

"I do. They actually live quite near." She stood up and headed toward the windows just past the sitting area. She settled on a settee, looking out at the lake, a frozen expanse beyond a stone retaining wall forming a barrier between the lake and the house..

Katie and Jeremy sat on a nearby upholstered bench.

"There is an island ten miles out into Lake Stanley," she said and that's where Lena and Celia's family reside."

Jeremy's brow furrowed with the same question that rocketed through Katie's mind. "Why on earth would they live there?"

"Because they love it," Nealie said. "They love the solitude most of the time but when they want to come to the city, it's a short commute. I visit often and it's one of the most gorgeous homes I've ever seen. The island is a couple miles across so they have horses and stables and a menagerie of other animals. And there's plenty of room for the extended family."

Katie was completely flummoxed and could see that Jeremy was in a similar state of incredulity. Something was off about what they were being told but she had no idea what it was. In spite of Nealie's calm explanation, she could think of no plausible reason for Francine's daughters to have lived at such a remote spot their entire lives.

"So they were adopted?" Jeremy inquired.

"Not officially but there were legal and binding provisions put in place."

"Do they have husbands and families?"

Nealie held them in her placid gaze. "No. I believe their abandonment by their mother had a rather profound effect on their psychological development. That's to be expected in such cases." She allowed them to ponder this for a time before she carried on.

"I can see that is all very perplexing for you. I think the best thing is for you to go to see them yourselves. I have a snowmobile you can use. The ice is plenty thick this time of year so it's perfectly safe."

Jeremy considered her with some relief. "That would be great. Can we go now? Can you tell us how to find the island....?"

"Certainly. But fog often moves in toward evening and hangs over the lake at night. It's better to wait until morning after it's burned off. Then there's no danger of getting lost out there."

Jeremy leaned back, frowning. "All right." He glanced at Katie. "We should go find a motel."

"No need for that," Nealie said. "As I mentioned earlier, we've been expecting you and Hettie's prepared the guest rooms. We would love you to stay here with us tonight, then my caretaker Ivan will guide you across the lake in the morning."

"We don't want to impose," Katie said.

Nealie gave a hearty laugh. "Oh, mercy no. I've been waiting for this for a very long time. It's terribly exciting to finally have Lena and Celia reunited with their blood family. They're going to be ecstatic to meet you and if they can help their sister, they will be positively over the moon.

"Now that we have that settled." She rose gracefully from her chair and stood looking out over the lake. "See what I mean about the fog? Already it's gathering."

They went to stand beside her, noting the change in the weather. The brilliant blue sky was tempered now by clouds, thickening across the ice..

"You must be bone tired and should have a nap before dinner. Come, I'll show you up." Nealie marched to the landing where another staircase led to a third story. She hurried ahead, her speed belying her age. "Here, we are." She grasped a brass knob and flung open the door to a wallpapered chamber made quaint by the angles created by a wide dormer window facing the lake.

She paused with her hand still on the knob. "There's another prepared room just there." She nodded across the wide hall. "But I'm sure this one will suffice," she added with a wink. "I shall ring my bell when dinner is served." Then she was off, fairly scurrying down the steps.

Katie looked at Jeremy and they both collapsed laughing onto the bed where they lay staring up at the ceiling, overcome by released tension and delight in Nealie. Jeremy turned his head toward her. "What the devil do you think we're going to find out in the middle of that lake?"

She rolled closer. "After what we've heard so far, it's hard to imagine."

He raised his hand to trace the side of her face, his eyes alight with joy. "Imagine, I have two sisters...."

"Incredible, isn't it?"

He moved his mouth the way one does when they're close to weeping but needing to cover the fact. "She made it sound like there's something not right about them." His tears ran down into the bedspread. "Like maybe they're mentally ill...."

"Honey, we don't know that. Let's just think that you have more family and they may be able to help Becca." She slid into the circle of his arms and kissed the wet from his face.

He held her tight and she snuggled her head beneath his chin, giving in to her drowsiness. They both slept until the faraway ringing of Nealie's bell brought them back to the darkening bedroom.

"Oh, God," Jeremy groaned, moving a little away from her, kissing her as he went. "I think we're being summoned...."

Katie got up and went into the bathroom to splash her face with cold water. She dared a quick glance in the mirror and saw she looked as bad as she felt, like she hadn't slept in weeks. Jeremy appeared behind her, combing his fingers through his tousled hair.

With a mutual grimace, they descended the stairs to find Nealie waiting for them at her desk. "Well, now that you've had a bit of rest, we'll have a nice dinner." She stepped past them to the staircase.

At the bottom, they walked toward the formal dining room they'd glimpsed when they arrived. "Your home is magnificent," she said as Jeremy seated her, then turned to hold Nealie's chair.

"Thank you so kindly. I was blessed to inherit it from my mother." She unfolded her napkin and spread it primly over her lap, then rested her chin in a delicate hand and slanted herself toward them. "My gran, of course, built this house when this area was first being developed. This was one of the first homes on Lake Stanley." She smiled. "It's always nice for later generations to inherit a home that has settled." She waved her hand airily. "That is my own term – you know it takes time, several years after people take up residence, before the trees and shrubs mature and a place settles into itself. Occasionally a spirit or two come to live and that's part of the settling also.

"Are any spirits residing here?" Jeremy asked drolly.

"Yes, I have Mr. Duncan in the attic. I've tried my best to help him move on but I'm afraid he's quite stuck. He was Gran's beau after my great grandparents died. They came here from Killibegs in Donegal when Gran was eleven. Sad story as they died in a wagon accident some five years hence, after they had built this house. Gran was an only child so she was left here with a houseful of servants. But she was a resourceful young woman who also had the Sight so she was soon a great success doing readings. Mr. Duncan came for that purpose and immediately fell hopelessly in love with her. She hadn't the same feeling for him but she did let him a room in the attic. He became so distraught over her rejection that he committed suicide on night with his Civil War revolver. He couldn't leave so his soul is still up there."

She looked up when Hettie arrived with dinner on a cart, everything snug under silver covers. "Oh, dearie, I quite thought you'd forgotten I quite thought you'd forgotten us," Nealie observed.

The maid ducked her head in apology. "Sorry. The chicken needed a bit more time in the oven." She served the prepared plates and set an ice bucket holding an opened bottle of wine on the table. She propped the tray nearby, then served Jeremy wine and waited for his approval.

He took a sip and lifted the glass with a nod. "Perfect."

She curtsied and moved on to fill Nealie's glass, then Katie's.

"Thank you, dearie," Nealie said, dismissing her with a brilliant smile. "Now back to Mr. Duncan for a moment. Don't let him frighten you if he should be on the prowl tonight. He gets bored sometimes and comes down from his room. I've told him countless times that most people don't enjoy his company but he persists." She pursed her lips in annoyance. "If you hear him on the stairs, don't give it a thought. He'll soon tire of his mischief and retire."

Katie considered the Mad Hatter aspect of the meal. If she hadn't recently had her own collision with a ghost and manifestation of her twenty-year-old nightmare, she would have probably been completely undone by Nealie's paranormal world.

As it was, the entire experience since they had arrived at the house, seemed perfectly normal and expected. Nothing more than the culmination of their peculiar journey since Francine's death. Observing Jeremy, she saw he was possessed of the same accepting composure.

"When can we leave in the morning?" he asked.

"Just as soon as the fog recedes. At least by seven I should think. I've already spoken to Ivan and he will be here first thing." She sat back and sipped her wine. "I am very thrilled for you. I know you're going to be pleased beyond measure when you meet your sisters after all these years. So do look toward it with happy anticipation."

When they had declined dessert and thanked Nealie, Katie and Jeremy excused themselves and headed to bed. They'd barely started toward the stairs when Jeremy turned back. "I need to call home. Is there a phone I can use. I'll pay for the calls, of course."

Nealie turned her head to grimace dramatically at Katie. "I will accept no payment but you may use the phone on my desk." Chuckling, she patted his arm as she swept out of the room.

Leaving Jeremy to make the calls, Katie went on to their bedroom. She moved to the window and looked out at Lake Stanley which was indeed shrouded by thick fog that gave the scene an eerie, supernatural look. Very appropriate.

She lingered there, staring into the winter night, her brain sorting through all that had happened today. A fierce optimism had settled around her. After the astonishing hours they'd spent with Nealie, she was convinced matters were now out of their control. Destiny had taken over and she had no doubt all was unfolding as it was meant to. Her worry faded into a sense of inevitability.

She lost track of time until Jeremy wrapped his arms around her from behind and Katie leaned her head back against his shoulder. "Maybe Mr. Duncan will come visit us tonight," he said.

She giggled. "Maybe. But it sounds like he's too shy for that."

"I'd like to ask him what it was like to fight in the Civil War."

"How's everything at home?"

"Excellent!" He turned her to face him. "Sweetheart, Becca's better."

Her eyes narrowed and tears sprang to her eyes. "Like how better?"

"Like she's responding to the chemo finally. Patrick said her white cell count has dropped dramatically."

"Oh, my gosh!" She laughed, all the time, hugging him, paying no mind to her tears. "Thank you, Jesus!"

He released her, chuckling as he watched her, then grabbed her again and kissed her passionately. At last, he pulled back to inspect her. "I'm so glad you're with me on this adventure."

"Me too."

"Oh, guess what, our bags are still in a closet downstairs where Hettie put them this afternoon. I'll go get them."

She watched him go on her way into the bathroom where she turned on the shower. When she emerged, she was grateful to discover he'd put her bag inside. She found a nightgown, then dried her hair.

When she slid into bed, Jeremy went to take a shower. She was asleep so quickly she had no memory of him joining her. If Mr. Duncan came to visit, she missed that as well.

They were both awake early the next morning and soon up and ready to leave. Once they'd ventured downstairs, they found Nealie waiting with coffee and hot cereal.

Shortly after they finished eating, Ivan, the caretaker arrived, a tall, stolid man with a bushy white beard. Katie was sure he must play Santa Claus every Christmas. After introductions, he handed them snowmobile suits. The one he wore was jumbo size. "Nealie thought you probably forgot to bring your own," he said with an affable grin.

"Thank you, Ivan," said Jeremy.

Shortly they were ready. Nealie, attired in Victorian garb similar to what she'd worn yesterday, had observed them closely all through breakfast. Now she came to embrace them. "Godspeed, my dears."

Squeezed in the tiny lady's arms, Katie felt her strength that did a lot to dispel her rising nerves.

"Thank you so much."

"We're burning daylight," Ivan said with a jovial tilt of his head covered with a ski mask. "Let us be off. Goodbye, my dear Nealie. I shall guard these two with my last breath."

"Oh, get on with you!" Nealie replied, herding them all toward a rear entrance.

Outside, two snowmobiles waited at the edge of the lake.

"Nealie said you two should go on one sled," Ivan said as they walked.

Katie said a silent thanks for Nealie's insight. She had never driven a snowmobile in her life and this was not the day to begin.

They were underway across the ice and soon lost sight of the shore. Now they headed into the blank void of sky and lake meeting. Ivan apparently had uncanny navigational skills in his head or else he was using a compass. They never veered from a straight path and perhaps ten minutes later, the shoreline came into hazy focus ahead. As they drew nearer, Katie made out the outline of a hulking stone building perched above the rock-strewn embankment rising from the lakeshore.

Without fanfare, Ivan pulled his machine onto a wide strip of beach and cut the engine. Jeremy followed suit and a deep silence came down around them. Katie couldn't recall ever experiencing such absolute quiet with no traffic or voices or even wind.

They followed Ivan up a flight of stone stairs negotiated the steep incline, ending at a slate patio wrapping around the entire rear of the huge house.

They soon stood before sliding glass doors and Ivan rang a bell.

Katie's heart had begun beating frantically when the complex came into view and now it seemed like the others could surely hear the raucous pounding. She gripped Jeremy's hand and dared look at him. His acute anxiety was evident in his tense and pale features. He met her gaze and managed a faltering smile as he squeezed her gloved fingers.

A tall figure appeared inside and slid open the glass door. "Ivan, good morning." A dark- haired woman stepped forward to embrace him. "Come in."

"Please meet my good friend, Alexis," Ivan said.

As he made further introductions, Katie studied Alexis, slender in jeans, her brunette hair cut in a stylish bob. "So nice to meet you."

Her huge brown eyes brimmed with mischief. "I'm just so excited to have you two here at last. And the girls are beside themselves." A slight frown surfaced. "That's what we've always called them. They were girls when they came to live with my parents but that's certainly not the case now. In any case, we mustn't keep them waiting."

"I gather Nealie's been in touch on the radio," Ivan said as Alexis ushered them through a room as large as some people's houses.

Shafts of sunshine spilled through skylights in the beamed cathedral ceiling, puddling at intervals on the tiled floor where an assortment of dogs and cats slumbered on Navajo rugs. An outsized dream catcher centered the floor-to-ceiling frosted glass fronting the magnificent chamber. In spite of its size, the entire room exuded warmth and comfort.

As they continued, Katie glimpsed massive bookshelves and an entertainment center that took up a good portion of a rear wall. Three people sat on a wraparound sectional couch overflowing with a motley variety of big pillows.

Two slim women of perhaps forty sat so close together they appeared at first to be one.... Katie faltered to a stop, gripping Jeremy's hands with all her strength. Shock shot through her body like a sudden change in temperature. She felt Jeremy stiffen next to her.

"Come, girls," Alexis urged. "They're here! This is your half-brother Jeremy, and your niece Katie."

The two women shot up from the sofa and launched themselves toward them, both faces filled with pure delight. They paused a second to study Jeremy then caught him in an rapturous hug.

Katie was flummoxed to the point of faintness. Panic throbbed in her chest. If she didn't sit, she was going to pass out. She veered to the couch and sank onto it, gasping for breath.

Alexis stood nearby, shooting concerned glances at her even as she watched the blissful meeting of the twins and the brother they'd never seen. After an uncertain span of minutes, Jeremy led the women to the couch where they sat beside Katie. All three were weeping and Katie struggled with the urge to join them.

In the interim when they weren't paying any attention to her, Katie observed the narrow, pretty faces, so like Jeremy's. They shared the same olive skin and pewter gray eyes as well as brown hair burnished with gold. There was no doubt they shared the same blood.

She forced her eyes lower, seeing what her mind had denied until that moment. They were twins – conjoined twins. A thousand questions were answered with that knowledge.

Abruptly aware of her scrutiny, they clamored over Jeremy, coming to wrap her in their arms. Two arms, one belonging to each of them. She continued studying them until she realized she was staring. "I'm sorry. I'm being very rude...."

"We're used to that," the one on the left said. She shrugged her arm, grinning. "After all, people are curious. If I were in their place or your place, I'd be too." She smiled. "We've been staring too. At you. You're gorgeous."She leaned in to kiss her cheek. "I'm Lena. Hello, Aunt Katie."

"I'm Celia," the other said, beaming. "I'm so glad you're finally here. We've be waiting so long."

Katie felt an unnamed tugging in her soul. She enfolded them close. Presently, they stepped back as Alexis took up her role as hostess again. She beckoned at two young girls who'd stopped reading to take in the proceedings. They were maybe ten and twelve and quickly came to stand beside the others. "Here are my own girls, Gwen and Patty. My husband Dan is in the barn but will join us very soon."

The girls responded politely to their mother's introductions, each mirroring her eager smile. Gwen soon edged closer Celia, hooking arms and laying her head on hers. Soon Patty did the same with Lena, the four standing in a haphazard line, obviously loving being close to each other. Katie marveled at the infectious goodwill that seemed to permeate the whole house.

"Now, let's all sit down so we can learn something about each other," Alexis suggested, herding everyone toward the sofa.

Katie and Jeremy ended up sitting on a settee opposite the others.

Lena laughed, appearing unable to contain her pleasure at seeing her brother. "You are so handsome," she said. "You're a lucky lady, Katie."

"I know," she agreed. "And you two are beautiful. It's not hard to see that you all have the same father."

"Who was our father?" Celia asked. "Alexis told us your grandmother is our mother but we don't know who our father is."

"He was also my father," Jeremy interjected, then attempted to explain their family tree.

"It's just so cool that we're all together now." Lena smiled, reaching across Patty to squeeze Alexis's hand.

Alexis slid forward a little on the couch. "I think Jeremy and Katie might appreciate knowing a little about you two."

"Like how we're put together and that kind of thing?" Lena inquired with a teasing tilt of an eyebrow. "Yes, that and whatever else they'd like to know." She looked back at Jeremy and Katie. "I think you should know we're very open and honest about everything. We've found it's the best way. The twins know that their mother just wasn't able to deal with raising them herself so she made it possible for them to have the best possible life here."

"Don't waste any time pitying us," Celia said. "We are the luckiest twins that ever lived!"

"Tell us why that is," Jeremy urged.

Lena gestured around the huge room with her hand. "Look at the fabulous house we have. We've had every advantage in our education, all the latest resources in electronics. And a brilliant teacher who's provided us both with the equivalent of two Ph.Ds. Our technology is a bit limited out here but we've had computers for as long as they existed for the general public. We've had all the books we've ever wanted and kept every one so we now have a really extensive library."

"We've also spent days and days in galleries and museums in Denver and Chicago and New York City and Washington, D.C.," Celia added. "And traveled to London, Paris and Rome."

"How splendid," Katie said.

"What do you do for fun?" Jeremy wanted to know.

"We have horses and all these pets." Celia indicated the menagerie still sleeping all over the room. "And we *love* movies. Ivan brings us all the tapes as soon as they're out. Sometimes, we go to theatres just for the fun of it."

"Do you ride English or Western?" Jeremy asked.

Lena gave him a sidelong look. "English, of course. It's so much more elegant."

He stood and in one stride went to slap her hand. "Your mother is ecstatic wherever she's looking down from!"

She and her sister shared a silly laugh, clearly

enraptured by their dashing brother.

"Now we'll tell you how we're put together," Celia said and they both stood up for inspection. "The most astonishing thing about us, is that we are two different people with two brains and two personalities. That said, we are identical which means we came from one egg that divided.

"We have two hearts, two spines, four lungs, two esophagi," Lena carried on, saying the word again. "Esophagi, say *that* a dozen times really fast." Glimmers of humor surfaced in her gray eyes. "So continuing on, we have three kidneys, one ribcage, one liver and we share everything from the waist down. And that's what Lena and Celia Foxworth are made of." They gave a grand bow.

Alexis clapped and the rest followed suit.

"Thanks so much for telling us," Jeremy said.

"May I take everyone's picture?" Katie asked, going for her camera bag lying with their outer wear that had been neatly laid over the end of a bench.

"Yes!" the twins said in unison. "Alexis said you are a professional photographer," Lena added. "Do you photograph celebrities?"

"Not very often."

Alexis had herded everyone into a group with Lena and Celia in front. "Ah," she said, "here's Dan. Come on, dear, get in our picture."

A tall blonde man strode in from a rear hall. "I see our guests have arrived. Hello, everyone." He put an arm around Alexis and they stood together at the rear of the group.

When Katie had taken several shots, Dan took her camera so she could be included. Then Alexis and Patty went to bring hot chocolate from the kitchen.

Lena and Celia settled themselves in the curve of Jeremy's arm as everyone sat again.

"So Dan, what breed of horses do you have here?" Jeremy asked.

"Thoroughbreds. We do a lot of jumping and dressage. All the girls would love to show but we haven't tried that yet. We may get to that this summer." He smiled wryly. "Getting those huge beasts to a show from here isn't as simple as loading them in a trailer."

"How did you get them here?"

"By boat but they were weanlings at the time."

"We just need a bigger boat," Lena said.

Ivan came from the kitchen with mugs of hot chocolate on a tray. Alexis followed with cookies. With a wink, Ivan stepped to a nearby hutch and came back with a bottle of bourbon that he added to everyone's cup except for the younger girls.

Lena raised her mug. "To finding our brother at last." She tapped his cup, then leaned up to kiss him.

"And our aunt Katie," Celia said, raising her drink.

As the others drank their own toasts, Katie tried to decide how old the twins were. From her hazy knowledge of when her own mother was born, she finally deduced they must be in their early forties.

Since meeting them, her initial shock had quickly given way to respect for their gutsy acceptance of who they were. She recalled the forthright way they had spoken about themselves earlier. There was so much more she wanted to know about them but one thing was certain, though Francine had essentially abandoned them, she'd made sure they were raised by caring people who'd given them a remarkable life.

After an hour when Lena and Celia insisted on hearing everything about *Radbourne,* Alexis and Dan wanted to know exactly why they were there after nearly half a century with no word from any family.

"We knew nothing about you until a few days ago," Jeremy said, then went on to recount the circuitous saga that had brought them to this house in the middle of Lake Stanley.

"And your daughter Becca has ALL," Celia ventured. "Acute lymphoblastic leukemia. Alexis told us and said maybe we can donate bone marrow for her."

Jeremy looked into their concerned faces. "The thing is, we're running out of option. We've been searching for a donor match for weeks now but haven't found one."

The twins threw out their hands in a shrug. "We're her aunts so I bet we're a match," Lena said. "When can we get tested?"

He grinned. "Right away.."

That afternoon, Katie sat in a waiting area at Denver Health Medical Center. Jeremy accompanied Lena and Celia to the lab to have their blood drawn. It had started snowing earlier and now Katie walked to the bank of windows fronting the room and stood watching the flakes swirling in the streetlights below.

Her eyes settled on an enormous lighted star

attached to some towering building somewhere far beyond the hospital parking lot. Outlined in gold, the star stood stalwart watch in the winter night, apparently a forgotten Christmas decoration or else one that was just left up all year because it was less trouble.

Christmas. She hugged herself. How had Christmas come and gone without her even noticing? No mystery there. Jeremy had been at the hospital in Billings for over a month. It was the first week in January when Francine died and now another week was nearly past.

When she stopped to really think about the rapid passage of time, she felt slightly disoriented. Events had come so fast that she hadn't been able to fully consider each one before the next was upon her. She was certain Jeremy was caught in the same time warp.

Even as her thoughts turned to Jeremy, she was aware of a disquiet far back in her mind. She hadn't had the opportunity to closely examine this constant perception of something off kilter, or perhaps she'd just avoided thinking about it in detail. It likely had its roots in the same old conflict between them, his inability to leave the past behind.

Even during the headlong rush of recent days, he had found time to visit Evelyn. On one hand, she could understand his need to share his grief and worry with Becca's mother. On the other, there was still the reality that Evelyn was far beyond understanding anything he might tell her.

She knew the matter must be sorted out but that would have to wait until a later date. Now all she could deal with was Becca and the jolting discovery of Jeremy's sisters. Her brain still hadn't gotten up to speed on that.

The twins were nothing short of a miracle in every sense of the word. The supernatural path, she and Jeremy had followed to reach them left no doubt in Katie that their bone marrow would be a match for Becca. Earlier while the twins and Dan had taken Jeremy to the barn to see their Thoroughbreds, Alexis had used the time alone with Katie to further educate her about conjoined twins, the Foxworth ladies to be specific. It seems Lena and Celia were among the rarest such births in the world. Conjoined twins occur once in every 200,000 births. The chance of them surviving was one in a million. To be so well-adjusted and high-functioning was virtually unheard of.

Alexis further explained that a trust had been set up for the babies' care within six months of their birth, funded in equal parts by Charles Foxworth and Francine. Over the ensuing years, the money doubled and tripled so there was always an unlimited supply to pay for everything that gave the twins access to the world. Despite the astronomical price tag, they had computer technology from the time they were twenty years old and actually became computer savvy to the point of being qualified to serve as consultants to developing technology companies.

"No wonder they think they're the luckiest women in the world," Katie marveled.

"It's true, all made possible with money paid to assuage guilt."

Katie considered the words. "Did Charles ever consider raising them himself?"

"Not as far as I know. He'd met Jeremy's mother in the interim after Francine found out she was pregnant and then when the twins were born, they were both freaking out to put it in modern terms. Francine's father died about the same time so she inherited *Radbourne* and was much too eager to begin importing her Arabian horses to care to deal with her inconvenient daughters. I've had to remind myself often over the years what the culture was like in 1962. Otherwise I can get very disillusioned when I think of Francine just turning her back on her newborn twins. But considering how the world was then, I *can* understand why she did it. Segregation was still status quo and she probably remembered the nightmare of Eugenics where anyone with physical and mental disabilities could be sterilized. When she first saw her twins, she was probably staggered to her soul and because of her own reaction, she no doubt knew they would be considered a monster or a girl with two heads. I'm quite sure that in her shoes in 1962, I would have wanted nothing so much as to shield them from the world's cruelty. So I can't say I wouldn't have done exactly as she did.

"I have no doubt Jesus was guiding her through the entire ordeal because without his help, I doubt she would've found caretakers like my parents who devoted their very lives to nurturing those tiny children. They never saw their limitations but only their capabilities to learn and love. Lena and Celia were their fulltime job and the girls truly blossomed in their care. I was two years old when we came to live here so they were my sisters, all of us growing up together. Needless to say, I accepted them completely as two more members of our family, never questioning the unique way they were put together. We were all homeschooled here and it was only when we started going on field trips to Denver when they were eight that I had to deal with the way others saw them.

"But no matter how people stared or made comments, my parents never reacted in any way. They just ignored it all unless confronted directly and then they answered questions as simply as possible and soon the girls were dealing with the unwanted attention themselves. With complete aplomb," I might add."

She smiled at Katie. "While it was happening, I never paid any attention to the way they learned to function as one. But looking back on it, I see how remarkable it is that they could communicate and coordinate their two separate bodies. When I started swimming and dancing and riding horses, they were right there with me, never turning from a challenge.

"Were they under a doctor's care?" Katie asked.

Alexis nodded. "Dr. Pride in Denver delivered them and he was enthralled with them from the start. While my parents were grappling with the question of how to deal with the public's reaction he offered to come out here regularly to handle their vaccinations and routine care. By the times they were teens, they handled the public with ease and started visiting a clinic in Denver and they still go there today."

"Was dating and the rest of it just never an option for them?"

"Not in their world at the time. If they were babies today, I'd say there would be no limit to their experiences." She shrugged. "It would have just been too hard back then and their lives were so full, it just never seemed to be something they considered. Not that they don't love romantic movies and novels."

When the others returned from their tour of the barn, Katie and Alexis' talk had ended. Now Katie turned from the waiting area windows and sat on a sofa, glancing at her watch. They had been at the hospital for nearly two hours.

Her impatience had become palpable now and she couldn't stand sitting there a moment longer. She hadn't been allowed in the lab waiting room because she wasn't a part of the twins' immediate family and that started to annoy her.

She decided what she needed most was to move so set out along the hall outside, walking at a brisk pace in an effort to banish her tension. She'd made four circuits of the immediate area when she spotted Jeremy and the twins approaching. She jogged toward them and was nearly knocked over when the women ran into her arms.

"We're a match!" Lena said, and they both pulled Jeremy and Katie into an ecstatic little jig.

"Isn't that just the best?" Celia asked, her eyes finding Katie's"

"I can think of nothing better," Katie agreed. She shifted enough to wrap one arm around Jeremy. "Now, Becca can get well."

He moved his face to kiss her. "God, I can't believe it...."

"Believe it, hon."

"We can be the reason she gets better," Lena declared. "How amazing is that?"

"It's way past amazing," Jeremy said and buried his face in Katie's neck, weeping.

Celia and Lena disengaged themselves and stood happily observing their brother while he got himself together. "We're going to take you to dinner now," Lena announced.

Jeremy inspected them. "I have a better idea. Why don't I take us to dinner?"

They both shook their heads. "No, no," Lena replied. "I've got it covered. We just have to find a good place." They immediately headed off toward the elevators.

They soon found an Italian eatery near the front entrance to the hospital. Seated in a booth, they surveyed menus. "Lasagna," Celia announced.

"Risotto," said Lena. "And salad."

"No salad." This from Celia.

Katie watched the exchange, fascinated by their give and take and final arrival at a decision mutually satisfactory.

"When do we give our bone marrow?" Lena asked when they had all ordered.

"We'll know more tomorrow after I talk to Becca's doctor." Jeremy raised his hand to flag down a bar maid. "Who wants a drink? Or should we have a bottle of wine?"

The consensus was for wine and the girl hurried off.

"But we'll go to Billings for the transplant?" Lena asked, moving the conversation back on track.

"Yes."

They settled back contentedly. "So we can go

to *Radbourne?"* Celia wanted to know.

"Of course."

CHAPTER NINETEEN

After dinner, they returned to Stanley Island to spend the night. They'd opted to rent hotel rooms but the twins wanted none of that and insisted that they come home with them.

As soon as they arrived, Jeremy phoned Dr. Cusack to tell him that donor bone marrow had been found. He explained the familial connection.

"Ah, Jeremy, that is positively stellar news. And, I must say, Becca is now responding so well to the chemo, I should think she can have the transplant sometime in the next two weeks."

"That's wonderful."

"Yes, indeed. We have to do some procedures in preparation. And we'll need the donor here ASAP as she too will undergo a battery of tests...."

"Actually, there are two donors in one body. The women are conjoined twins...."

There was silence on the line.

"Did you hear what I said?"

"Yes, yes I did. I was just thinking a moment. This is no problem," he added hurriedly, "but all the more reason we need the ladies in here soon."

"We can be there tomorrow."

"Excellent."

Jeremy hung up the receiver and scanned the expectant faces around him. Alexis, Dan, Katie, Lena and Celine waited.

"All systems are go." He clasped his sisters' hands. "We need to fly to Billing tomorrow because they need to do tests before the transplant."

Celia's face tensed. "They won't find something that keeps us from being donors, will they?"

"Celia, our little worrier," Alexis said.

Jeremy bent to kiss Celia's cheek. "I have every confidence that you two will be perfect donors. Let's have a little faith, huh?"

Celia ducked her head, glancing at Alexis, a bit embarrassed. "I do, I will....but I do worry sometimes."

"*All* the time," Lena groaned.

"No more worrying." Jeremy wagged his finger at them.

"We have to go straight to the hospital?" Lena asked. "We can't stop at *Radbourne* first?"

"Honey, the priority right now is getting Becca well," Alexis said, placing her arm around them.

"There'll be lots of time to see *Radbourne*," Katie said. "You two can come stay as long as you like."

"Can we ride an Arabian?"

"That's what we do at *Radbourne*," Jeremy said. "Now we'll see when we're going to Billings." He picked up the phone to call the airport.

They were underway back across the ice on snowmobiles as soon as the sun cleared the lake of the usual fog the next morning. The twins rode behind Ivan with an ease that indicated how familiar the commute had become to them. Their flight to Billings didn't leave until noon but they had left early so they could spend some time with Nealie before they went to the airport. They had kept her abreast of developments by phone but Katie was looking forward to seeing her again.

Upon reaching the beach in front of Nealie's house, Ivan bestowed a bear hug to each of them and kissed the twins. "May God be with you all. Go on with you now. I'll see to the sleds."

"Thanks, Ivan." Jeremy shook his hand. "For all you help."

"That's what I do," he said with a grin.

Celia and Lena had followed Katie toward the rear entrance but suddenly stopped and hurried back to Ivan. He gathered them close, seeing their tears. "What's all this?" He inspected them.

"I'm scared," Celia admitted. "What if something goes wrong?"

"That does happen sometimes," he allowed, rubbing his whiskers with a mittened hand. "But I feel very confident it won't in this case."

Lena was fidgeting, clearly impatient for her sister to pull herself together so they could get on with it. "That's what a told her, a dozen times."

Ivan chuckled and squeezed her shoulder. "We know nothing scares you. But your sister is a bit more cautious. Nothing wrong with that. But this is important business you're doing now. Since there's no way, one of you can do something without the other, you know there are times when you just have to buck up and forge ahead on faith if nothing else." He chucked Celia under the chin. "Got it?"

She nodded and gave him a meager smile.

"Good. Now that we have that settled, don't keep your brother and Katie waiting. "You have people to see and places to go."

They both giggled and traipsed on to join Jeremy and Katie as they neared the house.

The door flew up and Nealie stood with her arms spread in greeting. "My guests have returned. How lovely! Come in." She embraced the twins and led the way to the dining room where Hettie had set out breakfast.

Muffins fresh from the oven, sausage and coffee smelled delicious. They were all starving after their trek across the lake in the cold so everyone tucked into the food with relish.

Nealie had plenty to say to the twins about the course they were on to help their newfound niece. "You must be so excited you can scarcely stand it."

"I am!" Lena agreed. "I think Celia's getting cold feet."

"No, I'm not! I was just a little nervous but I'm fine now." She smiled at Nealie. "I'd never let Becca down."

Nealie squeezed her hand. "Of course, you wouldn't but that doesn't mean it's not normal for you to be frightened. Anyone with any sense would be."

"Except me," Lena couldn't resist saying.

Nealie frowned at her. "Yes, but you are just our freewheeling girl with more guts than good sense."

"True enough," Lena agreed amiably. "But maybe if it wasn't for me, we couldn't do all the things we do. Maybe we'd just be a big lump and have to be hauled around in a wagon."

"You paint a compelling image," Nealie said drily. Katie curbed her desire to laugh at Lena's irreverence. Clearly she was the dominant twin in more ways than her head and trunk forming the central column of their shared body while Celia's head and arm appeared more as an appendage.

One reality was clear to Katie, the two were a miracle of humanity. She felt more and more privileged as she learned the scope of their personalities and abilities. She felt a huge sorrow that Francine had chosen to never know what delightful people her oldest daughters were.

When breakfast was finished, Nealie asked Katie to go upstairs with her. Katie had no idea what she wanted but she welcomed the chance to talk with her alone.

Jeremy and the twins settled in a sitting area to watch *Regis and Kathy Lee*. Katie followed Nealie to her bedroom. upstairs.

Seated at her desk, Nealie appraised Katie. "Now that you've had the opportunity to interact with Lena and Celia, what do you think?"

"I've seldom known more beautiful, engaging women. They boggle the mind."

"They do that." She picked up a small, framed picture from the desk, looking at it intently. "Did you notice how delicate and perfect their limbs are?"

"I did. Any woman would be happy with long, slender legs like theirs."

"Indeed. Perhaps what I marvel at most is how much they cherish each other. Lena has always been the leader and quite fearless. When they were about seven or eight, she decided they should be separated surgically. That was never a realistic possibility but naughty girl that she was, she tormented poor Celia with the idea for a year or two. Celia was just sick with worry despite the rest of us assuring her such a thing would never happen.

"Yet, Lena persisted until Susan...Susan and George Evers are Alexis' parents who originally cared for the twins...finally took Lena to task for her behavior. She told her plainly that she was to stop scaring her sister, and for good measure, she gave her hair a good yank that made her cry. That was Susan's means of discipline when either of them misbehaved. In this instance, Celia cried because Susan had pulled Lena's hair and made *her* cry. In any case, the incident made a lasting impression, and Lena's never brought up separation again."

"Did they have therapy of some kind to teach them coordination? They are so comfortable and move in perfect concert."

"That all came naturally. Susan and George showed them how to do something, like riding a horse, and they took it from there. They learned to ride a tricycle when they were five and they still ride a bicycle. They can drive a car if they ever decide to live somewhere other than their island. Ivan towed one of those cars little kids drive over here on a small barge he built, and taught them how to drive it."

"They're really excited about seeing *Radbourne* and the Arabians. Do you think they would ever want to live there?"

Nealie pondered the idea. "They've lived on the island since they were born and there's much about it they love. But they've been far from sheltered from the world and have traveled quite a lot. They're actually very sophisticated and endlessly curious. At the very least, I think they will want to live at *Radbourne* a portion of the year. This is heady stuff they're dealing with. A brother who looks like that superb British movie star, Jeremy Irons, and an aunt who's stunningly beautiful, both of whom treat them like royalty. And access to a couple hundred gorgeous Arabian horses. I should think staying on the island would look pretty boring in comparison. At least until some of the magic has worn off."

They both fell silent, Katie thinking about all Nealie had said.

"You're probably wondering why I asked to see you alone," she said presently, granting Katie a blithe smile. "You have been very much in my mind since you showed up the other day. That's how it is with me. My psychic insights settle *in* my mind. As soon as I set eyes on you, I was aware of turmoil. Aside from this avalanche of events that you've become buried in recently, I'm speaking of some unfinished business that has pursued you for some months now." She sat still and Katie waited for her to go on. "I see that you were pulled to *Radbourne,* back to your beginnings by something dark and dangerous."

Her eyes took on a remoteness that deepened the green. Tension drifted over the well-bred planes of her ancient features as she seemed to be wrestling with some unspoken mystery.

Abruptly, the perplexity eased and she smiled. "You were brave and faced down an evil force, defeated it. That was an extraordinary feat. You freed yourself from something that had held you captive for years. "Well, done!"

Katie felt like she was being praised for a good report card. She found Nealie immensely entertaining. She suddenly wished her grandmother could have known her.

"I can't seem to figure out exactly what the force was that followed me from *Radbourne.*"

Nealie sat quietly, evidently gathering data from wherever her source of inspiration was. "An evil spirit attached itself to your subconscious the night you killed your mother. You must understand there are multitudes of malevolent beings on the other side, just waiting for some means to become part of earthly souls. In the New Testament, Jesus and his disciples recount many occasions when they exorcised these demons from people."

Katie sat staring at her blankly. "I had *that* kind of thing going on?"

"Yes," Nealie replied with total calm. "You were a perfect target because you were completely vulnerable. If someone had been knowledgeable enough to bring you to me or someone else with my abilities, you would've been spared all those years of suffering. I could have removed the spirit right away."

"How would you have done that?"

"The same way you and your grandfather did in the end. You had gained tremendous strength in the months before the final confrontation. You and your grandfather's spirit simply overpowered it."

Katie felt the same keen triumph that had

filled her the night in the library when the terror had been banished.

"Yes," Nealie said, reading the drift of her thoughts, "you should be proud.. It takes a great deal of self-awareness to accomplish what you did."

Katie waited for her to continue.

"There's another dilemma now in your life," Nealie said after a little span of silence. "On one level, you're enjoying a splendid relationship with Jeremy. Whereas there is an insurmountable obstacle on the other." She squinted in concentration. "The word insurmountable is Jeremy's term, not mine....She brightened as though the sun suddenly shone on her face and clapped her hands in delight before growing sober again.. "I knew the moment I met you both that something very near your heart was troubling you. I didn't see this other connection to Jeremy until just now."

Katie was jolted by her discernment. She started to speak but Nealie's upraised hand silenced her.

"There's another woman who is the obstacle." Her eyes met Katie's. "There's serious illness...."

Katie waited for her to put the last piece together.

"Jeremy has a wife who is very ill."

Katie laughed in spite of herself. "Good heavens, you're amazing."

Nealie merely appraised her for a time. "I already told you I have the gift of my mother and my gran."

"I see now why you've had such success with that."

"I was never given any choice in the matter.

My sight was bestowed upon me in the same way as the color of my hair and the number of years I will live on this earth."

"Do you have a daughter with the same sight?"

"Unfortunately, no. I was never blessed with a man to love. In my humanness, I couldn't accept that for too many years. I raged at God for this lack. But eventually, I came to see that I was given a gift to enable me to help all the people who sought me out. That was my calling and I couldn't have fully devoted my life and heart to it if I'd also been given love and a family." A hint of sadness crept into her voice. "So the sight that has been nourished and protected by the women in my family will end with me."

"Don't you regret that?"

"It's the way it was ordained. I've never had any say in the matter."

Katie marveled at her grace.

"Now I must finish what I brought you up here to tell you. You mustn't settle for what Jeremy has decided he can give you. He's a very loyal man as well as stubborn. He thinks he can't break the bond with his wife. But the truth of the matter is that he's deluding himself.

"He's being selfish and it's up to you to change his mind. He adores you and will be unable to live without you. So you must force him to see that. You will find a way. You have no idea how angry you are with him. When the time is right, you will show it. That is what I wished to tell you. Jeremy is an old soul with compassion and ethics. He is all you believed he was when you fell in love.

But before you commit your life to his, he must be free." Her gaze hardened. "See to it that he is."

Katie stared at her, speechless.

"The way will be laid for you and you will find the strength and the words," Nealie assured her. "Now, I must let you go. You all have a hard span of days ahead. Please keep in touch and kiss dear Becca for me." She rose and bent to drop a kiss on Katie's forehead. "Come now, you have a flight to catch and you can use that time to think over what I've said."

She lead the way downstairs where they found Jeremy and the twins asleep and the television still on. They all came awake when they entered the sitting room.

"It's time for you to be off," Nealie said briskly. "I hate to see you go but I know you must."

They put on their coats and gathered at the front door to say their goodbyes to the astonishing little Irish woman who's heart was as big as her Gift.

Sometime later, Katie woke from a nap. She took in her surroundings. Jeremy sat next to her on the commuter plane. Across the aisle, Lena and Celia were entranced, peering out the window.

When they had picked up their tickets, she and Jeremy had learned one more rule governing the twins' life. Jeremy had handed them one ticket and been told by Lena in no uncertain terms that they were two people and always got two tickets for whatever they set out to do – see a movie, a concert, attend the opera...

Jeremy had quickly returned to the counter

and remedied the situation by purchasing another ticket. As they made their way to their gate, Katie wondered anew at the women's refusal to compromise their principles. She knew few other women would stand up for themselves at the risk of making a scene. Hurrying to catch up with the twins, she gave them a quick hug of approval.

Jeremy had fallen asleep again. She realized the past days had taken their toll, exhausting him. She situated a travel pillow against his shoulder and cuddled close. Her mind slid back to her time with Nealie.

She'd had scant previous experience with psychics, little more than a gypsy at a renaissance festival back when she was a teen. That bejeweled woman clearly had no legitimate power to commune with the spirit world and some of Katie's rowdier friends had threatened to come back and egg her wagon. The woman had threatened to put a hex on them.

Nealie's insight had been the real thing, Katie had no doubt. The woman clearly had a direct line to the supernatural. Katie believed what she told her about Jeremy's stubborn tie to Evelyn. What she didn't know was if she had the fortitude to settle for nothing less than Jeremy unencumbered.

Patrick met their plane. Jeremy had told him about Lena and Celia so he was well prepared. "Hi, Lena, Hello, Celia," he said when they had deplaned. He gave each a kiss on the cheek. "I'm so happy to meet you. Becca's going to be pumped. Ever since I told her you were coming, you're all she's talked about." He turned to greet Jeremy and

Katie, then led the way to the parking lot and the Honda.

The twins seemed a bit dazed by the effusive welcome and were very quiet while they joined him in the front seat. They finally regained their composure as he left the airport and sped along the Interstate.

"So how is Becca today?" Lena asked.

"She's great. Now that the chemo is working, she's almost in remission."

"She has to be in remission before the transplant," Celia said. "And she also needs to have empty bone marrow."

"Tell us about that," Jeremy urged from the backseat.

"That's another purpose of the intensive chemo. It's called ablative therapy because of the effect on the bone marrow."

"Bone marrow produces most of the blood cells in the body," said Lena. "Ablative therapy prevents this process of cell production and the marrow becomes empty."

"An empty marrow makes room for the new stem cells we'll give Becca in the transplant," Celia volunteered.

Patrick craned his neck to look at them. "How do you know that?"

"We have a medical degree."

"No kidding." He shook his head in wonder. "I'm impressed."

"We might become GPs and go into practice," Celia said.

"Or not," Lena said.

When they reached the oncology unit, the

twins were placed in a sterile room because the prevention of infection was so critical. Not being able to see Becca right away dampened their spirits. Yet, because of their medical training, they knew what to expect so were very accepting of what lay ahead. Even Celia appeared to have put her fear to rest.

"We'll be back in awhile," Katie said before they parted.

"Thank you, my man, for taking care of Becca so we could have the time to find her those amazing donors," Jeremy said, hugging Patrick with one arm as they headed along the hall toward the elevator.

"Now *that* was some coup!" Patrick said. "Gives one a new appreciation for the power of prayer. I don't know about you but I've been talking to God pretty much nonstop since I got here. I think he understands that we just couldn't ever let her go."

"He got the message," Jeremy said, "and led us to my remarkable sisters."

"Francine was something to pull that off." Patrick could only shake his head. "I knew she was a formidable lady but I'd have never thought in a million years, she could turn her back on her own children. That takes some kind of cheek."

"She did with me," Katie interjected.

Patrick put his arm around her. "I've never been able to wrap my head around that either."

"I think she was totally self-absorbed at the time," Jeremy said. "My dad had already made it clear that he didn't want to marry her, and she was faced with the twins' that just rocked her world.

Conjoined twins were considered a true abomination of nature at that time. They were the kind of thing that usually ended up in circus freak shows because the parents couldn't deal with them. It's little wonder she just couldn't take them on."

"When I first came here, I would've been the first to condemn her but not anymore," Katie said.

"But for the grace of God...." Patrick added.

"Amen."

They stopped in a waiting area and bought lukewarm coffee from a machine.

"Thanks again for helping us out with Becca," Jeremy said.

"Believe me, it was my pleasure." Patrick rested his elbows on his knees, staring at the floor. "I can't tell you how worried I was. I was sweating blood." He glanced up. "This thing is really going to turn out okay, isn't it?"

"Definitely, yes," Katie declared..

"We'll be here now," Jeremy said. "Probably until after the transplant at least. You should get back to *Radbourne*."

He drained his coffee with a grimace. "Great stuff, huh?" He got to his feet. "I already said goodbye to Becca before I left for the airport. She's pumped. I think she'd going to break all records for recovery after the transplant."

"I agree!" Katie threw her arms around him. "Thanks so much for coming here and taking care of her." He hugged her, laughing, drawing Jeremy into their embrace. "I love you guys. Give Becca my love and tell her I'll be back Sunday to check up on her. Is there anything else I can do? When I get home?"

"You've already helped us more than I can ever repay. You're the best, buddy." Jerry shook his hand. "Thank you."

"You could check on Jekyll," Katie said. "I'm sure he's fine with Pearl but he'd love it if you took him out for a run while you're riding."

"I'll do that. Be sure to tell Becca I'm going to keep him with me. Maybe I'll bring him with me when I come back Sunday. I know he can't be with Becca but I think he'll really like the ride."

"He will. Thanks for one more thing." She stood on tiptoe to kiss his cheek.

They walked him to the elevator, then went in search of someone who could tell them when they could see Becca. Within half an hour, they were garbed in sterile clothing and ushered into her room.

Except for her totally bald head, she looked like her old self again, sitting cross-legged on the bed. A chemo I.V. line looped down from a stand and disappeared under a loose t-shirt.

Her eyes lit with joy when she saw them.

"How are you?" Katie asked, encircling her in her arms.

"I'm getting better! Dr. Cusack says my cancer cells are almost gone."

"That's what he told me," Jeremy confirmed. "That is the best news ever."

"And now my aunts are going to give me some bone marrow so I won't get sick again." Her gaze grew questioning. "Why don't I know my aunts already?"

"Because *I* didn't know them," Jeremy said. "I didn't know I had two sisters until a few days ago."

"But why?"

"Because Francine couldn't take care of them when they were born so she sent them to live with another family."

Becca inclined her head, clearly as flabbergasted as Katie had been when first told of the twins.

"It's very confusing, Katie said. "So confusing that I have to stop and think about how everyone is related to keep it all straight."

"But it makes me mad that I have aunts that I didn't know about," Becca declared. "We could have been loving each other ever since I was born....How come I missed all that?"

"Honey, sometimes this happens," Jeremy said. "Sometimes babies are born when their mothers just can't take care of them so they're adopted, and years go by when their mothers don't know where they are. That's what happened with your Aunt Lena and Aunt Celia. We're all really lucky that we've found one another. We'll have years and years to be together."

Becca mulled this over. "I'm still mad at Francine for giving them away so I couldn't have them in my life 'til now."

"I know," he said, sitting on the edge of the bed so she could climb into his lap. "I don't blame you for that because I feel bad too. I wish I'd known I have two beautiful sisters before now." He kissed her cheek through his mask.

"How come you have to wear all those clothes?" Becca grabbed Katie's gown to pull her closer. "I can't feel you."

"Now that the chemo has destroyed all the

cancer cells, you don't have much immunity so we have to be extra careful you don't get an infection, Jeremy explained. "Wearing these sterile gowns and masks keeps us from bringing any germs in here on our clothes."

She sighed and settled against him while she hugged Katie's arm. "All my hair fell out." Her voice was filled with sadness.

"But you still look pretty," Katie was quick to say. "Do you know that some people shave their heads because they like the look? Lots of men do."

"I don't like the look." Merriment slid into her eyes. "But the kids at school will think it's cool. Andrew will think I'm radical."

Jeremy laughed. "You are that, for sure."

"How's Jekyll? I miss him so much."

"He misses you too but Patrick said to tell you he's going to keep Jekyll with him until you get home," Katie said.

"I'm glad. I love Patrick. I think I'll marry him someday."

"What a good idea."

"He stayed with me a really long time. Even when I was sleeping. Whenever I woke up, he was still here."

"I know," Jeremy said, "and he's coming to see you Sunday."

She raised her head. "That's really nice of him. When can I go home?"

"Dr. Cusack doesn't know that yet. It depends on how fast the new stem cells make their way into your bone marrow and start making new blood cells."

"I have to be home when the new foals

come."

"I think that'll happen," Jeremy said, resting his chin against her hair.

"When will Aunt Lena and Aunt Celia come to visit me?"

"Not for awhile," Katie said, catching Jeremy's eye. "They're going to be busy with a lot of lab tests and that kind of thing."

"Do you have a picture of them?"

Unease jolted through her. She hadn't let herself think of how they would tell Becca about the twins. Now she decided without further thought that a straight forward approach was probably best. Despite her age, Becca had always proven herself capable of dealing with reality. She was a very old soul.

"It's in my purse and I left that in a locker when we put on these clothes. I'll go get it."

Jeremy absorbed her answer with equanimity and watched her leave.

In the hall, she found a nurse who encased the picture she'd taken at the restaurant in Denver in a sterile plastic sleeve. Back beside Back beside Becca, she handed it to her.

She studied it carefully, puzzlement creasing her forehead. After a time, she raised her eyes to consider Katie searchingly. "What's wrong with them?"

"They are conjoined twins. Have you ever heard that term? Maybe in science class."

Becca shook her head, tears trembling at the edge of her lashes as she continued looking at the picture. "What does that mean?"

"They're two different people who share one

body. They were born this way." .

"Why would God make them that way?" She looked up at him.

"I don't know but I do know how very special they are. They can do everything you can. They even ride a horse, a gorgeous Thoroughbred."

"Not an Arabian?"

"Not yet, but they want to as soon as we get back to *Radbourne.*"

"It's hard to get used to what they look like."

"Yes, it is, but once you see them, you'll forget all about that. You'll see they're just like everyone else and you'll fall in love with them."

Becca looked doubtful as she continued examining the picture. "How can they walk?"

"Pretty much the same as you do. They can also play the piano and drive a car."

"Wow," Becca breathed, slowly brightening. "Can't they come see me soon. I really want to see them and tell them how great it is that they're giving me their bone marrow."

"Just as soon as they have some free time we'll bring them to visit you," Jeremy said. "Maybe in a day or two."

"Where do they live?"

"In Colorado. And they have a zillion pets. Dogs and cats and their horses. We'll go visit them there sometime."

"Cool." She pulled up her baggy t-shirt to expose the catheter that had been surgically implanted in her chest. "Look what they put in. It's a central venous line." She grinned at being able to say the name. "I love it because they don't have to stick me with needles all the time.

Everything goes in here."

"That's awesome," Jeremy agreed as she pulled down her shirt. "You're very brave."

Her eyes closed.

"Do you want to lie down so you can take a nap?" Jeremy asked.

"I'll just stay here." She cuddled closer without opening her eyes.

They continued there, caught in the pleasant reality of hope. There was no longer reason to grapple with the horror of possibly losing this extraordinary child. Somehow they were spared the fate of unending sorrow.

Katie's felt incapable of grasping the enormity of this gift.

CHAPTER TWENTY

The transplant team coordinated each step with the greatest precision until the day of the final procedure. Ten days after they entered the hospital, Lena and Celia's stem cells were harvested in an operating room. They were anesthetized and needles were placed in their hip bones and sternum to extract their marrow.

Jeremy and Katie were in the recovery room as they came out of the anesthesia. Dr. Cusack stopped by to assure them the twins had come through the process without incident.

They waited next to the bed. Lena was the first to open her eyes. "Is...it o..over?" she asked groggily.

Jeremy gently touched her arm. "Yes, and you two did great."

She smiled a little before drifting off again.

Celia didn't awaken for another fifteen minutes. Her features immediately clenched in pain and fear filled her eyes.

"You're okay," Jeremy said, leaning down close to her face. "You're both fine. Tomorrow Becca will get your stem cells."

"It hurts," she gasped.

Katie stepped into hall to find a nurse who quickly came to add pain medication to their I.V. line. "That will help," Katie said soothingly when the woman had retreated. "A little pain is normal after the procedure you had."

Lena still slept and Celia gradually relaxed as her pain eased. After another hour, they were moved back into their regular room and they were soon sleeping.

Jeremy and Katie removed their sterile scrubs and went to the cafeteria for coffee. "I hurt for her," he said when they were sitting in a booth.

Katie nodded, taking his hand across the table. "This won't take much longer now that Becca's going to get the transplant tomorrow."

"I'm just thankful she won't be under anesthesia. The transplant shouldn't be any worse than a blood transfusion. A piece of cake compared to the harvest."

Kathy's gaze drifted to the bank of windows along one side of the cafeteria. Outside, it appeared to be a perfect February day, recent snow melting in the sunshine. A flock of birds swept up from the lawn and disappeared between some buildings. "Looks like spring." She gave him a smile. "I'm as anxious for the foals as Becca."

"I am too." He turned over her hand to caress her fingers. "I think by this time next month, we'll all be back at *Radbourne*."

They had been so preoccupied in recent days that they'd forgotten it was Sunday and Patrick had planned to visit so they were a bit startled when he appeared beside their table and pulled out a chair.

"Patrick," Jeremy said, shaking his head. "I forgot you were coming."

"I remember that feeling when I was here. All the days running together. So how goes the war?"

"Good," Katie said, reaching out to squeeze his hand. "Couldn't be much better really." She told him about all that had happened over the past week. "So tomorrow is transplant day. Day zero as they call it in the transplant protocol."

"Wow, that was fast."

"Becca's cancer free and Lena and Celia are totally free of health issues so those two factors have moved things up," Jeremy explained.

"Thank God." He pushed his chair back. "Can I see Becca?" he asked, glancing at his watch. "I didn't get off this morning as early as I wanted so I don't have much time."

"Let's go." Jeremy drained his coffee cup and got up. "She's going to love seeing you."

They had soon donned their head-to-toe aqua outfits and entered Becca's room where she was curled against a pillow reading a book encased in plastic. As she looked up, she tossed the book aside and scrambled to sit on the edge of the bed.

"Patrick! I thought you forgot!" She flung her arms around him.

He held her, laughing. "I'd never forget my best girl." Leaning back, he considered her. "I hear tomorrow is day zero."

"Yes! My aunts' stem cells may make me a little sick but I don't care. I want to get the transplant so I can start growing new blood cells and then, I can go home!"

"And then, you can start riding again."

She beamed at the idea, then looked at him sharply. "How's Jekyll?"

"He's wondering when you're coming home but he's having fun too. Whenever I ride up the mountain, he gets to have a long run."

"Thank you for taking good care of him," her voice had grown wistful."

"You are welcome and I had an idea as we were driving up here...."

"You brought him with you?" she broke in. Her eyes flew to her dad. "Could I?"

He shook his head and her shoulders sagged.

"But guess what?" Patrick said, tipping up her chin. "You *can* see him. That's my great idea. I'm going to bring him around to the lawn out there and you can see him through your window."

She glanced behind them to the window. "Thank you so much! Bring him up close."

"I will." He laughed at her excitement.

She wrapped her arms around Jeremy and Katie on either side. "I can see Jekyll."

"That's so great," Jeremy said, rubbing her back. "You've been very brave without him."

"But I miss him so much." Sudden tears spilled down her face as she rested her head against Patrick.

He hugged her tighter. "I can't stay long today so I'm going to go get him. You watch for us, okay?"

She smiled at him. "Thank you."

"You're welcome, my little friend."

He stepped back and said goodbye to Jeremy and Katie before he headed out, stopping at the door to wave at Becca. "Watch for us!"

"Why don't you come stand on this," Katie said, pushing an armchair close to the window. She went back to roll the I.V. stand while Jeremy carried Becca to the window.

"Come on!" She'd started dancing in the chair. "Come on, Patrick, bring my Jekyll..."

Katie delighted in her happiness, wishing she could somehow store it up to see her through any of the symptoms that might plague her after the transplant.

"There he is!" she shrieked, jumping up and down against the restraints of her dad's hands. "Come here, Jekyll! I'm over here!"

Patrick walked along the edge of the building and stooped down to let the shepherd loose. Jekyll trotted forward, then honed in on Becca and raced to the window.

He leapt up to put his front paws on the glass, then seeing her, he jumped back and raced in a joyful circle before he stopped to look at her with his head turned to one side. Becca called his name over and over between her peals of laughter.

He cavorted about the lawn for some minutes, always going back to lean on the glass, wiggling in an effort to get close to her. Becca clapped her hands with delight, then threw up her arms, sending Jekyll off on another gleeful circuit.

Finally, his energy spent, he came to stand still before the glass, looking mournfully at Becca. Patrick came to reattach his leash and rub his back, his gaze settling on Becca. "Gotta go," he finally mouthed and turned to lead Jekll away.

Becca's happiness gave way to sobs as she leaned against Jeremy. He picked her up. "Sweetheart, it won't be long until you two are back together."

Her thin shoulders shook but then she straightened, looking into his face. "I love him so much."

"And he loves you just as much. Jeremy said he's being brave while he can't be with you. He'd want you to be the same."

She slowly nodded. "I am."

He carried her back to bed while Katie maneuvered the I.V. stand into place. Becca was subdued now and settled beneath the covers and fell asleep.

"I'm going to check on the twins," Katie said, trailing her hand along Jeremy's arm. "Do you want to come?"

His gaze remained on Becca. "I think I should stay here. It feels like she's so fragile right now, she might break."

"See you soon."

When she reached the nurse's station near the twins' room, she was informed she must strip off the scrubs she was wearing and replace them with newly sterilized ones. Swallowing her irritation, she complied.

In reality, she was grateful for the caution. Drug resistant germs and viruses were becoming more and more common in hospitals and the last thing they needed now was for either Becca or the twins to contract some super bug.

Once she was dressed again, she proceeded to Lena and Celia's room where they were sharing a bowl of soup."

"Well, you two are looking chipper."

"Celia smiled, still holding her spoon. "We're fine, Katie. And so relieved. At least I am." She took another bite of soup and put the spoon down." She looked hard at Katie. "I was sort of freaking...."

"You were totally freaked," Lena interrupted.

"And how about you?" Katie asked, sitting on the bed next to her. "How did you get through that whole ordeal?"

"It didn't bother me. We've had a lot of surgeries."

"Have you? Like what?"

"We were born with a third arm coming out our back. So that was removed."

Celia scowled at her. "We were really little then so we don't remember that surgery."

Lena gave her an annoyed look. "Or the others for that matter." She rolled her eyes for Katie's benefit.

"Are you two getting on each other's nerves tonight?"

"It happens." Lena shrugged. "But we have to be careful about that kind of thing." She glanced pointedly at Katie. "What can we do about it?"

"Not much," Celia said as if on cue. "I do go to sleep sometimes when I can't stand listening to her any longer."

"I guess that gets the point across."

"She hates it."

Lena managed to look a bit sheepish. "I do."

Katie wondered how she would manage if she had another version of herself attached to her forever. She'd always heard that identical twins often fought as children because they couldn't deal with looking at themselves every day. What Lena and Celia had to deal with was far more radical than that.

She realized they were both studying her

quizzically. "I think you two are just fabulous, darlings."

They reacted with raucous laughter.

"Now tell me, have either of you had any more pain since we saw you?" she asked when they'd recovered a little.

"No," the nurse said we should have enough pain meds to be comfortable," Celia said, "so we've been asking more often."

"Well, that's good then."

"How's Becca?" Lena wanted to know.

"The waiting seems to be getting to her a little. Otherwise, she's fine and anxious to get the transplant over with so your bone marrow can start making new blood cells."

"She said that?" Lena asked.

"She did."

"I'm with her. We just want her to get better so we can all go to *Radbourne.*"

"That can't happen too soon for me," Katie said.

At seven o'clock the next morning, Jeremy cradled Becca on her bed. Katie sat beside them holding her hand while they all watched the I.V. line where the twins' stem cells were being transfused into Becca's central venous line. "When will my new bone marrow start making new blood cells?" she asked, preoccupied with the subject because she understood what had to happen before she could go home.

"It may happen in a couple weeks or it could take a month," Katie explained. "Maybe longer."

"What's it called again?"

"Engraftment."

"If they put on those blue clothes, can Lena and Celia come visit me pretty soon."

"Maybe in another week or two." Katie said. She and Jeremy had already talked about it being less of a shock for Becca to first see the twins' swathed in gowns. Their curiosity and personality would quickly win her over before she had to deal with the rest of it.

"I hope so," she said. "We can get acquainted while I get better."

"They'll love that," Jeremy said.

After the transplant, Becca improved daily, amazing Dr. Cusack and the entire transplant team. She managed to avoid most all the possible conditions that could have slowed her recovery – infection, bleeding, nausea, weakness.

Lena and Celia were discharged from the hospital and settled into a nearby motel, their room next to the one shared by Katie and Jeremy. When Katie went to the motel to take them to lunch a week later, she couldn't find them.

After searching their room, the halls and grounds and the adjacent restaurant, she called Jeremy who quickly joined her in the hunt for his wayward sisters. They had gone over the same route Katie had followed three more times before they watched a taxi stop before the motel doors. Celia and Lena climbed out, paid the driver and hurried toward them.

"Sorry we're late," Celia apologized. "Time got away."

Katie was ready to yell in her overwhelming need to know where they'd been. But then she remembered these were not children they were dealing with but adult women.

They came to a stop before her. "We decided to go see some of the town," Lena explained. "We've been in that motel room for five days and just had to get out."

Katie draped an arm around their shoulders, managing a smile. "Next time, please let us know beforehand. We were getting frantic."

"I know," Celia said. "We didn't think. We're just so used to going out on our own in Denver when we visit Nealie or Ivan."

This was news to Katie. "I'm sorry I overreacted. So are you ready for lunch?"

They all filed into the restaurant. "So how did you like Billings?" Jeremy inquired when they were seated.

"Not much to get excited about," Lena said. "Sorry."

He chuckled. "That pretty much sums it up, I guess."

"Dr. Cusack says you can go see Becca if you want," Katie told them. "Are you up for that after lunch?"

"Finally," Lena said with a big smile.

"I can't wait," Celia concurred.

An hour later, they were ready. Jeremy and Katie led them into Becca's room.

They hesitated inside the door, watching as Becca put down her game and peered across the room at them. They slowly went nearer. "Hi, Becca," Celia said as they reached the bed. "How do you feel?"

"Great. Thank you so much for helping me."
She sat studying what little of their faces she could
see below the masks. "I'm so glad you're my
aunts."

"We are too," Lena said as they embraced
her. "You're so pretty."

She reached up to touch her head where her
hair was just beginning to grow again. "Thank
you."

The twins settled into a chair beside the bed
and continued talking to her for half an hour during
which she occasionally broke in to tell them about
Jekyll and Juniper and the other horses she'd been
riding before she got sick. In turn, they regaled her
about their Thoroughbreds and all their dogs and
cats.

Jeremy and Katie watched from the couch by
the window, hardly daring to believe how well they
were getting on. Katie was still a little uneasy about
their vanishing act earlier. She realized she and
Jeremy had a lot to learn from these capable
women.

Becca was released from the hospital at the
end of February. Jeremy and Katie were given
extensive instructions about her care at home. As
they all headed home to *Radbourne,* Lena and Celia
shared the backseat with her. They chatted like old
friends until Becca fell asleep. The twins' could
barely control their excitement at being so close to
finally seeing *Radbourne.*

Patrick had briefed everyone at the ranch on
the details concerning Jeremy's twin sisters so there

was no awkwardness when he, Janel, Scott, Pearl and Jekyll greeted them in the driveway upon their arrival. Katie had wondered how Becca would handle the division of attention that had always been hers alone. But with her usual evenhanded outlook, she was gracious in the face of everyone's interest in the twins. Actually, she was more concerned with enjoying her joyful reunion with Jekyll who frolicked in circles around her until he eventually calmed down enough to be properly introduced to Celia and Lena.

"He's very beautiful," Lena said while they hugged him.

"He's my very best friend," Becca said, dropping her arm over his back.

"You're so lucky to have him."

"He's a service dog," Becca explained.

"Why do you need a service dog?" Lena wanted to know.

"Daddy thought someone might kidnap me. So he got Jekyll to guard me all the time."

The twins digested this, eyeing her with new respect.

"You can go see the horses," Becca offered.

"Aren't you coming?"

"No, I'm tired."

"Janel and I would love to show you around," Patrick suggested. "Let's start by visiting Bordeaux." He pointed across the frozen stream where the stallion stood watching them.

"Is that okay?" Lena asked Jeremy.

"Absolutely. We'll see you later."

"Great." They hugged him before following Patrick and Janel down over the snowy lawn.

Jeremy and Katie took Becca's hands, leading her up the terrace steps with Jekyll, Scott and Pearl following. "We'll have five guests for dinner, including my sisters," Jeremy told Pearl before they headed upstairs.

Becca insisted on climbing the staircase herself and the others came behind, converging on her bedroom where she and Jekyll crawled onto her bed. Scott sat down to take her pulse and listen to her heart. "You are an amazing transplant patient," he told her when he was finished. "How do you feel?"

"Good as new. But I don't want to get sick again so I need to get plenty of rest."

"Very wise," he agreed, then considered Jeremy and Katie sitting nearby. "And how are you two?"

"Very grateful to be home," Jeremy said with a weary smile. "I for one feel like I've been riding a merry-go-round in the middle of a war zone. Too many changes with too little time to absorb everything."

"That about covers it," Katie agreed.

"All those sudden twists and turns do tend to send one's stress level off the charts," Scott said. "I don't think there's much I can do to help you adjust." He gave them a wry grin. "But if you think of something, let me know."

Becca had fallen asleep, curled next to Jekyll with one arm thrown over him. Looking at them, Katie was overcome by her own exhaustion and stretched out, holding Jeremy's hand. He and Scott continued talking but she soon lost track of the exchange.

The light had shifted from sunshine to shadows when she awoke. Opening her eyes, she saw twilight outside the windows. Becca and Jekyll still slept. Someone had spread a blanket over the three of them.

Katie felt relief that they were home. Reflecting on the past three months, she acknowledged once more the huge miracle that had visited itself upon them during that time. Yet, disquiet mingled with the rest, something incomplete. She knew the source was Jeremy. Nealie's candid words came back to her and she knew the matter must be addressed soon. She hated to think about challenging him. It would be so much easier to continue as they were but she knew she could no longer settle for part of him. Their bond was too precious.

They had weathered the trauma of Becca's illness with good humor and no faltering in their steadfast dependence on each other. Their growth as a couple and deepening love accounted for that. Nonetheless, she'd periodically been aware of her increasing anger. She'd consciously assigned it to a separate part of her mind, much the same as she'd compartmentalized the haunting fear shadowing her all those years. She'd become adept at the subterfuge in order to function day to day..

She'd known what she was getting into when she began a relationship with Jeremy. She had thought she was strong enough to be satisfied with what he could give her. Since that October day over a year ago, she had known such joy but she'd also watched him withdraw from time to time. She'd watched him go off to the nursing home to spend time with comatose Evelyn....

Her troubled reverie was interrupted when Jeremy came to the bedroom. Sitting beside her, he leaned over to wrap her in his arms. "Did you get some sleep?"

"Yes, it was lovely. I'm so glad we're home." She turned her head to meet his lips with her own. "Where've you been?"

She felt him tense as he buried his head in her neck. "I went to talk to Evelyn."

"Umm." She rolled out of his embrace and sat up.

He considered her. "I don't think that's out of line considering what's happened with Becca."

"Maybe not but I don't think it was necessary either."

He collapsed back on the bed, staring at the ceiling. "Is this the way it's going to be now that we're home?" he asked tiredly.

"I don't know, Jeremy." Before she could say anything more, she was relieved when Becca woke.

"How you doing, kiddo?" Jeremy asked, turning his head to inspect her.

"Good." She snuggled close.

"Are you ready for dinner?" Katie asked them as Jekyll jumped off the bed.

They soon made their way downstairs to the dining room. The twins sat with Patrick, Janel and Scott.

"So how do you like *Radbourne?*" Jeremy asked when he sat beside Lena.

"We love it! And we've never seen horses so beautiful as your Arabians."

Celia rested her head against her arm braced

on the table, craning her neck to see him around Lena. "You are so lucky to live here."

Katie took a seat between Becca and Patrick, struggling to smile and join in the animated conversation. Fortunately, Becca and the twins monopolized the talk and Katie didn't have to interact for long. After apple pie, she excused herself and led Becca upstairs to bed.

Once she was in bed with Jekyll beside her, Katie went to her own bedroom. She took a shower and got into bed. The room felt lonely after the nights she'd spent in Jeremy's bed while they searched for clues to help Becca.

Her exhaustion wasn't diminished by her earlier nap and she was on the verge of sleep when she heard the door open and then Jeremy came to encircle her in his arms, bringing his face close to hers.

"You still angry with me?" He nuzzled her nose with his.

She swallowed the sharp words she wanted to shout at him. "Jeremy, we have to talk...."

"So talk."

"Not right this minute. We need some time and privacy to discuss where we're headed."

"I thought we decided that a long time ago."

This was hopeless, she realized. He hadn't an inkling what was bothering her and they were both too worn out to think clearly, let alone discuss something as serious as their future.

She lifted her hand to trace the fine planes of his face. "I love you so much."

"So I'm back in your good graces?" He pulled back to study her in the dim light. "Katie, we've gone though some pretty hellish weeks and I couldn't have gotten through them without you. You are the most important part of my life."

"You know how much I love it here with you and Becca."

"We both adore you. You know that. And now there are two more people who need you in their lives."

Katie's thoughts lurched to Celia and Lena. "I want to be part of their lives. They're a pure delight."

"Then just love us the way we all love you."

"You know I do."

"Now go to sleep. If you want to sleep until noon, go for it. I will keep everyone entertained and fed."

"Thanks." She didn't want him to leave. "Do you think if we left the door open and turned on a lamp we could get by with you sleeping here?"

He grinned. "I'm willing to endanger my reputation if you are." He disentangled himself from her and went to bring blankets from a bathroom closet and stretched out beside her atop the comforter. Within minutes, she was asleep in his arms, the disquiet set aside for the night.

CHAPTER TWENTY-ONE

After sleeping around the clock and then some, Katie awakened shortly after noon feeling restored. She no longer felt like her nerves were frayed and she could fall apart as the slightest provocation.

She thought about Jeremy coming to her after dinner, his tender concern and finally the way he'd held her close all night long. She didn't know when he'd left. She no longer felt any urgent need to confront him.

Certainly they must talk. There was a great deal she must say to him but there was time to deal with that. For the immediate future, she needed to deal with Becca and the twins, helping Jeremy as she'd been doing for a long time now.

After a shower, she hurried downstairs where Jeremy, Becca and the twins were eating lunch in the solarium. Jeremy got up to hold her chair, giving her a kiss. "You look like sleep did wonders for you."

"It did." She tousled Becca'a hair and sat beside Lena. "So what's everyone been up to while I was sleeping the day away?"

"Patrick let us ride in the arena!" Celia said. "Becca said it was okay if we rode Juniper. He's such a good horse."

"Becca's trained him really well," Lena added. "And he's so beautiful."

Becca smiled, hugging Katie. "When do you think I can start riding again? Daddy says in a week. Patrick says in three days. Daddy says we have to ask Scott."

"We should definitely ask Scott," Katie said, "but I think you could ride for ten minutes this afternoon."

Becca grinned at her. "That's what *I* think."

Katie glanced at Jeremy who turned his gaze on the twins. "What do you two say?"

"Ten minutes," Lena said with a grin and Celia nodded.

"It looks like the majority says you can ride for ten minutes." He leaned closer and kissed her cheek.

"Whoo...hoo!" Becca said and jumped down to throw her arms around Jekyll. "When can we go to the barn?"

"As soon as I eat this." Katie said, pointing at the sandwich Pearl had put before her.

Shortly, they all tromped through the snow to the arena. On the way, Lena and Celia stopped to feed Bordeaux the carrots they'd brought.

"They've quite fallen in love with him," Jeremy told Katie as they continued.

In the arena, Patrick schooled a young gelding and they watched for awhile before he dismounted and led him through a door. A few minutes later, he returned with Juniper.

"I thought you might like to ride your old friend," he said and lifted her into the saddle. "Does it feel good to be back.?" He gave her a thumbs up.

"I love it!"

"He's all warmed up so show us your stuff."

She picked up the reins and Juniper moved out with his usual animation. Katie was amazed at how confident Becca looked in the saddle.

She circled the arena for fifteen minutes instead of ten, urging Juniper into a trot, then transitioned smoothly to a canter. Lena and Celia clapped as she passed.

When she pulled up, they were eager to tell her how great she'd looked. "I wish we could ride as well as you," Celia said.

"If you stick around here long enough, you can do that," Patrick said.

Both she and Lena studied him. "Really?"

"Absolutely."

"Thank you, Patrick," Becca said as she followed the rest outside.

"You're welcome. You'll be back at your lessons in no time."

On the way back to the manor, Jeremy asked the twins if they wanted to live at *Radbourne*.

"You mean forever?" Lena asked.

"Well, that's one option. If you want to live here, I'm sure that can be arranged."

"I would miss Alexis and Dan and the girls," Celia said. "And Nealie and Ivan and all our animals...."

"Your horses and the rest could come here with you," Katie pointed out.

They had reached the terrace and filed inside, finally sitting around the table in the sun porch.

"That would be nice," Celia went on. "Otherwise we'd miss them too much." She studied her brother. "But Alexis and the others probably couldn't come live here."

"They *could,*" Jeremy amended. "We'd have to talk about that."

"Or maybe you could divide your time between Stanley Island and *Radbourne,*" Katie suggested.

"There's too much to think about," Lena said. "Do we have to decide right away?"

"No, there's no rush. There's plenty of time to figure out what will make everyone happy. Just remember that you're always welcome here."

"Thank you," Celia said, "and you are our family."

"Yes, we are" He hugged them with a wink.

Everyone settled into the rhythms of *Radbourne* as spring approached. Becca's recovery continued steadily.. She returned to school for half days and resumed daily riding lessons on Cassandra.

Lena and Celia also rode Juniper in the arena every morning. They were enchanted when the first foals were born and began spending more and more time in the foaling barn.

Katie concentrated on the responsibilities of the ranch and attempted to keep the unresolved issues between her and Jeremy consigned to the far reaches of her mind. But each time Jeremy went to the nursing home, sometimes staying for hours, her control grew more shaky.

Her patience fell away entirely one warm evening in March. After a full day, Becca and the twins were ready for bed early so Jeremy asked Katie to ride with him to the cabin. A full moon edged up, bathing the mountain in a silvery-blue luminosity that was different from anything Katie had seen during other visits to Francine's hideaway. The stillness closed around them.

As they climbed the steady incline from the ranch buildings, Katie knew this was finally her chance to set matters right between her and Jeremy. They had managed to regain much of their delight in each other while spring settled over the ranch with all its magic and promise.

Nonetheless, the status quo reigned and Jeremy drove to Sheridan several times a week to see Evelyn. Katie tried to grant him grace in the matter, assuming that because he hadn't been able to visit the nursing home for such a long stretch, he felt compelled to go more often now. Yet, despite her goodwill, her anger at him intensified.

Glancing at him, relaxed in the saddle, she saw he was as clueless as ever. She hated to consider blowing up the perfect night but she wanted this over.

While they continued through the ethereal moonlight, she was overcome by the enormity of what she had to do. Tears sprang to her eyes when she realized this might be the last time she and Jeremy came here. She hoped she could commit to memory every detail of the hours they'd spent there, holding them in her heart for the rest of her life. But she was so sick now with anxiety and dread, all she could do as they neared the cabin was cry silently.

Once they were inside, Jeremy surrounded her with his love and tenderness which only caused her to cry harder. He lit the prepared kindling in the fireplace, then led her to one of the chairs. He sat and drew her onto his lap, holding her again as he watched her intently. "Tell me," he said softly.

She drew a quavery breath and took the handkerchief that he handed her. Wiping her eyes, she struggled to locate some of her common sense. "Jeremy, I love you so much. I love my life with you here." With effort, she met his troubled gaze. "But I can't go on the way we have been. I've been searching my heart for months, knowing how loyal you are to Evelyn. I've finally come to a decision. I can't stay at *Radbourne*." She scrubbed frantically at new tears.

"What the hell are you saying?"

"I...I truly thought I could settle for part of you. But I can't, knowing that your heart is still with Evelyn. Do you have any idea how it hurts me when you go to her and stay for hours...?" She trailed off to blow her nose, angry with herself for her lack of control. She lifted her eyes, seeing that his heart was breaking.

"You belong here."

"Not if we must grow old as lovers but never husband and wife. For God's sake, Jeremy, I want to have your baby! It's not fair, damn it! I wish I could be satisfied with less, and for awhile I was. Being loved by you is such a lovely gift. But I'm too selfish to share you any longer. I must stop before I start hating you...."

Jeremy was so still that she felt an icy shiver inside. She hoped it didn't show.

"I can't give you what you want," he said at last, his voice breaking.

"I knew you would say that...." She could think of nothing more to say.

Still silent, he stared into the fireplace for some minutes before he gathered her close and carried her to the bed where he lay her down and wrapped her in a blanket and held her protectively.

She still couldn't stop weeping and he lay with her while she cried. His gentle concern and lack of anger unnerved and saddened her even more.

Much later when her tears were spent, she felt him drawing into himself, away from her. Her thoughts careened in opposite directions when he moved back to the armchair.

His withdrawal, putting distance between them chilled Katie but what did she expect? She pushed herself up against the headboard and pulled the blanket around her. "Thank you, Jeremy, for taking care of me tonight. You always do."

"I always want to."

"I love that...I've no idea how I can live apart from you."

"You have a responsibility to *Radbourne*."

"Francine was very wise and she altered her will so I would be protected whatever might happen. I'm certain she spent some time pondering just this kind of unforeseen development. That's why she made you manager of *Radbourne*. She actually spelled that out when she told us I am her heir, that her beloved ranch would endure whether or not I live there...."

"That wasn't what she was saying," Jeremy said. "She wouldn't have been so adamant about you realizing how precious *Radbourne* is if she hadn't believed you belong here."

"You may be correct about that, or not. In any case, I can't stay!" She flung back the covers and jumped out of bed, then furiously wadded up the blanket and hurled it at him. "Evelyn is never getting well!"

"I can't abandon her." He looked on the verge of tears now.

"At this point, having a life is not abandoning her. No matter what you do, her life won't change." She sank into the chair opposite him. "Even Becca knows you don't have any future with her mother. Jeremy, let it go. You can't do any more for her."

"I can honor my marriage vows."

Katie sat staring at him. "You've lost your mind. If memory serves, that's already a moot point. What does your therapist say about that?"

He looked away. "I stopped going."

"Oh, what a good idea." She leapt up and practically flew to the door.

"You knew the rules."

"But it wasn't a fair-minded game, was it?"

"It was never a game, Katie! You know that."

She hesitated only a moment more, then wrenched open the door. "If you think it'll help Evelyn, then why don't you go lie down with her in her hospital bed and stay there for the rest of her life!"

She rushed outside to the stable. Her shaking hands found the lantern inside the door. It seemed forever before she'd saddled Murphy and mounted.

As she guided the gelding along the familiar trail, she saw Jeremy silhouetted in the cabin doorway, one arm braced against the jamb, evidently waiting to watch her ride away from him. Although she knew it was false, his calm provoked renewed tears and she could hardly see as Murphy picked his way around boulders. She gave him his head, trusting him to get them safely down the mountain.

So many times she and Jeremy had made this journey when the moon hung low. Those rides were intimate extensions of their time at the cabin. A couple times, Jeremy had insisted she ride double with him while Murphy followed reliably. He'd held her all the way down. Now she'd left all the magic in ruins.

Halfway to *Radbourne,* she longed to turn Murphy around and go back but she realized Jeremy would be unapproachable by this time. With painful awareness, she realized she couldn't return in any case.

By the time she entered the lighted stable yard, the night had given way to a mother-of-pearl glow above the barns. The stable boy who appeared at the sound of hooves on the cobblestones stared at Katie, then took the reins. "Where's Mr. Foxworth?"

"He'll be along." Katie dismounted and put up her jacket collar against the chill. Until now, she hadn't noticed how cold it was.

She walked down the shadowy footpath, her turmoil guiding her closer to the stream. A rustling preceded Bordeaux, back in his summer quarters. He nickered and Katie held his muzzle, leaning against the stolid bulk of him. Tears dripped onto his nose. If the soft rumblings in his throat were any indication, he sensed her distress.

Bordeaux symbolized Jeremy's history at *Radbourne,* and the two of them were inexorably entwined in the ranch's present reputation. When Katie first came there, Jeremy's devotion to the old stallion mystified her. She now comprehended the depth of the cherished bond.

Loneliness overtook her as she continued along the water instead of going directly to the house. Bordeaux followed until she disappeared in a thicket of willows. She presently emerged in a clearing affording a broad view of the ranch headquarters. Dawn sent tawny rays undulating through the tree branches. She surveyed all that belonged to her, all that nurtured her soul.

There was no joy now in looking down from this spot. She let herself think about the future, knowing she must somehow find a place where she could be nourished by the same things that enthralled her here. The magazine in Boston no longer held appeal so one of the first things she would do is resign her position there. Then she would begin the search for something to do the rest of her life Perhaps she would look into other Arabian ranches. Her riding ability would qualify her to train and show. And she would be working with the exquisite horses she'd come to love so much.

Having touched on possible options, she felt a bit stronger, able to function. She soon headed back to the manor where Becca, Lena and Celia ate oatmeal in the solarium.

"Is Daddy still at the barns?" Becca inquired.

"He rode up the mountain."

"He didn't have breakfast?"

"Hard to believe, huh?" Katie dropped a kiss on her cheek.

"Did you hear any meadowlarks?"

She sat down, looking at her. "You know, I'm not sure. I had other things on my mind."

"Is it warm out?" Celia inquired.

"It was chilly earlier but I think it's going to be a glorious day."

"We thought we might lie out."

Katie studied them. "That sounds nice. The terrace is good for that. Maybe I'll join you later."

She watched them finish the bowls of cereal before them. Like all their day to day activities, they had worked out remarkable coordination in this as well. They each held a spoon and ate from two bowls, feeding themselves with faultless synchronicity.

Katie had been even more impressed when she saw them eat steak. Celia held the fork and Lena the knife and they cut the meat flawlessly. If one took a roll, the other buttered it. The cooperation between them was nothing short of inspiring.

Now, they laid down their spoons and excused themselves before going to their room to change into a bathing suit. "See you, kiddo." Lena touched Becca as they went past her.

"Are you and Daddy going to get married?"

Becca's inquiry careened through Katie's bruised mind. "Your dad's already married to your mom. You know that."

She rolled her eyes. "Well, yeah, but not really now. It'd be okay if they weren't married anymore."

"I may not be able to marry Patrick. I think he loves Janel."

"Really. I hadn't picked up on that."

Pearl appeared at that moment. "Good morning, Katie. Is Jeremy on his way?"

"I doubt he'll be back for awhile. I'll just have coffee."

"Very well." She left a pot and disappeared.

The twins returned with towels. "Do you have sunscreen? We didn't bring any because it was winter then."

"Look in that cupboard...."

"I'll get it," Becca jumped down and opened a nearby door, then handed them a tube.

"Thanks." They hurried out the door to the terrace.

"So what are you going to do this morning?" Katie asked Becca.

"I'm going riding up the mountain with Patrick and Janel at nine o'clock."

"I'm going to look at the new foals. Want to come?"

"Not right now. Pearl and I are going to give Jekyll a bath. He doesn't smell too good."

Katie drew her close for a hug, then headed out. She wanted to talk to Patrick and let him know what was happening with Jeremy. Sometime later, she found him lunging a yearling in the arena.

"Katie," he said when she stood beside him, "everything okay?" He studied her.

"No. Could we talk?"

"Sure." He reeled in the filly with the long line and tied her to a post before joining Katie on a bench. "What's up?"

"It's hard to know where to start..." She turned to look at him, seeing his concern. "This has been coming on for awhile now. I've given

Jeremy an ultimatum."

His gaze faltered and he put his hand on hers.

"I can't go on any longer the way we have been."

He looked at the ground while his fingers rubbed hers. "I don't know how you've handled it this long."

"I knew what I was getting into. Jeremy never misled me. Maybe I somehow believed he would change his mind but I know now he won't. He's made that very clear."

"He's not seeing the situation realistically. Evelyn is no longer his wife in any sense of the word and never will be again." He glanced at her.

"That's the way I see it," she agreed. "I can't understand why he thinks a divorce would be a betrayal. One can't betray what no longer exists. He doesn't see it that way."

Patrick nodded. "I've seen other friends throw away happiness with both hands because of their principles. At times, principles can get in the way of common sense."

"Well, in any case, I wanted to be the one to tell you I'll be leaving *Radbourne*. I could never continue living here, having only part of Jeremy. I should never have begun what I couldn't continue. I feel badly about that but it doesn't change the fact that I can't stay."

"What will you do?"

"Needless to say, I've given that a lot of thought. I'd have a hard time living without Arabians now that I know what makes them so incredible." She spread her hands. "I may see if I can work at another breeding operation. I'm sure I could earn my keep training and showing."

Patrick shook his head in frustration. "No question there. Jeremy's going to love that idea. Now that will be ironic, *Radbourne's* owner riding for the competition."

"Do you have any better ideas?"

"Only that you need to stay here. I can't believe Jeremy won't realize that sooner or later."

"I wouldn't count on it. You have no idea how loyal he is to Evelyn."

He pondered this. "He is a bullhead as Francine used to be fond of saying. All I can say is I'm so sorry. I can't imagine life around here without you. But I also know how much he loves you so I'm not going to give up on him yet."

"Thanks for listening."

"I wish I could do more."

"By the way, Becca seems to think you and Janel may be in love."

He grinned. "Does she now? Well, I wish it was so but she's still quite smitten with Scott. That's got to be way over before I'll make any move. My guess is she'll marry Scott."

"I wouldn't underestimate Becca. She's got some of her father's ESP."

"Speaking of Becca."

Katie saw her and Jekyll coming toward them. "Jekyll looks quite spiffy after his bath," she said when they stood before them.

"He smells good too. We used lavender shampoo on him. Pearl says it will make him calm."

"That's always a good thing."

"Well, ladies, time to get back to work."

Patrick kissed Katie's cheek. "I'll say a prayer," he whispered before going to collect the filly.

Katie waited with Becca until he returned with Juniper and one of the stallions in training. Janel soon appeared as well with her mount. Katie followed them into the stable yard where they mounted and moved off along the trail angling toward the mountains.

Too late, she wished she'd gone with them but then she realized she still could. She beckoned to a boy and asked him to saddle Murphy for her.

Soon enough, she was cantering up the incline and within a few minutes had overtaken the others who greeted her with waves and shouts. She guided Murphy alongside Becca who reached out to grab her hand.

After a couple of hours, they were riding back when Katie saw Jeremy's horse ahead, already descending the trail to the ranch buildings. Her heart cramped as she watched him.

When she'd left the barns and walked toward the house, she noted that Jeremy's Accord wasn't in the carriage house. *Figures. He would be with Evelyn.*

She heard running behind her and turned to see Becca and Jekyll approaching. She put her arm around Becca as they neared the terrace steps.

"Wasn't that a nice ride?" Becca asked as they entered the rear hall.

"Yes, it was. I loved it too. Now it's time you went up for your nap."

She frowned.

"That was the deal," Katie reminded her, "you can ride twice a day but you have to rest twice also."

"I know," she reluctantly agreed. "See you at lunch." She headed for the stairs with Jekyll marching behind.

Katie went back out to where Lena and Celia were sunbathing on a lounge chair at the rear of the terrace. She slumped into a rocking chair. "Are you getting some color?"

"No," Lena said quickly, "we put on too much sunscreen so we're white as ever."

"But it's really nice out here. It feels like summer."

Katie tipped her face to the sunshine, her thoughts turning to Jeremy. Dread lay in a heavy layer somewhere just out of reach. She searched for her anger, wanting to be enraged with him so she couldn't feel the pain.

It was no use. No matter how she tried to distract herself, she ached for him, wanting his company, his tender care, his love. She felt her resolve lessening. How would she ever live without him with any kind of purpose, let alone joy? Very likely she would drown in her sorrow. She had never believed anyone could die of a broken heart but if the way she felt right now was any indication, she thought it was possible.

She startled when she heard someone approaching up the terrace steps. Was he back?

Janel walked toward her. "How about an early lunch in town?" she asked, sitting beside her.

Katie noted she was dressed in tailored pants and cotton sweater, a coral and yellow scarf knotted stylishly at her throat. "That sounds lovely," she answered at last. "I could use about three martinis as well."

"I shouldn't wonder."

Katie considered her. "I guess Patrick filled you in."

"He did. I'm so sorry, Katie. Men are a conundrum, are they not?"

"I'd say." She smiled. "I'm grateful you rescued me in the nick of time. I was dangerously close to thinking I've made a terrible mistake."

"We can't have that. Now why don't you go change and we'll be off. In the meantime, I'll visit with these two lovely ladies." She turned her attention to the twins.

Katie hurried upstairs, looking forward to some female commiseration. Looking in on Becca, she saw she was sleeping. Much as she hated to admit it, she still needed a lot of extra sleep.

Katie went to her room to shower and dress. On her way to the terrace, she stopped in the kitchen to tell Pearl where she was off to, then rejoined the ladies outside. "Have a great lunch and have fun," Lena called after them as Katie descended the steps with Janel. They drove to the Sheridan Inn where they settled in for a leisurely meal, preceded by lemon martinis and followed by a bottle of Chablis. Memories of happy times there with Jeremy and Becca served to stir Katie's present grief and worry.

"I truly believed I could have a quote "casual" unquote relationship with Jeremy," she confided at some point, bracketing her fingers. "How stupid, was that?"

"At that point, you probably had no idea that you'd be here permanently," Janel surmised.

Katie stared at her wineglass. "That's true. I

could think no further than solving the mystery of why I was sent away from *Radbourne.*" She glanced up. "Do you know about that?"

When Janel shook her head, she proceeded to give her an abbreviated version of her hunt for the truth. "So at that point, I had no interest in *Radbourne* and was really angry with Francine so I wanted to leave as quickly as I could. I planned to return to my life in Boston." She sipped her wine.

"But Francine was just as determined to keep me here and I'd come to realize it was going to take some time to unravel the mystery of my short time at *Radbourne* as a child. So the months went by and my love for Jeremy and Becca and the ranch grew ever deeper. I became very comfortable here and when Francine named me her heir, I realized I no longer resented that. I was happy with the decision and everything was just about perfect on all fronts.

"Once the matter of my past was resolved, I no longer wanted to leave. And then Becca got sick and I become an equal partner with Jeremy in searching for a donor and we ended up finding Lena and Celia. That in itself was a life-changing event for both of us. It was such a time of joy and hope, yet very stressful as well. I had just come to the end of my endurance in a way I couldn't analyze for a long time." She fell silent and sat looking into Janel's beautiful, understanding face.

"I finally realized I was becoming so angry with Jeremy. Ever since we became a couple, he would leave me for hours at a time while he went to the nursing home and spent time with Evelyn. I'd accepted that as part of our deal for so long but recently, it just sent me into a rage. I knew I could no longer accept our present state." She drank the rest of her wine and set the glass down with a thud.

"So that's where we're at."

"Just let me say, I admire you tremendously," Janel said in belated reaction. "I doubt in your shoes, I could make the decision you have."

"Last night, my anger gave me courage. Today, I'm a wreck." She pressed a napkin beneath her teary eyes. Janel didn't press her to say more. "Remember, we're all here for you and we'll help you any way we can."

"Thanks."

They stayed there for a time, finishing the rest of the wine while once more, Katie prepared herself to return to *Radbourne*. When Janel parked in the carriage house, Katie noted that Jeremy's car was there.

After saying goodbye, Katie approached the house. Climbing the terrace steps, she tried putting her wildly scattered thoughts in some sort of order. Two crows scolded her from a nearby light post.

In the rear hall, she was confronted by a pile of Jeremy's belongings beside the door - packed saddle bags, a coat and jacket. The sight sent new dread through her. He was evidently planning to leave again, although not by car which encouraged her slightly.

It was time to find out what he was up to by this time. Resolutely, she strode to the kitchen where Pearl was preparing slicing vegetables on the butcher block.

"Have you seen Jeremy?"

Pearl nodded, her gaze troubled. "He packed some food and said to tell you he's in the drawing room."

When Katie entered, he stood staring out a rear window. She stopped some distance from him.

Eventually, he turned his head. "I'm riding to the cabin." At least his voice was civil.

"When will you be back?"

He returned his attention to the rear lawn beyond the window. "I have no idea actually. I just can't be near you right now. It's too bloody painful." He glanced at her. "You're really going to do this?" he asked, his meaning clear.

She looked steadily into his gray eyes that had no edge of steel today, only a huge sadness.

"Are you trying to force my hand? Is that what this is all about?"

Her back stiffened. "Jeremy, you know what this is all about." She gripped her hands together in an attempt to keep her voice from trembling. "Strange as it may sound, your loyalty to Evelyn makes me love you even more."

He stood still, studying her until Becca and Jekyll burst through the door .

Becca went to stand beside him, reaching for his hand. "Where are you going, Daddy?" she asked.

"To the cabin for awhile."

"By yourself?" She consulted Katie.

"Yes."

"But when will you come back?"

"I don't know yet. Probably a few days" He cupped her face, looking down at her. "Will you be okay while I'm gone?"

"Well, yeah. I'm not scared. Katie and I have

Lena and Celia and Patrick and Janel. We'll be okay."

"I know you will." Bending, he lifted her into his arms, hugging her close before he set her back down. He came toward Katie, taking her hand, his eyes tender. "Please take good care of her."

"You know I will."

"Thanks, Katie." He brought her hand to his lips. Strangely, his gentleness hurt more than his anger would have.

He left without looking back.

Becca came to grab her hand, visibly uneasy. Katie led her along the hall and out onto the terrace where they watched Jeremy walk down over the lawn to give Bordeaux the carrots he'd brought.

He soon moved on. The saddlebags slung over his shoulder reminded Katie of that first picnic on the mountain when she'd discovered what a sensitive, caring man he was. The memory stirred huge, aching loneliness.

CHAPTER TWENTY-TWO

Katie's grief and sorrow did not lessen as the days of Jeremy's absence crept by. Determined to keep up a positive front for Becca, she threw herself into busyness so she had little time to think.

With the reality of her relationship with Becca possibly ending in the near future, she gave much of her attention to her. Becca clearly loved this and appeared to keep her worry about her dad at bay. It was obvious that she found the situation perplexing but she didn't ask what was wrong. Katie identified with her silence. As long as neither of them talked about why Jeremy had left without them, they didn't yet have to face any troubling developments.

Lena and Celia also picked up the vibes of discord and Katie overheard them grilling Pearl a few times, but they too didn't ask Katie anything directly. They gravitated toward Patrick's calm and zany personality and began spending more and more of their time in the arena.

They rode with Becca during her lessons and hung around afterward, watching Patrick and Janel training the various horses. Observing them, Katie realized with new insight that they were bored although they were far too polite to say so. Whatever her own future held, she must discuss the twins with Alexis and Dan and determine if they should be working toward their goal of being doctors.

None of them could continue in the indeterminate state where they'd resided since coming to *Radbourne* from Billings. When Jeremy got back, he would have to deal with many decisions regarding his family. Katie was unsettled by this reality but also anxious for whatever resolution was coming.

While the twins were occupied with Patrick and Becca was a school, Katie began exercising horses on the mountain. She rode with the desire to become so tired she could sleep at night, pushing the horses in long, conditioning canters that weren't conducive to thinking.

She loved the exercise and the sense that she was accomplishing something worthwhile but the activity did little to ease the turmoil of her nights. Her vivid dreams reminded her of all the years when the old nightmare had stalked her.

Now the troubled dreams had nothing to do with that time. She and Jeremy were caught in demented conflicts and she was awakened many times between bedtime and dawn, sweating, with every nerve strung tight with nameless tension.

One night late in the week, she was yanked from sleep by a shattering clap of thunder that left her shaking. She leapt from bed and ran for Becca's room.

Becca was sitting up, clinging to Jekyll with both arms. "Katie, that scared me," she said when she saw her.

"Me too. I'm going to stay here with you until it's over."

"Oh, good," she agreed with her usual

philosophical acceptance. "I like the thunder," she said when she was settled between Jekyll and Katie. "But that one was too much."

"You're right." Rain was pouring now, the noise a low roar beyond the windows.

"I love the rain." Becca climbed out of bed and ran to the nearest window, Jekyll pushing close as she peered out at the sheets of water swirling across the lawn. "Look at it! It's so cool!"

Katie followed and sat in the rocking chair to pull Becca onto her lap. Jekyll seated himself close by, a rock of calm.

As the downpour continued, lightning flashed, one bolt touching down just outside, causing them both to jump. Becca laughed. "That was a good one!"

Katie smiled, a little taken aback by her gutsy enjoyment. Her mind turned to Jeremy. He was surely all right but the thought of him alone on the mountain unnerved her.

Perhaps half an hour passed before the storm grew less violent and the rain gradually became lighter. Slowly the foggy mass of it thinned so they could make out the trees outside.

"I hope Bordeaux went in his stall," Becca said. "Sometimes he's so dumb, he stays out in the rain."

"Yes, he does. I think probably he does that because he's like you. He gets such a kick out of the ferocious thunder and lightning, he wants to be sure he's out in the middle of it."

Becca giggled at the idea. "I think that's it but he better watch it or he'll get zapped and that would be horrid."

"You are right about that." Katie drew her closer. "How about going back to bed now?"

"Okay, I love to listen to the rain. It puts me right to sleep." She slid down and returned to her bed.

Katie stopped to cover her and give her a kiss before continuing into the hall.

Back in her own bed, she was still worried about Jeremy. He seemed so close and somehow she thought he might be hurt. She decided she would ride up the mountain in the morning to make sure he was okay.

She was rigidly awake for a long time. When she dozed at some point, she didn't fall into deeper sleep but was caught in dreams splashed with blood.

Jeremy's shallow sleep was also distressed, splintered by nightmares. His own voice, calling out, jarred him awake. He lay shaking, his body sweating, yet chilled. A chaos of pictures swamped his mind, a kaleidoscope of faces, turning, tormenting – Evelyn, Katie, Francine, Lena, Celia....

He'd been alone at the cabin for days, an eternity of introspection. Nights brought horrific battles. His body craved rest and release.

This night, he lay drenched in perspiration, his every nerve wrenched tight and he knew there'd be no more sleep. He lifted his watch from the nightstand. Two-thirty. Groaning, he got up to find a towel and clean underwear. A distant crescendo of thunder rent the night as he toweled off his clammy skin.

Dressed in t-shirt and shorts, he sat on the

bed, thinking about Katie. Was she sleeping? No. Some dim perception alerted him to her turmoil that flooded him with another dimension of sadness.

It had started to rain, the drops pattering on the roof. Any other night, he'd have found the sound restful.. Now it only sounded cold and wet. The room's chill eventually prodded him to the hearth where he poked the glowing logs until undulating light mingled with the gloom.

He picked up his jeans and sweatshirt from where he'd dropped them earlier and pulled them on. He sank into an armchair. Each night found him here, staring into the fire, remembering and weeping.

This rite, hidden in the dark, was familiar now, comforting on some bizarre level. He longed for Katie but more so, for Evelyn.

He reached for Evelyn's portrait he'd brought from his office, tilting the frame to make out her face in the flickering illumination. The fire wasn't bright enough tonight and panic shot through him. In a heartbeat, he was on his knees, crawling toward the hearth. He brought the picture closer. Slowly his pounding heart slowed and the terror eased as her face materialized. Still, his breathing was erratic and it was several minutes before he willed himself to relax

Turning to lean his back against the stone ledge of the fireplace, he let the portrait rest in his lap. He closed his eyes, creating Evelyn's face in his brain, her delicate bones brushed with firelight. But it was a contrary process tonight. Her pretty features repeatedly slid away, pushed aside by the intruding horror of the specter in the nursing home.

His renewed panic crashed over him and he battled his failure. *I won't forget.* Again and again, he brought the photo into the light, forcing back the other image. This is Evelyn, not the other.

Closing his eyes, he concentrated on the fantasy that always eased his sorrow and brought her back. Deliberately, like a painter bringing a scene to life, he remembered Evelyn lying with him in their bed, her bare skin warm and fragrant with her special perfume.

Another memory encroached on the first. More than once, Katie had found him working in the barns and they ended up making love in a freshly-bedded stall, their excitement heightened by the risk of discovery. No matter how great her desire, Evelyn would never have done that.

He shifted against the rug and the stone ledge. Tears spilled down his face, soaking his shirt already damp from earlier crying. Evelyn's sensuality, her laughing, passionate mouth and dancing eyes eluded him tonight.

Unbearable agitation built in him. Intent on escape, he laced on running shoes, grabbed his jacket and rushed out into the rain. He walked for awhile with no sense of direction, his tears icy on his skin in the bitter cold. Then he ran, swallowed by the sodden night that obliterated all thought. He had no idea how far he'd gone when his breath sawed painfully into his lungs. Agony knifed through his chest before trembling legs put him on his knees, fighting for breath. *God, he was having a heart attack!*

He was soaked and shaking and it took some

time to recover enough to stand again. Even then, his entire frame ached and it still hurt to breathe. Finally, he tried running again but immediately fell, sprawling into rocks that tore his jeans. He felt warmth spreading down his wet legs even as he struggled up. He ran on, maybe for half a mile before he stumbled to a stop.

Slowly he raised his arms to the rain, shouting Evelyn's name. He screamed until his throat was raw and he'd lost every ounce of his remaining strength. He collapsed to the ground, so stiff and exhausted he doubted he could get up. Whatever damage he'd done to his legs throbbed. He felt ninety years old.

He was aware after a time that the rain had stopped. Closing his eyes, he felt sunshine bathing his body, warming him a little despite his wet clothing. He had no conception of time passing but bit by bit, his mind cleared and he spoke softly. "Evelyn, I'm so sorry but I can't make you better...I've tried so hard...." New tears ran down into his ears. "...I have to let go or I'll be destroyed with you....I want to live the life I have now...It's a good life, Evelyn...Becca is happy...I can be happy. I want to be happy again. It's been so long...I...tried to keep you with me...." He turned his head to one side to ease the choking knot of tears blocking his throat, drawing a labored breath.

"...I loved you so much, Evelyn but I can't anymore. I'll die if I do. The world where you and I lived isn't here anymore...." He lost track of where he was as he verbalized everything he'd been afraid to say until this moment in time. He cried so hard, his stomach felt like it was tearing inside. He vomited. Fumbling in his jacket, he found a handkerchief to wipe his face, then lay back again.

"I...I know you can't ever again be the way you were. I...wish I could set you free...but all I can do is pray that God will take you soon. I will always cherish you in my heart...."

Katie's tumultuous lack of sleep drove her from bed early. The twins were still sleeping but Becca and Jckyll soon joined her in the sunroom.

After their quick breakfast, Becca followed her out into warm sunshine. The morning was fresh-washed and glorious. Meadowlarks sang in the grassy paddocks beyond the stream. Becca spun in circles, reveling in the perfect weather. Jekyll capered around her.

"It feels like spring," Katie said. "I've been saying that but it *really* feels like it this morning."

"Tomorrow it *is* spring!" said Becca. "The spring solstice."

Katie smiled at her high spirits. She remembered her own girlhood joy at the official end of winter. Balmy days after interminable ice and snow. The coming liberation from boarding school with the promise of summer fun.

When they reached the arena, Katie asked a stable boy to saddle Murphy for her. "I'm going to go see how Jeremy survived the storm last night," she told Patrick.

He granted her a curious look. "That's good. I think. Anything new there?" He glanced at Becca who'd already mounted and was riding Cassie at the other end of the arena.

"No."

"Well, keep the faith." He gave her a legup and opened the gate for her.

"Thanks." Katie rode past the cottages where Janel was jogging with Breighton along the trail ahead. What a gorgeous Golden Retriever he was, she thought, waving as she continued up the slope.

Her worry for Jeremy increased as she cantered across the meadows, becoming a frantic pounding in her head after she reached the cabin and found no sign of him. She checked the stable where an elegant stallion appraised her from his stall, then ran back to Murphy, remounted and turned back toward the higher peaks, silvery against the deep blue sky.

After half an hour, she found Jeremy lying flat on his back, bruised and bloody on the ground. She scrambled out of the saddle and rushed to him.

He appeared unconscious when she knelt beside him, searching his face, shouting his name. Then he startled, his eyes flying open. After a bit of adjustment, he grinned, reaching for her hand.

Somehow she knew there'd been an extreme shift since she'd last seen him. "Sweetheart, what happened to you?" She squeezed his fingers, wincing at all the blood.

He reached up to touch the dried blood on his mouth and face. "I was in one hell of a fight."

Fear for him surged through Katie but she tried to keep her tone light. "What does the other guy look like?"

"You're looking at him. I was battling myself half the night. I picked a great arena, don't you think? It's a wonder I wasn't struck by lightning." He grimaced as he managed to sit up, grasping a nearby rock.

Katie knelt down, unable to make sense of anything he'd said. Inclining close, she searched for clues to explain his condition. "How'd you get out here?"

"I ran." He rested his forehead on hers. "I've struggled all week to sort things out. I'm a slow learner but I did eventually come to the same conclusion the rest of you reached a long time back."

He slowly lifted his head to look at her, his eyes remarkably clear and filled with a profound calm Katie had never seen before. "I finally got in touch with the part of me who loves you so much I could never let you go."

She was held captive by his appraisal as she felt her heart opening. Though he was hurt and thinner, overall, he looked stronger. His eyes held the remnants of ungodly suffering, yet there was an ease about him that sent shivers of joy through Katie.

Bracing himself with one arm, he held her face still. "Are you okay? You look so tired."

"The storm woke us and then I kept having awful dreams about you."

"I picked up on that in the middle of my emotional wreck...."

"Jeremy, is it true what I see in your eyes?"

Tears welled but his mouth quirked in a smile as he drew up his legs and wrapped his arms around his knees, "It's true."

They were lost in the amazing process of assimilating all that was happening to them.

"I'm so happy," she managed after a time.

"Nothing else for us from now on." His lips brushed hers. " Do you think we can make it to the cabin?"

"We can but try." She went to fetch Murphy from where he cropped a patch of new grass.

She slid an arm around Jeremy's back and while he held onto the rock, they presently had him standing, albeit shakily. The next step was for him to be atop a slab of sandstone abutting the boulder he'd been clinging to. She brought Murphy closer so he could hang onto the saddle while he stepped up. When he looked somewhat stable, she mounted, then held the horse still while Jeremy slid on behind her.

She turned Murphy in the direction of the cabin. "You went all that way in the storm," she marveled after they'd ridden a couple miles. "Without a horse?"

"*Ran* all the way." He steadied his head against hers. "Running from the truth, you know," he added ruefully.

It took nearly an hour to reach the cabin. Katie helped him inside and onto the rumpled bed where she undressed him and brought a basin of water to tenderly bathe his wounds.

She found aspirin that she gave him with a glass of water, then dressed the worst of the abrasions with antiseptic and gauze. At last, she stretched out beside him, covering them with a blanket. Delayed reaction moved through her and she couldn't stop shivering. He rolled toward her a little, compassion in his face, the length of his body pressed close, "Darling, I'm so sorry." His eyes held her, searching, asking.

"I...truly believed it was over for us...It was the worst pain I've ever felt."

"Sweet, Katie, my love, my forever love...." He tenderly gathered her to him. "Can you forgive me?"

"I already have, Jeremy." Winding her arms around him, she gave herself completely to his sudden ardor.

Passion ignited between them, filling any remaining void. He kissed her mouth, her neck, the expanse of her stomach....His voice fell over her in an intermittent litany of healing. She clung to him, drowning in relief, knowing she would never be far from him again.

"I want to make love to you," he whispered, his fingers seeking the zipper of her jeans. .

She laughed, helping him remove the rest of her clothes. "You sure you're up to this...."

"Never underestimate me, my love...."

"I never would."

They made love slowly, very carefully, every move exquisitely familiar, every sound of their passion a balm to their weary spirits. They finally lay spent in each other's arms.

"Tomorrow, I'll talk to Bernard," Jeremy said after a time. "I'm not sure what a divorce in my situation entails, but he will." His disquiet conveyed something of the battle he'd fought. "I've let go, Katie."

She started to reply, to put into words her warring emotions of the past few weeks. Mixed with her joy was stark pain.

Jeremy, sensing her inadequacy, pressed his fingers to her lips. "We have a great deal to talk about and unlimited time to do it." He winked. "It'll likely take most of it for me to make up for all the grief I caused you." He tipped up her chin, his eyes imploring. "Katie, I just didn't know until now. I am so terribly sorry." He drew a long breath. "Sometime, I'll tell you what I went through this week. But not just yet." He swallowed convulsively. "It hurts too much."

She lay next to him and nestled her head on his chest. She could hear his heart beating. Drowsiness overtook them both and they fell asleep.

It was afternoon when they started for *Radbourne*. They pulled up before starting down the last stretch of the trail. The ranch headquarters offered up the vital intermingling of colors and textures Katie had come to love. Now the blended hues were softened and subdued by the pale greens of spring

Her eyes traveled over the stolid manor house that had looked so forbidding when she first arrived. Now she saw the grace that had likely guided Tyson Chamberlain when he first built it. Her heart swelled at the sight of wide meadows filled with broodmares and foals, the wonderful old trees and slate-roofed barns and stables. How she adored this place. How had she ever believed she could leave it behind?

As though drawn by their inspection, Bordeaux crashed out of the trees and stood gazing up at them. His trumpeting neigh echoed across the valley.

Jeremy laughed and Katie turned in her saddle to look at him, seeing his love for her, for this venerable ranch. And his commitment to build something fine here with her at his side. She was home.

EPILOGUE

Two months later

"I can see Daddy and Patrick." Becca stood with Katie, Janel and Jekyll on the circular stone staircase leading to the terrace from the tower. "They look very handsome."

Katie rested her hands on Becca's shoulders. "Don't they though." She surveyed them below with the young minister.

Striking in pinstriped morning coats, the two chatted with Lena and Celine sitting nearby with Alexis and her family. The twins wore a slender pink gown that set off their dark beauty. Next week they were heading back to Colorado to begin their internships in General Practice. Upon graduation, they would return to Wyoming and set up their practice in Sheridan.

Katie kissed the top of Becca's head within its circle of baby's breath. She and Janel wore baby's breath in their hair as well. Jekyll waited patiently near Becca to make his debut as ring bearer. Baby's breath adorned his neck with a poufy pale green bow.

A few steps behind, Katie's bridesmaid Janel wore lavender satin. Becca had been her choice for maid of honor from the moment the wedding was set and now twirled in her pale yellow organza, inspecting herself in the glass panels of a window.

While they watched the subdued activity on the terrace, Katie slid one hand over her stomach, savoring her secret. She'd wanted to tell Jeremy about their child right away but decided to surprise him on their honeymoon.

Nealie in a Victorian dress of purple watered-silk sat near the altar that was gracefully hung with white roses and purple hydrangeas. Most of the terrace was filled with friends, neighbors and employees.

Presently Pearl hurried to her seat next to Nick. They knew the ceremony was about to begin. Pearl had been cooking for most of three days to add favorite dishes to the buffet luncheon the caterers would serve.

Katie turned Becca around to inspect her one last time in her finery. "You look so pretty, sweetie."

"You too." She grinned up at her.

Katie visualized Jeremy's appreciation of her own beaded dress in sage green. Sleeveless and cut low in front, it clung to her curves in tiers.

Becca collected a satin pillow tied with the rings from a chair close by. Jekyll took it in his mouth as they'd practiced.

A string quartet played beyond the altar. Anticipation flowed through Katie when she heard the first thrilling strains of her very favorite piece of music played on a baby grand – *Mozart's Piano Concerto Number Twenty-one.*

She gathered four long-stemmed white roses and handed one to Becca, another to Janel. Becca started down the steps with Jekyll beside her. Janel preceded Katie.

Once she reached the terrace, Katie stopped to give Nealie a rose. The bottomless green eyes brimmed with merriment. "You're lovely, my dear."

She walked on to Jeremy who smiled and mouthed, *"I love you."*

When she saw his tears, her heartbeat quickened with love for him, this strong, gentle, honorable man. Her friend, her lover, her destiny.

She smiled through her own tears and he reached for her hand.

The End

ABOUT THE AUTHOR

Jeannie Hudson grew up on a ranch in Wyoming where her rapport with animals was nourished in a country environment. She attended Casper College where she was the only student to serve as editor of the student newspaper, *The Chinook*, for two years which included a full scholarship.

While at the University of Wyoming, she began writing full-time and began selling short stories to magazines. Over the next two decades she sold four suspense novels and raised Arabian show horses.

After a move to Minnesota, she continued writing and began raising show beagles. When she returned to the West, she took up watercolor painting which she has pursued along with writing over the past ten years. Now she lives in the Black Hills of South Dakota with her husband Adam and two rambunctious beagles, Murphy and Bailey.

Coming soon from Jeannie Hudson

Mariposa
The Yearning Tree